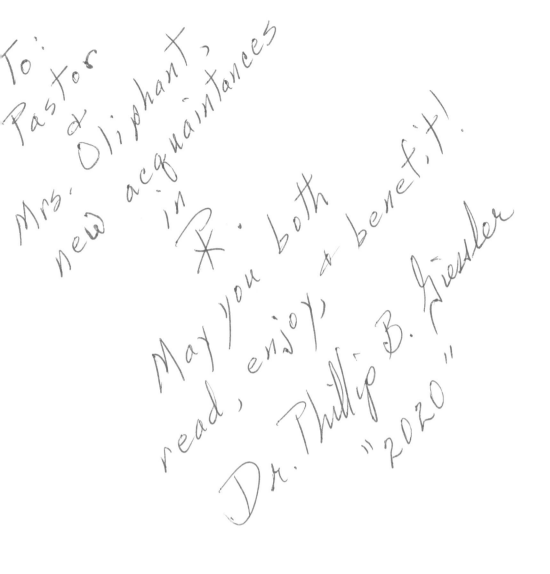

To:
Pastor &
Mrs. Oliphant,
new acquaintances
in P.F.

May you both
read, enjoy, & benefit!

Dr. Phillip B. Giessler
"2020"

W9-BAT-714

SOLVING NEW TESTAMENT MYSTERIES WITH OLD TESTAMENT CLUES

Evidence Just Too Coincidental to Be Accidental!!!

PHILLIP BRUCE GIESSLER

eFox Solutions Review

Copyright © 2020 by Phillip Bruce Giessler.
Revised and Updated with Corrections and Minor Additions, May, 2019, January, 2020.

All rights reserved. No part of this publication may be reproduced, distributed, or transmitted in any form or by any means, including photocopying, recording, or other electronic or mechanical methods, without the prior written permission of the publisher, except in the case of brief quotations embodied in critical reviews and certain other noncommercial uses permitted by copyright law. For permission request, write to the publisher, addressed "Attention: Permissions Coordinator," at the address below.

eFox Solutions Review
P.O. Box 133
Ishpeming MI 49849
efoxsolutionsreview.com

Hotline: 906-204-4763
Email: *efoxsolutionsreview@gmail.com*

Copyright © 1976 Mrs. William F. Beck. Old Testament Scripture quotations are taken from *The Holy Bible: An American Translation* (AAT). Osage Beach, Missouri: Lake Printing Company. Used by permission. All rights reserved.

Dr. William F. Beck developed this translation over a period of thirty years. It has undergone a series of careful revisions—major and minor—from the year 1976 to the present. Two great strong points characterize this Bible version: extreme faithfulness in the handling of the Messianic Prophecies relating to the coming of Jesus Christ, as well as "ease of reading" for English readers.

Copyright © 1990 Mrs. William F. Beck. New Testament Scripture quotations are taken from *God's Word to the Nations: New Evangelical Translation* (NET). Cleveland, OH: NET Publishing. Used by permission. All rights reserved.

This New Testament is a major revision of the translation work of Dr. William F. Beck's AAT (An American Translation). The major revisers were Greek specialists Siegbert W. Becker, Robert G. Hoerber, and David Kuske.

The NET's major contributions to the world of modern translations relate to updates of modern language for "ease of English reading," unique poetic layout, especially the book of *Revelation* by Rev. Jack Michael Cascione, containing a "*kai*" format unique to all other Bibles; built-in outlines that divide the texts of the various twenty-seven books of the New Testament, brilliant maps by Dr. John C. Lawrenz, superb informational appendices, and other front and back data of significance.

At times, the author has incorporated minor translation changes to Scripture quotations from the two above-mentioned Bible versions. These are in harmony with the principles of Dr. William F. Beck, who at times was this author's personal tutor. (Formerly, your present author had the privilege of writing the Prefaces to the Second and Third editions of the AAT and later served as Editor-in-Chief of the NET.)

Maps by Dr. John C. Lawrenz. Used by permission.

Ordering Information:
Quantity sales. Special discounts are available on quantity purchases by corporations, associations, such as, seminaries, churches, schools, and others. For details, contact the publisher at the address above.

Printed in the United States of America.

Library of Congress Control Number		2018962857
ISBN-13:	Paperback	978-1-7344785-0-1
	Hardback	978-1-7344785-1-8
	ePub	978-1-7344785-2-5

Rev. date: 01/25/2020

Dedicated

to all my missionary supporters and students,

past and present

in

Africa, America, Canada, Ecuador, and Finland

to the glory of

THE HOLY TRINITY

God the Father, Creation's *Building Architect*

God the Son, Creation's *Building Contractor*

God the Holy Spirit, Creation's *Building Inspector*

(See Appendix 14, page 276.)

ACKNOWLEDGEMENTS

The William F. Beck family members, especially Reu Beck, for permission to use the translation texts of the AAT and NET Bibles.

Vicque Fassinger for the initial editing of this book, as well as initial designs incorporated into the body of the text. Invaluable!

Virginia "ginnie" Renkel for insightful textual polishing of the Second Edition.

Alan Carlson, Rev. Michael Hageman, Jeff Kitzler, Jesse and Erica Kloos, Courtney Mosley, and "Davey" Scott for their valuable computer assistance.

Dr. Solomon Praveen Samuel and Dr. Alvin J. Schmidt for insights concerning the world of self-publishing.

Dr. John C. Lawrenz for use of his maps.

See Further Personal Acknowledgements for additional well-deserved credits on pages 285-288.

FOREWORD

As a seminary student nearly four decades ago, I first explored the Scriptures under the tutelage of Dr. Phillip Giessler. I remember imagining that the Bible would leap from my hands, miraculously coming to life through his amazing teachings. "Dr. Phil" combined powerful observational skills, an intense love and regard for the Scriptures as God's Word, and an insightful bent for the practical into an experience that has shaped my pastoral practice and personal piety.

Reading *Solving New Testament Mysteries with Old Testament Clues* recaptures that original excitement . . . and more. In some ways, perusing its pages is like reuniting with an old friend. There's Dr. Phil's passion for digging deeper, making unbelievably insightful connections, and inspiring a love for Scripture through solidly faithful teaching. At the same time, there is a seasoning that comes from his decades-long journey as a parish pastor, Bible translator and promoter, Bible study leader around the USA, and seminary instructor on four continents. What you hold in your hands is the culmination of God's lifelong "workmanship" (Ephesians 2:10) in the life of an adventurous, engaging, and inquisitive Scripture scholar whose mind and heart are captivated by the Word of God.

This book is written for inquisitive, investigative thinkers capable of evaluating amazing, incredible, and stunning data. It seeks readers who yearn to go deep and find hidden clues that lead to solving Bible mysteries.

You will be one of many who will enjoy the findings revealed on the following pages—benefitting greatly. That's a promise.

In addition, a special challenge to any Bible believer, atheist, agnostic, and endorser of macroevolution, plus *any* Scriptural believer or doubter: Read this book's data and see if you don't come to the realization that *Solving New Testament Mysteries with Old Testament Clues* is *Evidence Just Too Coincidental to Be Accidental!!!* In short, you will be discovering an abundance of Scripture's surprising connectives.

As the centerpiece of it all, you will discover that Jesus the Christ is truly the *pivotal* point of all Scripture. This basic truth will forever be burned into your mind on the pages to follow. You will see why some Greeks came to Philip the disciple and said, "Sir, we want to see Jesus" (John 12:20–21).

This book's catchy subtitles are fascinating. Just two examples: concerning Jesus's baptism—"Houston, the Dove Has Landed," and when comparing the First Adam to Jesus, the Second Adam—"Splitting the 'Adams'"!

For those of you who are a bit older, the example of the old "Mikey" commercial for Life cereal will resonate as you consider reading this Scripture production, "Try It; You'll Like It." For younger minds, the Sherlock Holmes motif of "clues" and "mystery" solving should hold intrigue.

Enjoy.

Rev. Thomas R. Ahlersmeyer, PhD
Senior Pastor, Holy Cross Lutheran Church—Fort Wayne, Indiana, USA
Previous President, Concordia University—Ann Arbor, Michigan, USA

ABOUT OUR AUTHOR

When presenting lectures and seminars, those introducing Dr. Phillip B. Giessler often desire to present his personal data—academic degrees, teaching experiences, and published writings. Giessler's reply to anyone introducing him is: "Don't waste time telling them about me and my background; just tell them I love Jesus, and let's get going with the subject at hand."

And so we shall!

ABOUT THIS BOOK

The adventure you are about to encounter is set within a mystery, detective, clue-finding format. It takes you from the first promise of the One called Jesus all the way through Old Testament hints and forward pointers on into the New Testament fulfillments of His birth, ministry, suffering, death, resurrection, and ascension.

But there needs to be more to entice you to read on!

What has just been said may seem like "old hat," yet there is way more than that. The information presented contains so many new details and ways of presenting old truths—also, many factors *not* contained in other books. By reading, you will be heading into a real treat of investigative discovery that others have not previously experienced.

That's a big-time promise, but one that you will find to be true.

Happy reading and detection of life-changing views concerning the One who claimed to be the Messiah, the Savior of the world!

PUBLISHER'S COMMENTS

This present publication is a self-publishing venture under the auspices of eFox Solutions Review.

Some unique and special features to be found in *Solving New Testament Mysteries with Old Testament Clues* are contained on the following pages. First, Chapter 1 lists all the questions to be answered in this book. Chapter 2 will prove a Godsend to anyone not very acquainted with the Bible; besides, teachers of Scripture also will find this chapter ever so valuable for use with persons asking questions about the Bible in general. Chapters 3 to 22 contain amazing data from the pages of both the Old and New Testaments. Readers will constantly say: "Why haven't I spotted that before?"

In addition, Appendices 1 to 15 will prove worth the price of this book alone. Pastors, Bible teachers, and readers with good Scriptural acumen will use the contents of these "15" over and over again to their own edification and to the advantage of others with whom they come into contact. Appendices 3, 5, 11, 14, and 15 will be quite understandable and exciting for a Bible novice. (Religious teachers will desire to use their contents to instruct people on all levels.) Appendix 10 and its section entitled "From Here to Eternity, will force readers to think as never before—though the *whole* of Appendices 10 and 12 are for the more seasoned religious thinkers and inquirers.

Second, the embedded footnote system makes quotation references *less cumbersome*; those sources can be located at the end of the book by finding the first letter of any reference under Bibliography with Reference Codes and noting the "code" that identifies any particular text reference.

TO THE READER

Hi there!

Thanks for placing this book into your hands either in hard copy or via e-book.

It seems the title caught your eye and caused you to take a peek. I hope the Foreword and other pre-matter has caught your eye and will intrigue you to read on.

My former day school and Sunday school teachers, coupled with superior professors in institutions of higher learning, have made this present work possible. (See Further Personal Acknowledgments on pages 285-288.)

Yet, my best teacher of all has been the Holy Spirit. He has been behind it all, laying a solid Scriptural foundation by opening my eyes as I studied His word over the years. Besides, He has provided a valuable talent to take the great biblical scholarship of others and make it very understandable to the English-speaking "Johns" and "Judys" in the marketplaces of this world—and even adaptable to the comprehension skills of foreign-speaking students in Africa and elsewhere.

At least 85 percent of the surprising truths revealed in *Solving New Testament Mysteries with Old Testament Clues* are unique—and, as far as I can tell, are solely based on *personal* research and contain *original* conclusions.

Some may think certain ideas herein are plagiarized. Be assured that non-referenced thoughts are not. Other writers may have had identical or similar ideas at former or later times, but they were *not* known to me.

After beginning the writing of this book, a work and compilation done by Professor Chad L. Bird came to my attention. It is effectively divided into two main parts: *Reading OT Narratives Christologically* and *Christ in All the Scriptures: The Biblical Typology of Luther & the Fathers* (B, *ROTNC*, 87 total pages). If an idea communicated in Bird's compilation was new to me, it is referenced via footnote. If not new, a previously noted idea from another writer is sometimes cited for reinforcement. Finally, ideas associated with a noted point in this present book but going in *unrelated* directions, well, such data is *not* cited. Additionally, current readers eager to see more *connectives* between the two Testaments are encouraged to consult Bird's work.

Note: *See* "Bibliography with Reference Codes" at the end of this book *to decipher code lettering and page references.*

I wish to acquaint readers with David Limbaugh's, *The Emmaus Code* (E, *EC*, 420 total pages). It contains brilliant research on Old Testament prophecies and New Testament fulfillments and falls into the top twenty-five of all books I have ever read. In a sense, this work could be viewed as a companion predecessor to *Solving New Testament Mysteries with Old Testament Clues*.

Also, I am thrilled to have come across a fantastic publication of *Genesis* ("188" theological meditations) by a deacon and preacher from Poland: Valerius Herberger (1562 to 1627), called the "Jesus preacher" (H, *GWG*, introductory page). This work came to my attention when 99 percent of the present book was ready for submission to my publisher. I wish I could have worked Herberger's comments on Genesis 4:1 and 49:8–12 into my research. His whole *Genesis* treatment contains a wealth of edification for those who realize that all Scripture is "Christ-centered"!

Also, at the very last moment I was introduced to a special book by Scott Hahn, *Joy to the World*. Though my views strongly differ on several doctrinal points, this book is one of the most readable ever and contains some really great insights into Scripture. Hahn has a special gift for putting things across in a memorable way. Two examples: "What happens in Bethlehem doesn't stay in Bethlehem" and when comparing Matthew's brevity concerning his report of the Wise Men to Luke's style of *much* info, Hahn writes that if Dr. Luke had included the Magi episode in his Gospel, then "We would probably know their postal addresses in Persia" (H, *JW*, pp. 13 and 117, respectively). Worth a big chuckle.

For years, it has been my privilege to teach the contents of my present book to various audiences. Over and over, post-lecture comments by attendees have reflected amazement. *Connectives* between the Old and New Testaments had not previously dawned on those hearers. These uncovered "mysteries," as you will see, were not and are not based on cultic fantasies or ideas that come from a wild human mind; they are just simple truths loaned by God to my inquisitive, Bible-searching mind.

God says, "Ignorance [lack of knowledge] destroys my people" (Hosea 4:6). We see this in society today when late-night TV hosts interview people on the streets. Many of these folks have not had the opportunity to be trained from little on up; they have so little acquaintance with Bible facts: history, geography, and doctrine. Therefore, they usually cannot be blamed when God's word remains a "mystery"—and little Bible "clues" here and there have not been picked up. *When read, this book can solve that problem.*

Christ Jesus once concluded, " . . . every student of the Scriptures who is trained for the Kingdom of heaven is like the owner of a house who continues to bring *new* and *old* things out of his treasure chest" (Matthew 13:52). This is the *goal* of my book: to present "old things" in a "new," fuller, and more insightful way, and at the same time, to line up "new things" with the "old" truths of the Bible.

As you, the reader, journey with me through this investigative book, you are promised surprise after surprise, enjoyment after enjoyment, but most of all, insight after insight.

Welcome to the biblical world of amazement. Expect *spectacular* insights, excitement, and personal benefits to come your way. I hope you find much encouragement on the pages of the following twenty-two chapters and fifteen appendices—a wealth of biblical ammunition to face life's challenges!

Addendum: Since I have been a foreign Bible teacher over the last eleven years, *primarily* in eastern Africa, certain oversimplifications will permeate many pages for purposes of clear communication to those for whom English is a *second* or *third* language. For example, Bible books will *not* be abbreviated for brevity of space; regularly accepted footnote format will be replaced by embedded *codes* in the text or by multiple *appendices*. Clarity of communication, not insult of intelligence, is intended for readers when, for example, seemingly unnecessary *italics*, *parentheses*, *bracketed* materials, and imbedded *boxes* are frequently added. Also, frequent departure from the standard *Chicago Manual of Style* (*CMOS*) is intentional, especially in terms of the unique usage of the *capitalization* of many names and terms. This overall iterary approach should also aid those readers who are *not* very acquainted with the Bible. Conversely, modern English colloquialisms are frequently employed to keep attention and add humor for our readers in the Americas and other English-speaking countries.

Dr. Phillip B. Giessler, Litt.D.
Contact info: *pbgfbnt@gmail.com*

TABLE OF CONTENTS

Appendices

Indexes

PART I

BEGINNING OUR INVESTIGATIVE JOURNEY

CHAPTER 1

QUESTIONS AND MYSTERIES TO BE INVESTIGATED IN THIS BOOK

To Whet Your Appetite

Who is the *Who* who sent the *Who* who came to earth's Whoville to rescue us "Whos"? (Chapter 3)

Did God predict the coming of Jesus to Adam and Eve in Genesis 3:15? Did they understand any of it? (Chapter 4)

Why is it interesting to know *the geographical route* Abraham followed when he went to Mount Moriah to sacrifice his "only son Isaac"? (Chapter 5)

Why is it important that it was Luke who reported the "virgin birth" of Jesus in greatest detail, the wrapping of Jesus infant body in "baby clothes" [KJV: "swaddling clothes"] at His birth, as well as the fact that Jesus sweat "blood" through His pores in Gethsemane? (Chapter 6)

Why is the *incarnation* of Jesus (God coming "in flesh") the *greatest* miracle reported in the Bible? (Chapter 6)

How does one explain the three weird citations of fulfilled messianic prophecies in Matthew 2:15, 18, 23? (Chapter 7)

Why did Jesus need to be a Priest "according to the likeness of Melchizedek"? (Chapter 7)

Why could Matthew the tax collector not accurately add to "14" *three* times in Matthew 1:17? (Appendix 4)

What do we learn about the Holy Trinity at Jesus's baptism, especially thinking "oil, dove, stayed"? (Chapter 8)

Scripture says that the First Adam was a "type" [a picture or shadow] of the Second Adam, Jesus. Name some of the ways that Adam *prefigured* Christ (see Romans 5:12–19). (Chapter 9)

Why did Jesus need to be led by the Holy Spirit into the wilderness for forty days at the *start* of His ministry—and not later? (Chapter 9)

Why did Jesus pick twelve disciples, not nine or fifteen? (Chapter 9)

What does Jeremiah 16:14–21 have to do with Jesus's extended ministry on earth? (Chapter 9)

Why did Jesus have to change water into wine at the wedding in Cana in Galilee as His "first" miracle? (Chapter 10)

Why was a new "equalizer" needed in NT days? (Chapter 11)

What quality of authenticity does John 7:31 pinpoint that had to be present in the coming Messiah? (Chapter 12)

In what way would Nathanael benefit by riding the Jesus-escalator? (Chapter 12)

Why in the world would Jesus call the "Canaanite" woman a "dog"? (Chapter 12)

How was the worldly Peter way off target in Matthew 18? (Chapter 12)

In what ways does the repeated word "better" in the book of *Hebrews* and "greater" in Matthew 12:41–42 provide an overview of Jesus's *superior* ministry when compared to the ministries of OT personalities? (Chapter 12)

What *kind* of bread did Jesus use to feed the five thousand? Why twelve and seven baskets of *leftovers* after the feedings of the "5,000" and "4,000," respectively? Who cares? Does it really matter? (Chapter 13)

At times, Jesus asks questions but gives no answers. Why? (Chapter 13)

Why did Jesus have to *walk on water*? (Chapter 13)

How does the leprosy of the OT Naaman tie in with Jesus's ministry? (Chapter 14)

Why did Jesus raise the boy of the city of Nain in the way He did? How does this connect with the resurrection ministries of Elijah and Elisha? (Chapter 14)

When did Jesus make an ax head float? (Chapter 14)

Why "five" stones when David fought Goliath the giant or why "five" porches at Bethesda or why "five" brothers in the episode of "The Rich Man and Lazarus," as told by Jesus? (Chapter 15 and Appendix 14)

Why did the prophets Moses and Elijah need to appear before Jesus on the Mount of Transfiguration, talking to Jesus about His upcoming death? (Chapter 15)

Why did Jesus take a special *out-of-the-way geographic route* to Jerusalem when He traveled there to die? (Chapter 15)

How do the words of Zechariah 3:9d ("I will remove the iniquity of that land in one day"), a significant prophecy concerning Christ's death, play into the whole Calvary crucifixion of Jesus, the Second Adam, as well as relate to the First Adam in the Garden of Eden? (Chapter 16)

What is the importance of knowing the "times" of day as to when Jesus was condemned, crucified, and died? (Chapter 16)

Where did Jesus *start* the most intense part of His suffering? *Significance?* (Chapter 16)

Why did Jesus repeat the same prayer three times in the Garden of Gethsemane? (Chapter 16)

In what way was the NT high priest Caiaphas parallel to the OT prophet Balaam? (Chapter 16)

What is the significance of the *name* Barabbas, the man who was on trial with Jesus? (Chapter 16)

Why did *God* make sure a "crown of thorns" was put on Jesus's head at His trial? (Chapter 16)

Why does Matthew say the soldiers of Pilate put a "scarlet" robe on Jesus, while Mark and John say it was "purple"? (Chapter 16)

Concerning the *time* elements of 2 Samuel 24:15-16, how do they relate to Jesus's death in Mark 15:34–37? (Chapter 17)

Where was Calvary located? (Chapter 17)

Why was Jesus crucified in the "middle"—between two criminals? (Chapter 17)

What's that "Paradise" statement from the lips of Jesus at Calvary all about? (Chapter 18)

How exactly was it predicted, some five hundred years before happening, that Jesus's mother, Mary, would be at the cross, but her husband, Joseph, would not be? (Chapter 18)

Why was it significant that "the sun stopped shining" for three hours on Good Friday as Jesus was on the cross? (Chapter 19)

When Jesus cried, "I thirst," is the prophecy in Psalm 69:21 the only passage fulfilled by Jesus's words? How does Judge Samson figure in? (Chapter 19)

Why should a Bible detective *tie together* the "first" and "seventh" sayings of Jesus on the cross? (Chapter 19)

Why was it necessary for Jesus to suffer and die on a *Friday* and not on a *Wednesday*? (Chapter 19)

Why did Jesus have to rise from the dead on a *Sunday*? (Chapter 19)

Why did certain "dead" people come alive on Good Friday *after* Jesus died—and not on Easter morning *after* He rose from the dead? (Chapter 20)

Does the "water and blood" that flowed from Jesus's side *after* he was dead refer to the biblical teaching of baptism and the Lord's Supper, or is there another meaning or an initial, primary focus? (Chapter 20)

Why was Jesus laid in "a *new* tomb, in which no one had yet been laid"? (Chapter 20)

What is the significance of Jesus being in the grave all day Saturday, the middle day of His three days in the grave? (Chapter 20)

What did Jesus do in hell's "prison" on Easter morning? (Chapter 21)

When Jesus returned to earth after His descent into hell, why is it strange that Scripture reports that He *first* appeared to *women*? (Chapter 21)

What is the significance of a *woman*, Mary from Magdala, seeing Jesus on Easter morning *in a garden*? (Chapter 21)

Why was it necessary for Christ to remain on earth for *forty* days after His resurrection; that is, before He was permitted to ascend into heaven? (Chapter 22)

Where did the term *private eye* originate? (Appendix 14)

What are the real implications of the story of David and Goliath? (Appendix 14)

Why is the "Joppa clue" important to an understanding of the Cornelius story in Acts 9:43–10:48? (Appendix 15)

CHAPTER 2

SOME BASICS ABOUT THE BIBLE

Just for Starters

You may have heard the phrase "It's all about the chicken!" The "Chicken Tonight" fast-food chicken chain restaurants in Uganda. Africa must start somewhere; probably wise to start with *chicken*.

The same is true when trying to understand the Bible. Simple knowledge must precede deeper comprehension. Probably best to start with some basic Bible facts! Thus, this present chapter will give some "elementary" data about the Bible, facts crucial and even fascinating for the Bible novice, even of interest to the Bible veteran for teaching purposes.

1. The Bible is divided into *two* parts: Old Testament (OT) & New Testament (NT)
   a. The OT was written in the Hebrew language; some Aramaic also;
   b. The NT was written in the Greek language.

2. "Bible" means "book" ["roll"]; (Greek: *biblion*) or "books" ["rolls"] (*biblia*). Collectively, Christians call the Bible "God's Book" or the "Books of Scripture," referring either to the whole collection in the singular as "the Book" or to all the books individually in the plural as "the Books." Since there are sixty-six [66] books in total, one can say, "God's Book is made up of sixty-six books."

3. The words "covenant" and "testament" are parallel words, and in my opinion, they are the very most important *common* nouns in Scripture. They reflect that the OT is the "Promise" and the NT is the "Fulfillment." This promise-and-fulfillment motif all centers in *Jesus Christ*. (Texts such as Luke 24:44–48; Acts 4:12, 10:43; 1 Corinthians 2:2 cement this *Christ-centered* idea. [See Chapter 6 below.])

4. Here is an *acronym* to give meaning to the word B-I-B-L-E:
   Basic
   Information (or) Instruction
   Before
   Leaving
   Earth.

5. Suggestion: If you are rather *unfamiliar* with the names of the books of the Bible, you will be aided in reading this present book by *first* taking any Bible, looking at the Table of Contents, familiarizing yourself with the books, and reading the names—one by one. (Do not worry about pronouncing them correctly.)

6. The Bible's *twofold division*, done mathematically, counting the letters of each word:

        3   9

a. **O-L-D**   **T-E-S-T-A-M-E-N-T** = ___39__ books

(slide the "3" and "9" together)

        3   x   9

b. **N-E-W**   **T-E-S-T-A-M-E-N-T** = _+_27__ books

(multiply the "3" by "9")

                                        ____

            TOTAL OF   **66 BOOKS**

"In and around" the Bible

1. In general, the OT constitutes over two-thirds of the whole Bible, while the NT makes up a little under a third of the Holy Scriptures.

   Have fun and do your own calculations. Google "Total words in Hebrew Old Testament," then click on "Old Testament—Biblebelievers.com" and read the data about "King James Bible Statistics."

2. The *history* of the OT covers about 4,000 years; the *history* of the NT about 90 years, which includes John's vision in Revelation.

3. The OT was written over a period of about 1,500 years; the NT in about 40 years. David Limbaugh reports that there were ". . . sixty-six books written by some forty authors over 1,500 years in three different languages" (L, *EC*, p. 8).

4. Genesis 1–11 covers as much time as the *whole* rest of the Bible from Genesis 12–Revelation 22. Astounding! The first 2,000 years of history are packed onto ever-so-few pages of Scripture! *Clues* galore between

the lines! The job of the Bible detective: Always follow the *God trail* to Calvary and the empty tomb (see #9. below).

5. The shortest chapter in the Bible is Psalm 117, only two verses.

6. The longest chapter in the Bible is Psalm 119, a whole 176 verses.

7. According to one popular calculation, the middle verses in the Bible are Psalm 118:8–9. Read these verses and note a clue that contains *"Evidence Just Too Coincidental to Be Accidental!!!"* It is this: Since the Scriptures teach that "trust" in God *saves*, it is significant that the Bible's middle verses warn you *not* to put your "trust" in people—or political leaders. Yikes, like a *wise* person in our day and age needs to be alerted to this obvious fact!

8. Toward what Human Being does the whole Bible point? *Jesus Christ* (see Acts 10:43).

9. There are at least 333 prophecies in the OT that predict the two comings of the Messiah. Google "333 prophecies" to verify.

10. Because Jesus is both *divine* and *human*, He is thus called the God-Man.

11. The name Messiah or Christ means Anointed or Chosen One, while the name Jesus means Helper, Refuge, Savior. Thus, Christ Jesus means the Anointed Savior or Chosen Savior, *anointed* in baptism by the Holy Spirit to be the world's *Savior, chosen* and endorsed by His heavenly Father to *save* people from sin (Matthew 3:16–17).

A Way to Divide the Books of the New Testament

The NT begins with the four gospels: Matthew, Mark, Luke, and John. This leads to a significant question: After reading the four gospels, why would one even want to cross over the "bridge" book of Acts (the NT's *post*-history narrative of Jesus's days on earth) into the Epistles or NT letters (Romans to Jude), which tell "what people are to believe, how they are to live, and that they are to tell others about Jesus," and then finally into the Bible's last book of Revelation, the "He wins; we win" book, *unless* Jesus truly was *who* He said He was? And so, the fuller answers to this crucial question remain a mystery, dear Bible detectives, until you use OT clues to unravel the NT mysteries of the four gospels. Shortly, we will tackle the next twenty chapters of our book, receiving sufficient answers that will lead us into the whole of the NT as outlined below:

1. The gospels – the four "Who Is He?" narratives
2. Acts – The "bridge" book
3. The twenty-one epistles – The "Acceptable Human Responses" *to* the four gospels
4. Revelation – The "Jesus Wins; We Win" Apocalypse!

Dividing the Old Testament [OT] Scriptures

The OT *Hebrew* canon was divided differently than we are accustomed to dividing the books of the OT today. It is of primary importance that we note the *ancient* division. This will especially help us to understand Christ's references to these writings. Let us therefore note the *Hebrew* formation and comment on its relation to a few NT texts.

A. Law (Tōrāh)

Pentateuch:	Genesis, Exodus, Leviticus, Numbers, Deuteronomy	5 scrolls

B. Prophets (Něvi'im)

Former Prophets:	Joshua, Judges, Samuel, Kings	4 scrolls
Latter Prophets:	Isaiah, Jeremiah, Ezekiel, The Twelve	4 scrolls

C. Writings (Ketuvim) [Scriptures]

Poetry:	Psalms, Job, Proverbs	3 scrolls
Rolls [scrolls]:	Song of Solomon, [Ruth], [Lamentations], Ecclesiastes, Esther	3 scrolls (or 5)
History:	Daniel, Ezra-Nehemiah, Chronicles	3 scrolls

Total Scrolls: 22 (or 24)

When one analyzes the *three* Hebrew words above and the underlined lead letter of each, then it makes sense that the Jews refer to the OT books as the TaNaK, often spelled *Tanakh*.

The twenty-two total agrees with Flavius Josephus, the Jewish historian. Josephus lived to witness the destruction of the Temple in Jerusalem (AD 70). He commented that the Jews had twenty-two books (J, *WJ*, *Flavius Josephus against Apion*, 1.8), that is, these were "scrolls" (rolls of papyrus), not *books* in our sense. (Later, a book-type copy of certain Scriptures was called a *codex*.)

This twenty-two division helps one understand the comments of Jesus and His followers when they speak of the OT writings. For instance, in Luke 24:44 Jesus says: ". . . everything written about Me in the Law of Moses, the Prophets, and the Psalms must be fulfilled." Here in a concise statement, Christ refers to all three major divisions of the OT. He says the OT spoke of *Him* in the Law, the Prophets, and in the Psalms. As such, the term *Psalms* is collective, including those books in the *third* section, called the Writings.

> Psalms is the *first* book in the third section of the OT Hebrew canon, and therefore, it is sometimes given the role of speaking for all the other books in this third category.

At the time of Jesus, it was a custom to refer to the entire OT either by the term *Law* or *Scriptures* (Luke 24:27; John 10:34). This is what Paul does when he writes to Timothy and tells him to remain faithful to the whole OT, since "all *Scripture* is given by inspiration of God" (2 Timothy 3:16).

It should also be mentioned that the total number, stated above, varies between 22 and 24. The reason for this is that at times the book of Ruth was counted with the book of Judges as one book, being recorded together on one scroll, that is, on the same scroll. This was also true of the book of Lamentations. It was written by the prophet Jeremiah; therefore, it was often included on the Jeremiah scroll. At other times, Ruth and Lamentations were counted separately, each having its own scroll, which made these two books easier to be carried and to be read at Jewish festivals. In any event, this separation away from Judges and Jeremiah brought the canon-count to 24 scrolls, not 22 as when Ruth and Lamentations were combined with Judges and Jeremiah, respectively. Now you analyze how these 24 books equal today's 39 OT books! It provides a good exercise as you recall all the books of the OT.

The Roman Catholic branch of the Christian church claims there are more than sixty-six books. Before the Reformation in the early 1500s, Roman Catholics and Protestants *both* held to the ancient, traditional count of sixty-six. After the RCC's Council of Trent, the number was increased (M, *EDV*, p. 36, pt. 10), partly due to Rome's need to enforce *doctrinal* teachings different than those taught by reformers, the likes of Drs. Martin Luther and John Calvin.

SOLVING
NEW TESTAMENT MYSTERIES
WITH
OLD TESTAMENT CLUES

EVIDENCE JUST TOO COINCIDENTAL TO BE ACCIDENTAL!!!

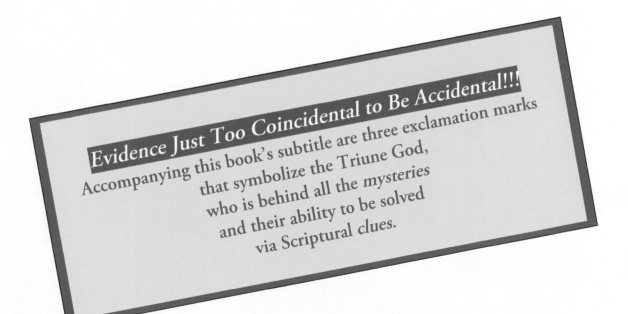

Evidence Just Too Coincidental to Be Accidental!!!
Accompanying this book's subtitle are three exclamation marks
that symbolize the Triune God,
who is behind all the mysteries
and their ability to be solved
via Scriptural clues.

Since we are investigating
the data of
the Scriptural scrolls,
and since
the Old and New Testaments
were originally written on
scrolls [rolls]
(cp. Luke 4:16c-17;
2 Timothy 4:13;
see B, *BP*, pp. 9-14),
you will find
the picture of a
SCROLL
at the
beginning of each chapter.

As you read Chapters 3–22, you will notice shaded boxes. The colors indicate the following: peach shading = definitions; green shading = fascinating data; gray shading = Bible commentators; yellow shading = reference to any appendix; purple shading = general information; blue shading = reference to an ancient church history personage; gold shading = crucial comments; **bold white** and non-bold white lettering with gray shading = each chapter's ending summary, entitled **Evidence room conclusion:**. (The same color coding holds true for the appendices to this book.)

CHAPTER 3

OUR INVESTIGATION OF MYSTERIES BEGINS: FIRST THINGS FIRST

Examining Clues in the Evidence Room

*Do the four gospels sufficiently validate
the messianic credentials of Jesus?*

Our Overriding Investigative Questions

The primary goal of our investigative journey is to explore the life and ministry of Jesus, the One identified on the pages of the Bible's New Testament as "the Christ" ["the Messiah"] (Matthew 16:16–17). In so doing, three ultimate questions must be posed: (1) How could anyone living twenty centuries ago have been absolutely certain that Jesus of Nazareth was the long-expected Messiah? (2) In fact, how can anyone living today know for certain that Jesus Christ—that first-century AD human personality—is the world's Savior? (3) Besides, why would anyone be moved to accept Scripture's allegation that this Nazarene really was the Redeemer, a person whose promised "coming" had spanned some 4,000 years of previous Old Testament history?

This book aims to answer these *central* questions.

How? By *Solving New Testament Mysteries with Old Testament Clues* (clues that provide *Evidence Just Too Coincidental to Be Accidental!!!*).

To solve such New Testament mysteries, Bible detectives must unscramble the life and ministry of the Lord Jesus. His life story is recorded in the four gospels of the New Testament:

Matthew, Mark, Luke, and John. But to grasp the details presented in those four Gospels, readers must simultaneously decipher the meanings of various Old Testament passages. As will be shown, the "clues" hidden in these Old Testament texts will marvelously help solve many mysteries surrounding the *words* and *miraculous actions* of Jesus in the New Testament. Listen to the words of the legendary theologian Augustine: "The New Testament is in the Old concealed; the Old is by the New revealed."

> The four canonical Gospels are the main records detailing the birth, ministry, death, resurrection, and ascension of Jesus. (Both Luke and Acts describe His ascension back into heaven.)

We now begin an investigative journey that examines the accounts of the earthly sojourn of Jesus.

The Key Mystery and the Location of Its Initial Clues

Our mystery investigation first and foremost revolves around the main character of human history, Jesus Christ. To start, we must gather vital "clues" to substantiate His predicted and claimed credentials. This book's title states that we will gather such clues from the Old Testament. Thus, it may seem strange that we take our *initial* clues from the first four books of the New Testament.

Why? Well, as odd as it may seem, those first four books are primarily reports of a transition from Old Testament times to New Testament realities.

What does that mean?

It means that the New Testament does not *start* until the near *end* of each of the four canonical Gospels. Only on the eve of Jesus's arrest and crucifixion did the actual time of the New Testament begin. In reality, it only began when Christ instituted the Lord's Supper by saying that the cup of wine His disciples were about to drink was the "New Testament"; that is, the "New Covenant" or "New Last Will and Testament" in His blood. In this way, Christ was telling His disciples that the fulfillment of the predictions of the Old Testament were now at the redemptive point of *imminent*

> John 13–17 reports words spoken by Jesus at the Last Supper, but *not* the special words connected with the bread and wine and the body and blood. See 1 Corinthians 11:25 for the Apostle Paul's reiteration of those exact words of Jesus, words that would later be reported in the first three gospels, Matthew, Mark, and Luke.

fulfillment—yes, New Testament times were now kicking in (Matthew 26:28; Mark 14:24; Luke 22:20).

What does this have to do with our investigation into the credentials of Jesus? Much!

When our clue-gathering initially begins in the New Testament's first books, it will really concern clues discovered on the basis of words spoken *before* the New Testament began. And so technically, these clues will be Old Testament clues!

Initial Clue-Gathering in the Four Gospels

Since we will be dealing with the *life* and *ministry* of Jesus, it is obviously wise to begin in the four gospels *before* backtracking to the Old Testament books for a more chronological approach.

To somewhat repeat, our primary investigative sources will be Matthew, Mark, Luke, John, and in one case, Acts, whose first chapter completes the four gospels, giving an account of the final days of Jesus on earth.

These initial New Testament writings can easily be referred to as "The *Who Is He?* Books" since they reveal *who* Jesus always was from all eternity, *who* He became on earth through His human birth, and *who* He now is to all eternity. Thus, we ask, *Who is Jesus?* Jesus is the God-Man, and He still

> Compare Revelation 1:8c–f: "the Lord, the One-*Who*-Is and the One-*Who*-Was and the One-*Who*-Will-Be" (also note 1:5).

possesses both a *divine* nature and a *human* nature in heaven (cp. Revelation 1:7–8; 5:6; 19:6–8); this the New Testament teaches.

"Who" Clues

As we consider *who* Jesus is, and subsequently *who* we are in His overall earthly and eternal plans, we will use an analogy to a popular children's book from the early 1950s: Dr. Seuss's *Horton Hears a Who!* Horton was a kind and trustworthy elephant with huge ears that enabled him to hear a small cry from the inhabitants of Whoville – a tiny, dust-sized planet spinning out of control. Horton recognizes the problem, intervenes, and saves the "whos" and their beloved Whoville.

> Perhaps Dr. Seuss's Horton idea was inspired by Psalm 8:4: "What is man that You [God] should think of him, or a human being that You should come and visit him?"

A Scriptural parallel between the Seuss's creation and Bible truth is easy to spot.

Planet Earth was spinning out of control *with sin*; God the Father recognized the problem and "loved the world so much that He sent His one and only Son so that *who*ever believes in Him [Jesus] should not perish but have everlasting life" (John 3:16). In the Whoville analogy, Jesus is the Horton who intervened and saved earth's inhabitants from spinning out of control and whirling away into earthly and eternal hopelessness.

About the Gospels' *Who Is He?* Motif

While we are looking for Old Testament clues to solve New Testament mysteries, a quick stop to explain the *Who* motif in the gospels will prove most helpful and enlightening.

When exploring mysteries in the four gospels ("The Who Is He? Books"), Bible investigators will notice right from the beginning of the ministry of John the Baptizer—the introducer of Jesus and the last of the Old Testament prophets—that religious opponents came to John to interrogate him. Three different times religious opponents inquired, "*Who* are you?" John repeatedly told them he was *not* the promised One (John 1:19–34). Then the journey through the gospels intensifies; over and over readers find the terms *who* and

> Appendix 1 is a listing of those nearly forty references.

whom referring to Jesus nearly forty times. Repeatedly, those four gospels bring up the question of Jesus's identity. Is He truly *who* He says He is?

The four gospels are in perfect sync. They verify the ultimate answer to the "who" questions.

To start, Matthew creates a tone-setting genealogy; he proves Jesus to be the promised One *who* has the needed messianic credentials (Matthew 1). Matthew further substantiates his claims with evidence gathered from Old Testament messianic predictions, showing fulfillment after fulfillment coming to pass via the words and actions of Jesus.

> Several of Jesus's miracles will be explored in depth later on during our investigative journey.

Mark, the disciple of Peter the apostle, verifies that Jesus is the One filling the bill. The miracles of Jesus show *power* beyond words. Mark's reporting makes his readers recall similarities and see parallels between the miracles of Jesus and miracles from the Old Testament. Connectives between the miracles of former prophets and those of Jesus are cleverly suggested. Mark

> To note Peter's influence on the Gospel of Mark, read Mark 1:21–3:30 and Acts 2:22.

purposefully directs his Gospel to Roman citizens, most of whom worshiped *power* (cp. chapters 1; 3; 5). If Mark could prove Jesus to be the most powerful human ever, a Roman just might listen to the Christian message and even come to recognize Christ as God, a being far superior to the fickle Roman gods and their earthly armies.

Dr. Luke, a physician, skillfully handles the scalpel of his words to present both the heavenly and earthly credentials of Jesus in his Gospel. He presents much *medical* data relating to Jesus's total ministry, and thereby shows Jesus to be the capable "Great Physician" not only of body and mind, but also of soul and spirit; Luke affirms Jesus's credentials as Savior of all humanity (Luke 2:10–11).

John solidifies it all, as his first chapter reaches back into eternity to tell us *who* Jesus was and still is—the eternal Son of God (cp. John 20:31; 1 John 5:20).

The Bible wonderfully weaves all this evidence together to aid us human mystery-solvers.

Out of the nearly forty Greek *who* and *whom* evidence-indicating yellow markers at our investigative scene, we'll explore nine of them in depth as definitive evidence that the four gospels are initially intended to identify the Person of Jesus as the God-Man—the Savior of the world (cp. 1 John 4:14–15).

More Key Examples of the "Who's Who" of the Four Gospels

Our first above-mentioned example was a *threefold* example, combining three references from the Gospel of John (specifically 1:19, 21–22). The thrice-repeated word *who* in these verses all pertain to John the Baptizer, so they are counted as one, making them example #1.

The second of our nine *who* and *whom* examples can be cited at both Jesus's baptism in Matthew 3:17 and at His transfiguration in Matthew 17:5, where we hear nearly identical words repeated in both passages. On these occasions, the Father in heaven

> Most of the "who" occurrences serve as OT clues, testifying to the true identity of Jesus, the sent One.

identifies Jesus as the One *whom* He has sent to planet Earth: "This is My Son, *whom* I love and in *whom* I delight."

Third, some forty days after Jesus's baptism, John the Baptizer lets his critics know the true identity of Jesus. Upon seeing Jesus returning from His wilderness temptation, John remarked, "A Man is coming after me *who* ranks above me because He existed before me" (John 1:30). Surely, John was referring to the *eternal* Jesus, since the earthborn Jesus was six months younger than John himself (Luke 1:26, 36).

As things progress in a revelatory way throughout the ministry of Jesus, the world of unbelief even gets involved. In a fourth example, King Herod Antipas—son of Herod the Great who tried to kill Jesus at His birth—asks "*Who* is this Jesus I hear about?" (Luke 9:9), and the further context in Luke 9 lets us know that it is Jesus, the miracle-working King *who* is preaching about His own Kingdom (cp. vv. 6, 11).

Turning to example five, readers of Scripture even hear the demons of hell getting involved in the whole *who* process. These evil spirits, whom Jesus is exorcizing out of a possessed man, say to Jesus "Have You come to destroy us? I know *who* You are—the Holy One of God" (Mark 1:24). Incredible spiritual knowledge those demons possessed!

Sixth, when Jesus pronounces forgiveness upon a repentant woman, we discover mystified dinner guests asking, "*Who* is this Person *who* even forgives sin?" (Luke 7:49). As we continue to investigate, we learn more about the identity of this *who* in Matthew 9:6a. He is the "Son of Man," the One *who* has authority from on high both to forgive and to heal on earth (vv. 6b–8).

With the seventh example, we explore a twofold *who* that encompasses the arrest of Jesus in the Garden of Gethsemane. Twice Jesus asks the arresting soldiers, "*Who* is it that you are looking for?" (John 18:4, 7). The reply: "Jesus from Nazareth." By this time, New Testament readers know the identity of Jesus, though the full extent of His work is not yet understood.

The definite identity of Jesus is revealed in a most significant *who* passage—#8 in our count. This passage tells what happened at the city of Caesarea Philippi. Jesus asked His disciples, "*Who* do people say the Son of Man is?" After a few bogus answers from other disciples, Peter proclaims, "You are the Christ [the Messiah], the Son of the living God!" Jesus concludes that Peter's revelation came from His heavenly Father, the first *Who* who sent the saving *Who* [Jesus] to earth's Whoville (Matthew 16:13–17). Although Jesus's claim was comprehended, the method of His victory-to-be was still a big mystery to everyone.

Our ninth example is the ultimate *Who* passage and comes at the end of the Fourth Gospel. We hear it in John 21:12 when the disciples, surprised by an early morning appearance of the resurrected Christ on the shores of the northern Sea of Galilee, identify Jesus as He says, "Come, have breakfast." And then, that ultimate comment in John's Gospel: "None of the disciples dared to ask Him, '*Who* are You?' They knew it was the Lord."

By this time, Jesus's disciples knew who the *Who* of the earthly Whoville was, but

Beyond this compelling "who" data, the four gospels also have the highest privilege of presenting:

- The history of Jesus's birth,
- His preaching and miracle ministry,
- His suffering,
- His death,
- His resurrection, and
- His ascension.

more clarity as to His overall Person and mission was still needed. That clarity came at Pentecost, fifty days after the Passover, the day on which Christ died (Acts 2:22–24).

And so, our mystery-solving has begun, and there is so much more to come. Are you ever going to be surprised!

The effectiveness of those events to come spell S-A-L-V-A-T-I-O-N for those *who* endorse Christ as their Savior from sin, via their faith. Matthew 9:22 reminds us of that "faith" factor when we recall that Jesus often said to those He healed, "Your *faith* has made you well."

Evidence room conclusion: Jesus stands out as the most important "Who" in the *Who's Who* of history.

CHAPTER 4

CHRIST'S FIRST ADVENT: INITIAL OLD TESTAMENT *GENESIS* CLUES

Examining Clues in the Evidence Room
*"Who" were the earliest Old Testament believers expecting,
and in whom did they put their faith?*

Concerning Predictive Prophecy

Predictive prophecy is one of the many fascinating elements of Scripture. Although many people dream of being able to foretell the future, the Bible insists that only God knows the future for sure; only God knows for certain what will happen in both the near future and the far future (Isaiah 41:21–23; 42:8-9; 44:6–8; 45:21; 46:9–13; 47:8–15).

After the first man and woman—both of whom were created by the direct hand of God (Genesis 1:26–27; 2:7, 18–22)—sinned by eating fruit from the forbidden tree, God's former prophetic threat took its toll. He had predicted, "The day you eat from it [from 'the tree of the knowledge of good and bad'], you will certainly die" (Genesis 2:17). That first human couple did die *spiritually* on the very day they ate from that tree. Later, they also died *physically*—like the rest of humanity that followed. Death came to rule all over planet Earth (cp. Genesis 5:3–31).

Then came God's Good News, His *proto-evangel*, His "*first* Gospel" promise. In His mercy and grace He prophesied the eventual birth of a boy-child who would save humanity (Genesis 3:15).

Michael E. Fuller, PhD, professor of early Judaism and biblical studies, gives a marvelous breakdown of the Genesis 3:15 messianic text (F, *UB*, pp. 223–224).

Did Adam Believe God's Genesis 3:15 Promise?

He did. After several consequences for the first disobedience were dished out by God (Genesis 3:16–19), the man gave his wife a proper name—Eve, which means *life.* An ironic name! A clue: The man named his wife Life right after she had brought "death" into the world. This shows without a doubt that this man Adam believed the *first* "Gospel" promise. How is this shown? Adam's naming of Eve indicates that he comprehended God's promise to send a "Life-giving" Savior, who would come from one of her descendants.

The first recording of the man's proper name "Adam" is not recorded until Genesis 5:1.

Remember that Jesus Himself later said: "I am the Way, the Truth, and the *Life*" (John 14:6). Yes, from Eve came "life" from one generation to another until Jesus was born. As the Gospel of John says of Jesus, "In Him was *life*, and the *Life* was the Light of mankind" (1:5).

Another New Testament mystery solved with an Old Testament clue. Astounding!

Did Eve Believe God's Promise of a Savior to Come?

She did. At the birth of her firstborn son, Cain, she exclaimed: "I have gotten a man, the LORD" (Genesis 4:1). Most English Bible translations have missed the importance of the Hebrew term *'eth* and have translated, "I have gotten a man *with the help of* the LORD," treating *'eth* in a prepositional way. Very doubtful. Another clue: *'eth* was an *appositional* indicator, defining *what* the "man"-child would be—both God as well as a human male, the God-Man.

While both Adam and Eve did believe in God's promise of a Savior to come, just how much did they understand about this coming Savior? Though it might seem appropriate to treat this complex question at this time, let's discuss it later when we

For further verification of the validity of the translation, "I have gotten a man, the LORD," refer to the fascinating, substantiating data recorded in Appendix 2.

explore Old Testament "types" in relation to Abraham's sacrifice of Isaac in Chapter 5. (Hold on! You *will* be surprised by the answer!)

In any event, the correct understanding of *'eth* in Genesis 4:1 indicates that Eve believed *her* son Cain was the promised Savior. What can be said of Eve's conclusion? *Right idea, wrong kid!* The world would have to wait on *God's* timetable—some 4,000 years later when Messiah Jesus was born!

Lamech, a Noteworthy Old Testament Believer

Lamech, a ninth-generation descendant of Adam who lived over 1,000 years after Creation, also mistook *his* newborn son, Noah, to be the Savior. Still another clue: "When Lamech was 182, he had a son, and he called him Noah, saying, 'He will *comfort* us as we work and are weary because the LORD has cursed the ground'" (Genesis 5:29).

> Noah: "Comfort."

This whole passage came to light for me when I heard that Reverend Richard Ramirez, *a pastor* at Messiah Evangelical Lutheran Church and School in Fairview Park, Ohio, USA, had connected Jesus's "crown of thorns" back to the "curse" God had put on Adam when He said,

> . . . cursed is the ground on account of you. Weary from work you will eat your food as long as you live. The ground will grow *thorns* and thistles for you, and you will eat the plants in the field. In the sweat of our face you will eat bread until you go back to the ground . . . (Genesis 3:17–19).

Suddenly the connective between Jesus's crown of thorns and Genesis 3:17–19 became so obvious.

Then Genesis 5:29 also popped into my head. Lamech was expecting the coming of the "Thorn-Take-Awayer" who would bring "comfort" by removing sin, a blood removal by Jesus, the "Curse Remover," who would eventually rid the world of the curse of *thorns*. (The "blood removal" aspect comes from Genesis 3:21 and 4:4; this concept will be treated in our next chapter.)

Once again, another Old Testament believer [Lamech] had the *right idea, wrong kid!*

> Notice 2 Corinthians 1:3–5, where both the Father and Son bring *comfort*. This "comfort" aspect belongs to the whole Trinity.

The *right child* eventually came, and He promised: "I will ask the Father, and He will give you another Comforter [Helper] to be with you forever. He is the Spirit of Truth . . ." (John 14:16–17). The obvious Comforter initially detected is the Holy Spirit, the Third Person of the Trinity.

However, insightful Bible detectives who are traveling with us on our investigative journey will notice that Jesus promises "another" Comforter. Implication: Jesus is also a Comforter, *the* Comforter Lamech was expecting!

Conclusion: When in heaven, curse-weary work will be over, sin will be no more, and every saved soul will have eternal *comfort*.

Clues, clues, clues—all solving New Testament mysteries with Old Testament data.

Evidence room conclusion: The earliest OT personages were expecting the coming of the One who would put an end to the original curses caused by sinful disobedience. They trusted God's first messianic promise (Genesis 3:15) and placed their faith in the promised One, looking forward to His appearing.

CHAPTER 5

CHRIST'S FIRST ADVENT: ABRAHAMIC OLD TESTAMENT *GENESIS* CLUES

Examining Clues in the Evidence Room
*Do varying Old Testament indicators
really point forward to Christ?*

A Crucial Discussion As We Begin Investigating Genesis 22

Welcome to Genesis 22, the account of Abraham's sacrifice of his son, Isaac. It is one of Scripture's more familiar stories that many will recognize. (Do yourself a favor and read Genesis 22 at this time.) This Bible chapter demonstrates what Scripture, at times, refers to as *types*. Such literary phenomena can also be described as predictive *pictures*, *analogies*, *parallels*, or *connectors* that prefigure persons, places, or things pertaining to the future. Sometimes "types" were designed by God to paint parallels that pointed ahead to Jesus and His earthly sojourn. It can be stated this way: God had Old Testament figures

> Have you detected any parallels to Jesus's life in Genesis 22? One group of my African students instantly detected eight *connectors*—with very minimal help! View these eight at the end of this chapter.

act out in shadowy, weakened ways what Christ Jesus—the prefigured, predicted One—later acted out in real and perfectly completed ways.

Types, Pictures, Analogies, Parallels, Connectors, and Fulfillments

Types are easy to spot and endorse when Scripture succinctly identifies them as such: Romans 5:14b: "Adam was a type [Greek: *tupos*; picture, comparison] of Him who was to come."

> Examine Kuske's insightful discussion of *type* in K, *BI*, pp. 99–102, also section 12 on p. 111.

The problem with typology, however, is that Bible interpreters sometimes go "hog wild" and find parallels not intended by Scripture. For example, when one evaluates types endorsed by various influential church fathers of the past, many of their conclusions seem "off the wall," while others appear legit (cp. B, *ROTNC*, Part II, 4–61). Emeritus New Testament Professor David P. Kuske of Wisconsin Lutheran Seminary-Mequon, Wisconsin, USA, a master Scriptural exegete, sounds several overall warnings concerning *types*. He strongly dismisses the number of "types" that have been cited by pastor and writer William Graham Scroggie (1877 to 1958) between the Old Testament Joseph and the New Testament Jesus (K, *BI*, pp. 101–102). At first glance, Scroggie's comparisons seem quite feasible, but a crucial question arises: Did God intend these similarities to be predictive of the coming Christ? Any careful interpreter must question the presence of definite clues that absolutely suggest this in the Scriptural account of Joseph. Certainly many will disagree.

Also, in contrast to our following treatment of Genesis 22, Kuske would again protest. He contends that the Genesis 22 context "only" warrants one true type (K, *BI*, p. 100)—the ram, which foreshadows Jesus, the Lamb of God (vv. 13–14).

> Charles Porterfield Krauth, a former champion of orthodoxy in the Lutheran church, writes: "A type is a person or thing divinely foreappointed as the symbol of a person or thing not yet revealed" (K, *CRT*, p. 716; cp. L, *EC*, p. 155).
>
> Those interested in an extensive treatment of "typology" will find Fairbairn's *The Typology of Scripture* (470 pages) quite enlightening. Note F, *TS* in this book's Bibliography.

As a Bible interpreter, I paint with a brush a bit broader than Kuske's. Yet, for the sake of carefulness, our present investigation will usually label the similarities between Abraham the father and God the Father, between Isaac the son and Jesus the Son of God, as analogies, applications, and parallels—and not as *types*, that is, *until* we look back through New Testament glasses.

Here is the dilemma: Many, like Kuske, react very negatively against the sad history of *eisegesis*. A rightful concern. Caution guards in favor of the Bible's warning that no one should "add" to Scripture (cp. Deuteronomy 4:2 with Revelation 22:18–19). However, there is another danger mentioned in those two passages, namely, "taking away" or "subtracting" from the depth of Scripture. To fail to point out the fuller meaning of a passage can also be negligence on a level

> *Eisegesis*: fanciful interpretation, or, in detective language, false investigative conclusions.

with the sin of "adding." Both the limiting and expanding of Bible texts finds an exegete on an interpretive tightrope, an investigator's nightmare, with a remaining demand to be totally faithful. (Note Norman Geisler's and Limbaugh's cautions about *typology* at L, *EC*, p. 157.)

In relation to the whole handling of types, pictures, analogies, parallels, and connectors, much emphasis has been put on the reality of "progressive revelation"—the teaching that God only *gradually* revealed more and more to His people over time. In part, this truth is substantiated by 1 Peter 1:10–12 when Peter states that the prophets of the Old Testament did not always comprehend what they had written. Hidden truths had been given to them by the Holy Spirit through a process known as inspiration (2 Peter 1:20; 2 Timothy 3:16), which affirms that the prophets were servants of God who were not in control of divine mysteries—God was!

So, we are told in 1 Peter 1:10–12 that the prophets had to go back and search through what they had written to try "to find out *what Person* and *what time* the Spirit of Christ in them was pointing out when He [the Spirit] predicted the sufferings of Christ and the glories [His resurrection and ascension] that would follow."

A fuller revelation culminated when God's New Testament people better came to understand the "fulfillment" aspects of Old Testament prediction via the Pentecost experience (Acts 2).

But not so fast. Does 1 Peter 1 say the Old Testament prophets remained in the dark even *after* their investigations? For certain, they never reached the total, fuller understanding that Bible readers have today as a result of the greater revelations written on the pages of the New Testament. Today's readers have so many more facts that constitute New Testament *fulfillment*.

However, concerning the possible reality of a fuller comprehension than is usually granted Old Testament personages, there is much more to be considered.

The J-E-D-P Crowd

If you are not familiar with the code J-E-D-P, each letter stands for a possible different writer of the Torah or Pentateuch; together the letters represent a theory of diverse contributors. The J stands for a writer who supposedly favored the Name *Yahweh* (Jehovah or LORD) in his OT sections. E favored *Elohim*, another name which is translated "God." D stands for the writer called the Deuteronomist, while P indicates those sections penned by one known as the priestly author.

It is all so subjective. The endorsers of the J-E-D-P theory differ among themselves as they wildly speculate. I once heard that one scholar speculated that there were sixty-four different writers for the first five books of the Old Testament. Though I never saw this verified, I do have a copy of Peter Ellis's *The Men and the Message of the Old Testament*. Ellis color codes portions of *Genesis* to *Deuteronomy*, indicating which verses were written by which writers, *even* splitting verses in half, saying they come from two different authors, *even* proposing an additional editor called a "redactor" who gave portions a final edit. (Ellis's whole color coding selection can be found at E, *MMOT*, pp. 57–71.) It's a real rainbow of colors—and it takes way more faith to believe this nonsensical approach than the Bible's claim that Moses penned these books, as Jesus said, Moses "wrote about Me" (John 5:46). (Some J-E-D-P scholars dismiss Christ's statement by saying that Jesus knew Moses had not written what the Old Testament Scriptures claim, but He didn't want to get into an argument with the authorities of His day, so He did not bring it up. Nice try!)

The J-E-D-P theory is now being proven to be outdated, false, and incorrect. See C, *RB*, 386 pages of irrefutable argumentation. Present advocates of the J-E-D-P theory can now find an illuminated path that reveals why this theory needs to be dismantled—and how it can be done!

Many Bible exegetes are called "higher critical" scholars. They deny the genuineness of *remote* predictive prophecy in the Old Testament. As a result, these interpreters are forced to reject the authenticity of biblical authorship of writers like Moses, Isaiah, or Daniel—and this is in spite of the fact that for centuries Christian teachers taught that such Bible writers truly were the authors, as claimed in their books.

But today a great number of seminary professors and pastors *teach that* these Bible books were really written by others. This contrary approach *teaches that* formerly assumed predictive prophecy is really *vaticinium ex eventu* (prophecy after the event). In short, it is said that many Old Testament books are fraudulent writings. They purport to be making predictions about the future when, in fact, they are merely pretending to make predictions of events that had already taken place.

Isn't hindsight great? Anyone can make predictions of events that have already happened.

Make no mistake about it, this type of interpretation empties Scripture of God's messianic predictions concerning Jesus, and, in turn, voids God of His ability to foretell the future, the very thing God insists He can do (read Isaiah 41–44).

This "higher critical" destruction of sound biblical evidence pertaining to predictive prophecy is a method of interpretation called the "documentary hypothesis" or in code letters: the J-E-D-P theory. This theory comes in many *contradictory* forms and assumes that more *advanced* Old Testament knowledge only came into vogue way later than the days of Abraham, Moses, or David, only near the *end* of Old Testament times.

Alongside this interpretive J-E-D-P hypothesis comes the *Sitz im Leben* deduction which assumes that ordinary Old Testament personages—and even God's prophets themselves—had a very limited knowledge of New Testament things. In other words, Old Testament people were basically unaware of any true depth pertaining to so-called predictive, messianic prophecies from the Garden of Eden forward through most of the years of Old Testament history. They could not have been told future things because predictive prophecy was a non-entity.

> *Sitz im Leben:* "life situation" or "setting" or "understanding" of an original reader.

The *Sitz im Leben* Lure

A greater folly follows: Many fine, conservative Bible scholars have fallen for some of the *Sitz im Leben* deductions. True, they believe and teach that God had the ability to relate facts about the future in the Old Testament, even future facts about Jesus—His coming, His person, His redemptive work. Yet at the same time, they hesitate to believe that men like Adam, Abraham, and David could have comprehended very much of the meaning of those messianic prophecies.

Even in regard to 1 Peter 1:10–12, many orthodox professors and pastors tend to believe that when Old Testament writers went on their "searches," they came up pretty much empty. Such Bible leaders have been swallowed up by the *Sitz im Leben* phenomena, deducing that the "life situations" or "settings" of Old Testament personages would make most messianic comprehension *impossible*. Oh, to be sure, they grant some of the more general knowledge, like Old Testament believers knew a definite "Someone" was coming to deal with physical and spiritual problems common to humankind—but nothing too specific about that coming One or His eventual work (Psalm 14:7).

Is that so? I beg to differ.

The *Sitz im Leben* data is flooded with "iffy" conclusions. Amos 3:7 says, "But the Lord GOD does not do anything without telling His secret plan to His servants, the prophets."

Whoa! We better hold our horses and avoid reaching rapid, hasty conclusions.

How can Bible readers know what Old Testament personalities really understood? Were any of them there to question Adam, Noah, Abraham, David, or Amos?

Also, does 1 Peter 1:10–12 say the prophets never received fuller answers when they contemplated what they had written?

Instead, Scriptural investigators are enlightened when they hear Hebrews 11:19—with its reference back to Genesis 22—reporting that Abraham believed in the possibility of "resurrection." How did Abraham learn of this rising-from-the-dead stuff? Had he learned it from Job 19:25–26 or from Genesis 3:15 or possibly from God Himself when the LORD may have instructed him concerning *resurrection* during His previous tent-visit (Genesis 18:1)?

In the Genesis 3:15 passage—the first promise of a Savior, it was predicted that the coming Descendant would have His "*heel* bruised," whereas, the serpent (Satan himself, cp. Revelation 12:9) would have his "*head* bruised." Did this indicate Jesus's resurrection from the dead, since one can recover from a "bruised heel," but no one survives a "bruised head," meaning a "*crushed* head" (definitely see Romans 16:20)? In short and in "seed" form, Genesis 3:15 predicted the ultimate decimation of the devil and the eventual resurrection victory of Jesus.

From another point of argumentation, we ask, Why could Abraham not have known about life after death? He certainly could have been informed of this during the lengthy conversation he had with his three heavenly Guests who came to his tent (Genesis 18), especially considering the implications of verses 1–8. (I was taught that some early church fathers taught that the three tent Guests were the Father, Son, and Holy Spirit.)

For certain, Hebrews 11 says Abraham believed God could do what humans think impossible (cp. Luke 1:37), namely bring a sacrificed Isaac back *from the dead*.

An Example: Two Mountains

To help solve some ongoing *typology* concerns, let's imagine viewing two mountains. From far away, they may appear very close to one another, but when the first mountain is reached, one realizes that the second mountain is still far off in the distance. Today's Bible investigators are like that; they are between two mountain locations—Jesus's first coming and His second coming. Looking back, they understand a sizeable amount of Old Testament data because they have New Testament explanations, but looking ahead they can only apprehend certain truths. Worldly "end things" and God's plans for the future, not so much. (1 Corinthians 13:12b: "Now I learn only in part, but then I shall know as He has known me.")

Now think for a moment.

Can today's people look back *onto* the other side of that "first coming" mountain and know all that was going on, the totality of what God had revealed to Old Testament believers? This does not seem likely. How can one be sure, then, that a person like Abraham could *not* have understood *types* and prefigured predictions in more depth than Bible scholars may assume?

Yes, the argument could be brought up as to why the Pharisees, even the disciples of Jesus, were so often in the dark as to the simplest of truths if the Old Testament personages had great enlightenment. Easy, threefold answer. First, the people of Jesus's time were so *law*-oriented that they could not see the truths of the Gospel when right before their very eyes truths that had been prophesied in the Old Testament.

Second, at times Jesus revealed truths (Matthew 13:17: matters possibly not revealed to the prophets of old), and at other times, He intentionally blocked understanding so people of His day could not, right then, interfere with God's eternal plans, plans concerning Jesus's crucifixion (John 2:23–25; 8:7, 30; 7:1–6; Acts 1:7). However, maybe these blocked facts had formerly been comprehended by Old Testament believers. Who knows?

There is yet another factor that holds much validity when interpreting the Old Testament, even when debate warns about seeing too much in a text. It is this: Moderns are people of the New Testament, and even if Abraham did not understand the importance of certain God-directed actions, why should today's Bible detectives not detect them—that is, after the fact—since they can now see fulfillments through the eyes of God Himself, the One who has revealed them more fully on the pages of the New Testament?

By this time in history, Bible sleuths can comprehend God's formerly directed messages to Abraham and Isaac through the prophetic actions recorded in Genesis 22, and as interpreted in the light of Jesus happenings in the New Testament.

Yet, we cannot look back *behind* the "first coming" mountain and know everything a man like Abraham comprehended; also, we cannot understand everything that will take place *beyond* the "second coming" mountain. Only those new revelations portrayed on the pages of the New Testament give us a super grasp of the meanings of certain realities *between* the Old and New Testament mountains—and only a limited grasp of realities *behind* the "Old Testament" mountain and *beyond* the "New Testament" mountain are available. Think about it, Bible examiners!

Interpreting Genesis 22 without Subtracting or Adding

God told father Abraham to take his only son, Isaac, on a three-day journey to the Mount Moriah range of hills. There he was to sacrifice Isaac on an altar. When they arrived on that third day, the wood to be used for the fire of sacrifice was laid on Isaac's back, and Isaac carried it up the mountain. When they both reached the mountaintop, Isaac was bound and placed on an altar to be stabbed to death with Abraham's knife. Just when Isaac's blood was to be shed before the fire was set, the special Angel or Messenger of the LORD called out of heaven to stop the sacrifice.

> This special Angel or Messenger was the pre-incarnate Jesus who often appears in the OT to protect His own genealogical line. See, for example, three OT locations as to His identity in Exodus 3:2, 13–14; Isaiah 63:9; Malachi 3:1.

Genesis 22 also tells about a ram that was seen caught by his horns in a bush; it had been provided by God as a *substitute* sacrifice for Isaac. Result: Isaac went free and eventually fathered Jacob [Israel] to keep the crucial messianic line alive so that Jesus could later be born to fulfill God the Father's divine plan.

The Genesis 22 account is laced with parallel pictures of the Christ to come, as well as intriguing predictive flavor that we should see when looking *back* through glasses wiped clear by New Testament fulfillment.

There are no less than eight (8) clue-like *types* and likenesses to Jesus, as well as New Testament salvation factors that reveal *"Evidence Just Too Coincidental to Be Accidental!!!"*

1. Abraham is told to sacrifice his "only" son Isaac; yet, Abraham also had *another* son, named Ishmael. In theological terms, however, Isaac was the *only* son of the "promise"—the promise that Jesus would later be born from Isaac's genealogical line (Genesis 21:12; Hebrews 11:18; Galatians 4:29–30), not Ishmael's. In view of this whole Abrahamic account, it is easy to see the parallel fulfillment of this Genesis 22 *type* when the New Testament calls Jesus "the one and *only* Son" of God (John 3:16).

2. Abraham was told to sacrifice Isaac on one of the hills that was on the Mount Moriah range (Genesis 22:2). The Temple in Jerusalem was later built on one of these Moriah hills (2 Chronicles 3:1) where lambs were sacrificed, typifying the later bloody death of Jesus. That hill where Abraham took Isaac would seem to be this later Temple hill.

Was this *also* the same hill where Christ was later crucified? No, that was Calvary—a different hill on that *same* mountain range, dictated by the fact that Jesus had to die "outside" the city of Jerusalem as our Scapegoat (Leviticus 16:22; Hebrews 13:12; John 19:19–20). More on this in a later chapter.

The fact that Abraham lived in the southern city of Beersheba at the time God told him to journey to Moriah (Genesis 21:30–34) is of interest. This meant Abraham's trip would have taken him right along a road that cut through the place where the *later* city of Bethlehem would be located.

By viewing OT truth through NT glasses, one would be justified to state a *theological* and *historic* truth, declaring, "All roads lead through Bethlehem to Calvary and onward to heaven" (Giessler). This "Bethlehem" conclusion was first picked up, in part, from an insight provided by Henry A. Harper (H, *AD*, p. 15). Perhaps this is more "*Evidence Just Too Coincidental to Be Accidental!!!*" Hmm?

---

3. Next, we need to note the *typological* parallel between *Abraham the father* and *Isaac the "only" son*, as well as *God the Father* and *Jesus the "only" Son*. Need more be said, literary detectives?

4. In Genesis 22:4 readers learn that Abraham and Isaac took a *three-day* journey to Moriah. The writer of Hebrews 11:17–19 sees significance in the fact that Abraham, "by faith," got Isaac back alive, even though it seemed certain

It is also most interesting that the Apostle Paul in 1 Corinthians 15:4 notes that the OT "Scriptures" had said Jesus would rise "on the third day." The Genesis 22 context, along with Hosea 6:2 and Jonah 1:17 (cp. Matthew 12:40) serve to be the very "Scriptures" to which Paul refers.

that Isaac would remain dead after being sacrificed. In this connection, there is something of great importance that should not be missed: Abraham received Isaac back alive on that "third day," the same day his three-day journey was accomplished. Did you catch that, remembering Jesus was given back alive to His Father after "three" days in the grave? Just another little clue along the way.

5. What did Abraham lay on Isaac's back for their trip up Moriah's mountain of sacrifice? Wood; yes, wood! Does that ring a bell concerning Jesus? He also carried the "wood" of His cross toward Moriah's Calvary.

While Abraham would *not* have made this parallel connection, it certainly would have been present in the mind of God from the beginning of His salvation plan, since God knows all things (cp. John 21:17b). Let's call it a "parallel" for terminology's sake. God is omniscient; therefore, we have every right to see certain textual parallels, even if certain *types* were only understood by God Himself in former times.

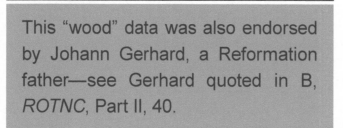

This "wood" data was also endorsed by Johann Gerhard, a Reformation father—see Gerhard quoted in B, *ROTNC*, Part II, 40.

Once again, today's Bible readers are people of the New Testament, where many veils have been removed (cp. 2 Corinthians 3:12–18).

6. Another interesting *type* relates to Isaac's obedience and willingness to be sacrificed. Years ago, I was taught that Jewish tradition says Isaac was 25 years old when he traveled to Moriah. If true, He could easily have overpowered his 125-year-old father (analyze this calculation in the light of Genesis 21:5). Instead, Isaac was *passively* obedient; he willingly permitted himself to be acted upon. The parallel: Jesus was also *passively* obedient to His Father when He permitted Himself to be arrested and crucified though He had the power to escape (cp. John 18:4–9); yet, He willingly drank the cup of suffering His Father demanded for our release.

7. One of the easiest types to be considered pertains to the *ram* that was caught and offered up in the place of Isaac (Genesis 22:13b: "instead of his son"). Clearly, the ram was a picture of Jesus, the Lamb of God, who was sacrificed *in our place*, as the *substitute* for our wrongdoings (Revelation 5:6, 9).

8. The final interesting type-like indicator presented here is communicated by the words, "Abraham named that place 'The-LORD-Will-Provide'" (Genesis 22:14). As Scripture concludes in John 3:16: "God loved the world [all people] so much that He gave ['provided'] His one and only Son . . . ."

> A tradition says the OT contains 333 promises of the coming Messiah! While some of these messianic prophecies will be explored on our investigative journey, they, along with other ones, are listed in chart form in Appendix 3. In addition, David Limbaugh's book also has a magnificent discussion of messianic prophecy (L, *EC*, see "messianic prophecies" page listings in his Index).

9. David Limbaugh adds another not mentioned above (L, *EC*, p. 39): ". . . Isaac becomes a type of Christ. Also significant is his [Isaac's] 'miraculous birth,' . . . ." For Limbaugh, it would seem, the miraculous birth of Jesus is a typological parallel. Obviously, he does not mean to say that Isaac's birth is an *absolute* parallel to Jesus's miraculous "virgin birth." It is just an interesting typological picture.

Evidence room conclusion: There were many *literary* indicators and action scenarios that God used to preview His Son's coming and to hint at aspects of the saving work Jesus would carry out. OT clues must be spotted to apply them to NT mysteries.

PART II

STARTING OUR JOURNEY INTO
THE NEW TESTAMENT

CHAPTER 6

INITIAL INSIGHTS GOVERNING NEW TESTAMENT INVESTIGATIONS

Examining Clues in the Evidence Room

*Does further data from the four gospels
solidify Christ's credibility?*

Acts 10:43: The Key New Testament Investigative Scripture Reference

Vital Old Testament interpretive groundwork—a basis for solid future investigative procedure—was laid in former chapters. Now it is necessary to provide a parallel New Testament foundation that can and will move us forward—with essential spiritual insight—into the *mysteries* of the life of Christ: His birth, early years, preaching and miracle ministries, His suffering, death, resurrection, and ascension. The remaining chapters of our book will use this firm foundation to unravel these mysteries with Old Testament clues.

Among others, one key indicator cements this foundation. It must be followed if solid evidence is to be gathered by Bible

David Limbaugh, agreeing with several other writers of the past, contends that " . . . we can see Christ on every page of the Old Testament as well as the New"—and in so doing, he again reminds us of the Augustine quote that reinforces it: "The New Testament is in the Old concealed; the Old is by the New revealed" (L, *EC*, pp. 3, 15).

investigators as they tackle numerous biblical mysteries. This important New Testament presupposition is given in Acts 10:43: *"All the prophets testify about Him* [my emphasis] that through His Name everyone who believes in Him receives forgiveness for his sins."* In other words, God's Old Testament spokespersons—all of them—talked about Christ's future coming and His work of redemption. They spoke of His person, His work, and the outcome of His earthly mission. All of this leads to the irrefutable conclusion that the whole Old Testament is *Christ-centered.* This is both a presupposition as well as a major factor for our investigation to prove as it moves from chapter to chapter.

Crucial info: Even *non-writing* OT prophets—like Elijah and Elisha—foretold the eventual coming of Christ. They also prove to be *Christ-centered.* How they accomplished this will be shown later in this book.

Matthew's Starting Point

The narrative in the Gospel of Matthew had a purpose: to convince Jews that Jesus of Nazareth was the Messiah they had been expecting for so many years (Matthew 11:3; cp. Luke 24:21; John 7:31). To accomplish this goal, Matthew began his Gospel with a "genealogy" of Jesus's family line. If Matthew could convince a Jew that Jesus was from the right stock—from Abraham, Judah, and King David's family—he had an ear that might listen to the rest of his presentation. Following that genealogy, Matthew then immediately writes, "This is how Jesus Christ was born."

A fascinating clue that revolves around Matthew's genealogical mathematics, as well as Luke's parallel genealogy of Jesus, has been relegated to Appendix 4.

Both Matthew and Dr. Luke endorse the truth of Jesus's "virgin" birth. Now *there's* a mystery to explore! Nobody would accept *that* notion (except by faith or pure stupidity, right?) Well, that's where our unconventional God comes in. He has Matthew, a Jew and disciple of Jesus, translate Isaiah 7:14 with the Greek *parthénos* ("virgin"), thus endorsing that virgin-birth doctrine which is so often massacred by unbelieving scholars.

The ancient *Ras Shamra* tablets found at the city of Ugarit record a word related to *almāh*, one that can only mean "virgin."

Such scholars love to say that Isaiah, who writes, "An *almāh* will conceive and give birth to a son," did not use the correct Hebrew term for "virgin." Rather, he chose a term that should be translated "young woman." They contend that the Hebrew *bethūlāh* means *virgin*, not Isaiah's *almāh*.

Nonsense! In Genesis 24:16, *bethūlāh* is defined with the phrase, "no man had lived with her," while Genesis 24:43 lets *almāh* stand alone when defining Rebekah as an unmarried *virgin* who is worthy to be Isaac's wife.

Additional evidence proving that *bethūlāh* could not be limited to a true virgin is found in Joel 1:8. It says, "Wail like a *bethūlāh*, girded with sackcloth, weeping over the young man she married in her youth." What, she remained a virgin during her whole married life? Most unlikely.

Best Attestations to Jesus's Virgin Birth

Matthew reports that Mary, the mother of Jesus, never had sexual relations prior to her pregnancy (1:18b). Dr. Luke records many more details about those virgin-birth aspects. He tells of God's angel Gabriel visiting Mary in her Nazareth home. He writes, "The virgin's name was Mary" (Luke 1:27b). After God's angel Gabriel informed Mary that she was going to have a baby, "Mary asked the angel, 'How can this be? I have had no [sexual] relations with a man'" (Luke 1:34).

Question: Why would Mary have had reason to lie when she was not yet pregnant and had minimal understanding of the depth of what she had just been told? Gabriel filled that gap of

> The verb tense employed by Dr. Luke (1:35) is a present participle ("being born"), as William F. Arndt (of Bauer, Arndt, Gingrich, Danker lexicon fame) notes: ". . . the conception which the angel announces was taking place at the very time when he [Gabriel] spoke to her [Mary]" (A, *GL*, pp. 51, 53).

mystery. He announced, "The Holy Spirit will come over you, and power of the Most High will overshadow you. And for that reason the Holy Being 'being born' [of you] will be called the Son of God." Of course, the whole biblical episode seems unbelievable.

Gabriel's declaration to the startled Mary demanded faith. Therefore, she was told, "There is nothing that God will not be able to do" (Luke 1:37).

> Luke also uses the Greek term *parthénos* which is universally acknowledged to mean "virgin," and *only* virgin; Matthew uses the same Greek term in Matthew 1:23.

But what about the greater context? The writer is Luke, a medical doctor (Colossians 4:14). Therefore, one should logically ask, What doctor in his right mind would ever have a woman come into his office and believe her wild story that she had become pregnant without the implanting of sperm from a male human being—without any sexual interaction? Only a quack doctor! Luke, however, was a highly intelligent physician, as the sophisticated Greek used in his two New Testament writings—Luke and Acts—proves.

Wow! That God of the New Testament is so stupendous! He uses seeming nonsense to make fools of the wise. God has a brilliant doctor verify a virgin birth. A mystery to be sure, but with powerful clues on all sides—and then He gets the last laugh!

> 1 Corinthians 1:20–25 describes the God of the Bible as One who is always ahead of the game, and Psalm 2:4a says He "sits . . . in heaven" and "laughs" at unbelief.

A Preliminary Miracle—God's Greatest

God had just pulled off the greatest miracle of all time—the *incarnation* (Latin: *in* = in; *carnis* = flesh). Yes, it is true. Jesus came to earth in the flesh (John 1:14), and this is certified to be a *mystery* of greatest proportion—even greater than God's act of Creation or the resurrection of Jesus! 1 Timothy 3:16: "There is no doubt about it (KJV:

> Appendix 5 (Christianity's Heart and Core) lists the "five reasons" that God the Father sent His Son to earth.

'Without controversy'), great is the mystery of our religion—He [Jesus] appeared in flesh . . . ." There's a *mustērion* for you! This time it comes via a clue given on the pages of the New Testament, providing more evidence for every alert Bible investigator.

> *mustērion*: In the Greek NT, this term indicates a "God mystery" that can only be *spiritually* comprehended, up to a point, by human followers of Christ (1 Corinthians 2:14–15).

The Actual Birth of Jesus in Bethlehem of Judea

Joseph—the legal (not actual) father of Jesus (Luke 3:23b)—was indirectly commanded by the Roman Emperor Caesar Augustus to travel south "from the town of Nazareth in Galilee to David's town in Judea, which is called Bethlehem, because he was of house and lineage of David" (Luke 2:4; cp. 1 Chronicles 5:1–2). This was done to fulfill Roman census-taking obligations which most likely involved taxation. Joseph traveled with his pregnant wife, Mary.

When they arrived, Jesus was born in that "little town of Bethlehem" (Luke 2:6–7; Matthew 2:1). Which brings us to an oft-overlooked clue—the term *Bethlehem*, the city of the Savior's birth, as foretold some 700 years before in Micah 5:2.

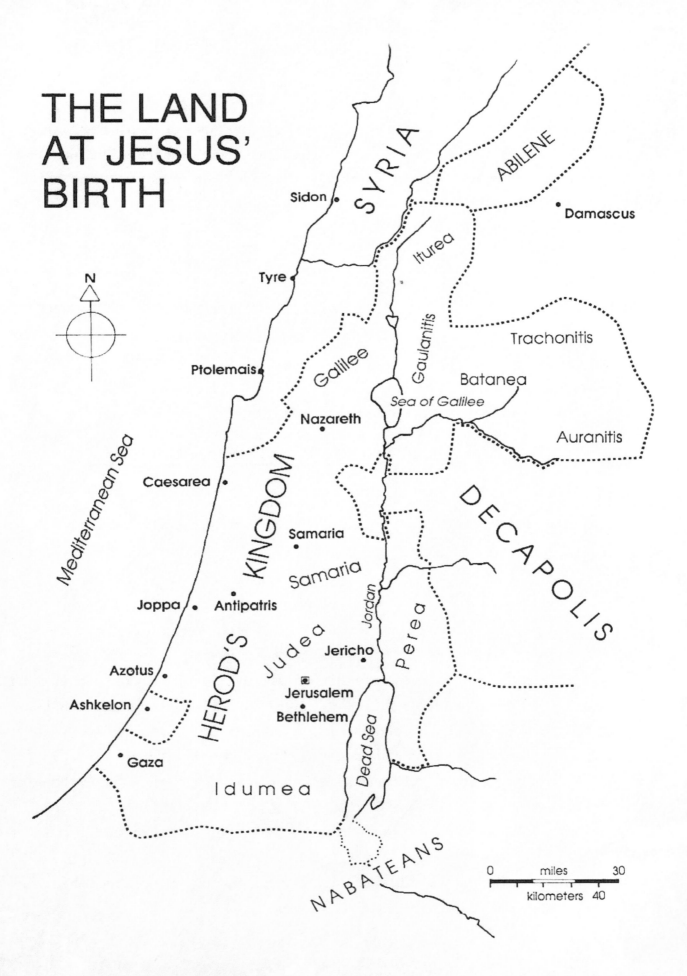

THE LAND
AT JESUS'
BIRTH

N

SYRIA

ABILENE

Sidon

Damascus

Iturea

Tyre

Galilee

Gaulanitis

Trachonitis

Ptolemais

Sea of Galilee

Batanea

Nazareth

Mediterranean Sea

Auranitis

Caesarea

DECAPOLIS

KINGDOM

Samaria

Samaria

Joppa   Antipatris

Jordan

Judea

Perea

Azotus

Jericho

Jerusalem

Ashkelon

Bethlehem

HEROD'S

Dead Sea

Gaza

Idumea

NABATEANS

0   miles   30

kilometers   40

43

"Bethlehem" has much significance! This city had not only been the birthplace of King David (Israel's greatest king up till then), but now it also became the birth city of Jesus, who became David's greater Descendant; God in heaven was Jesus's real Father (2 Samuel 7:11b–16).

Now for a *clue*-clincher that reveals the *geographical* importance of Jesus being born in a specified birthplace named "Bethlehem" (Micah 5:2): For you see, the name "Bethlehem" is made up of two Hebrew words: *bēth* (house); *leḥem* (bread). Thus, Jesus the "Bread of Life" (John 6:35) was born in the "House of Bread"!

"Evidence Just Too Coincidental to Be Accidental!!!"

Observations Concerning Jesus's Birth

The Christmas account in Luke's Gospel should be very familiar to most. Let's highlight a few interesting things.

> If you have not recently read that account of Jesus's Christmas birth in Luke 2:1–20, do yourself a favor and take time to digest it now.

Possibly you have heard the sentence, "There was no room for them [Mary and Joseph] in the inn" (Luke 2:7). No big Holiday Inn was present at the Bethlehem interchange. Bethlehem was so very small. Therefore, the town found itself overflowing with many visitors at census time. Thus, as early tradition has it, Jesus was born in a *cave* and laid in a "manager" (see H, *JW*, p. 17).

manger: a feeding container for use by animals.

Such caves are still around Bethlehem to this very day, and in Jesus's day inns were located near these caves. For the convenience of travelers, caves were provided by innkeepers to house their guests' ancient modes of transportation—horses, donkeys, and camels. Jesus was right at home with these animals; He had created them on the sixth day of Creation (Genesis 1:24–25; cp. John 1:3). Now that Creator had become a baby, lying in a manger, not in the penthouse of the local Bethlehem motel (cp. Colossians 2:9).

Of the many components of Luke's reporting that are significant, two are of particular interest. First, Luke shares that Jesus was wrapped in baby clothes. This shows Dr. Luke's pediatrician interests. Beyond warmth, this indicates wrappings that secured the baby so His bones would be aided in healthy growth (cp. Luke 2:40).

Second, Luke mentions "shepherds"—people often considered as being at the bottom of the Jewish food chain. Yet they served as God's representatives from that Jewish nation, Jews called by holy angels to worship His Son. And so it turned out that the night of the Savior's birth became the *"Jewish* Christmas"! Note: By using a "poor" class of people to be the *first* to worship Jesus, God shows Jesus as Savior of "all" (Luke 2:10).

> The "Gentile Christmas" is represented by the non-Jewish Magi ["Wise Men"] who came to Bethlehem at a later time.

> **Evidence room conclusion:** The promised One finally came and everything surrounding His birth verified that He was the long-expected Abrahamic, Judean, and Davidic Descendant, that human "Seed" of whom all the Old Testament prophets has prophetically spoken. This is verified by Galatians 3:16.

CHAPTER 7

FASCINATING FACTS CONCERNING JESUS AND HIS EARLIEST YEARS

Examining Clues in the Evidence Room

*Do the actions of Jesus during His early childhood years
with His family fulfill several Old Testament prophecies?*

Jesus's Circumcision

Eight days after His birth, Jesus was circumcised; this most likely occurred in the local Bethlehem synagogue or in the house that Mary and Joseph came to call home. On this occasion, He received His name JESUS [Helper or Savior] (Luke 2:21). Many astute Bible detectives correctly conclude that at this commanded event (Leviticus 12:3), Christ also shed His first drops of blood when He was circumcised. Ray Comfort, Christian author of more than forty books, including *Scientific Facts in the Bible*, notes that the eighth (8th) day was the best day for circumcision since it is the day "when the human body's immune system is at its peak" (C, *SFB*, p. 23). Another mystery of God uncovered!

JERUSALEM

The city of Jesus' day was totally destroyed by the Romans in A.D. 70. As a result, the location of many places must be considered tentative.

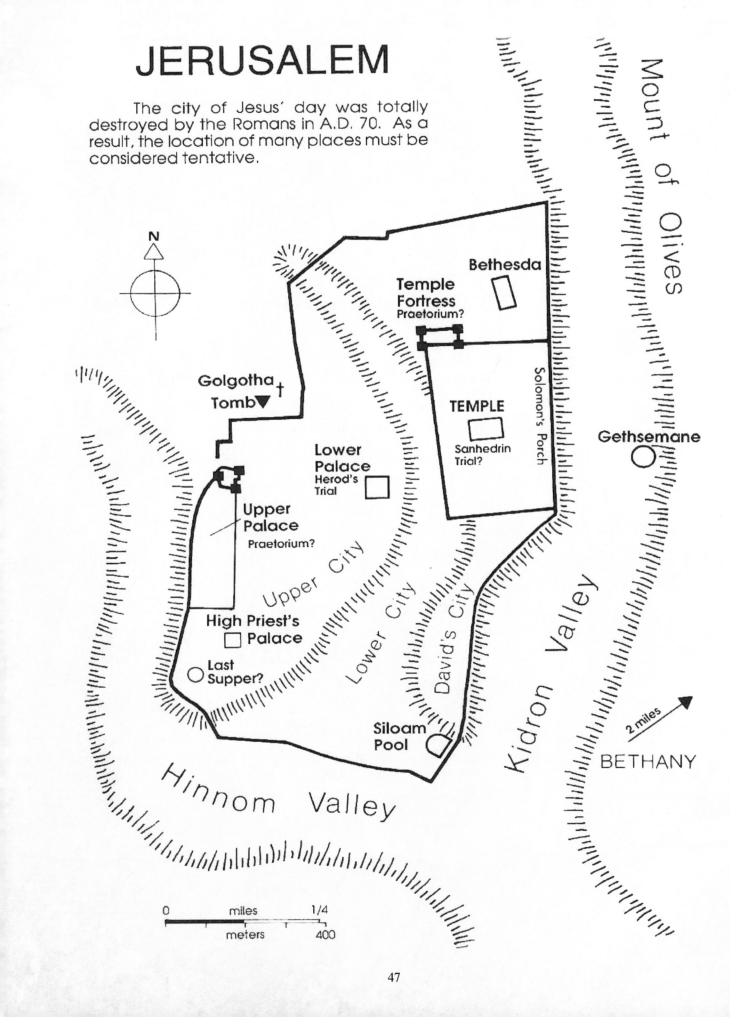

N

Mount of Olives

Bethesda

Temple Fortress
Praetorium?

Golgotha †
Tomb ▼

TEMPLE

Sanhedrin Trial?

Solomon's Porch

Gethsemane

Lower Palace
Herod's Trial

Upper Palace
Praetorium?

Upper City

Lower City

David's City

Kidron Valley

High Priest's Palace

Last Supper?

2 miles

BETHANY

Siloam Pool

Hinnom Valley

| 0 | miles | 1/4 |
| meters | | 400 |

Mary's "Purification"

Between forty days and one year after Jesus's birth, Mary was required to appear along with Jesus at the Temple in Jerusalem—six miles north of Bethlehem. Mary and Jesus, guided by Joseph, ventured to Jerusalem (Luke 2:22).

Mary's obligation was to go through a rite called "purification."

Women were considered unclean for forty (40) days after the birth of a son and eighty (80) days after the birth of a girl (Leviticus 12:1–6). Since this sounds chauvinistic today, another investigation is demanded.

When a mother gave birth, she brought a sinner into the world—whether male or female (cp. Psalm 51:5). Giving birth to a baby girl, however, was viewed as giving birth to one who would grow up and give birth to yet *another* sinner. Thus, the doubled number of days for uncleanness!

Once again, this does not sound fair to us moderns. Since sinful fathers impregnate women, it seems that they should get the blame, too. Isaiah 55:8–9 states God's perspective, whether we like it or not: "'My thoughts are not your thoughts, and your ways are not My ways,' says the Lord. 'As high as heaven is above the earth, so far are My ways above your ways and My thoughts above your thoughts.'" Oops, this investigative trail ends with "Let God be God." Little choice, unless we think we can win an argument with God!

There is a bigger concern here, however. Why would Mary need to be purified if she had just brought a *sinless* Jesus into the world (1 Peter 2:22)? One of two answers solves the mystery. First, Jesus may already have been carrying the sins of the world, even as a baby (2 Corinthians 5:21: "God made Him who did not know sin to be sin for us . . ."), or Mary may just have been fulfilling the prescribed Law to a T, just because it was commanded.

In any event, Mary offered up two turtledoves or two young pigeons as her purification offering (Luke 2:24). This was the accepted offering to be given by a *poor* family. A lamb was to be offered if a family could afford it (Leviticus 12:8).

Evidence alert, detectives! Since Mary did not offer a lamb, this means the Wise Men had not arrived in Bethlehem in the period of time before the trip to Jerusalem; otherwise, with the gift of "gold" from one of the Magi, Mary would have been able to afford to (and obligated to) offer a lamb.

Mary's "Presentation" of Jesus

Why did Jesus have to be "presented" (Luke 2:23)? The answer is detected in Numbers 3. Originally, each *firstborn* boy of all the twelve tribes of Israel was obligated to become a *priest.*

But God had a plan for His future human Son, who would become the ultimate Prophet, Priest, and King. We focus on the "Priest" aspect for the moment.

The biblical book of Numbers contains two numberings (census takings) of all the males of Israel—hence, its title (chapters 1; 2; 26). In it, God began to require every male of the tribe of Levi to become priests. With this change, the oldest males of the other eleven tribes of Israel now became free to hold whatever occupation they desired when of age. To affect this new procedure, God designed a tradeoff: the substitution of one Levite for every *firstborn* from the other eleven tribes of Israel. When the census of all twelve tribes of Israel was completed, the Levites numbered 22,000, while the non-Levite firstborns totaled 22,273, a difference of 273 persons (Numbers 3:39, 43).

Then God implemented His plan. Those extra firstborns from the non-Levite tribes could be ransomed for a cost of five shekels of silver (Numbers 3:46–48). Therefore, a five-shekel payment *unobligated* each firstborn, meaning non-Levite firstborns now became free; they were no longer required to become priests for life, unlike *all* the males from the tribe of Levi.

An inquisitive observer undoubtedly asks, "What does all this have to do with Jesus?" Much!

Jesus was from the tribe of Judah. God did not want Him to be a *Levitical* priest, but rather a priest "according to the order of Melchizedek" (Psalm 110:4; Hebrews 7:17). Priest Melchizedek, a non-Levite, lived long before Levi was born and before there were Levites (Genesis 14:17–20).

It's a long story.

In a nutshell, we now see how Jesus—from the tribe of Judah, not the tribe of Levi—could be set free to become God's Priest, not because He *had to be* a priest, but because He *chose to be*. In Christ, a *willing* heart, not a demanded heart, now entered the *eternal* priesthood to become High Priest, sacrifice for our iniquities, and also intercessor (Hebrews 7:25, plus vv. 26–27): "He [Jesus] always lives to pray for them [His people]."

When Mary presented baby Jesus to His heavenly Father at the Temple, she paid the five shekels of silver to ransom Jesus so He could ransom us for the Father's *pleasure*.

> In Old Testament times, priests never died in the place of lambs, but NT Priest Jesus changed all that. He sacrificed *Himself* as the Lamb of God, dying in the place of all His lost, human sheep to bring them back into God's flock.

Jesus later preached, "Do not be afraid any longer, little flock, because it is your Father's good *pleasure* to give you the Kingdom" (Luke 12:32).

Old Testament clues that solve New Testament mysteries just continue to pile up.

Wise Men (Astronomers) from the East

Matthew 2:1–11 (selected):

> Jesus was born in Bethlehem in Judea when Herod was king. Then Wise Men came from the east to Jerusalem. "Where is the Child who was born King of the Jews?" they asked. "We saw His star in the east and have come to worship Him."
>
> . . . Herod secretly called the Wise Men and found out from them the exact time the star appeared. As he sent them to Bethlehem, he said, "Go and search carefully for the little Child, and when you find Him, report to me so that I too may go and bow down before Him." [Hypocrite!]
>
> .The Wise Men. started out. And there was the *star* they had seen in the east! It led them on until it came to a stop over the place where the Child was.
>
> They went into the *house* and saw the little Child with His mother Mary. They knelt and worshiped Him. Then they opened their treasure chests and offered Him gifts: gold, frankincense, and myrrh.

Let's start in the "east"—in the Mesopotamia and Media/Persia areas where the Wise Men originated their journey. Tradition says there were twelve lead travelers. This makes a lot of sense since the larger the caravan, the less likely the possibility of highway robbery. Their entourage could easily have numbered a hundred or more. No wonder Herod became "alarmed" at their arrival (Matthew 2:3). He thought his kingship was in danger.

Inquiry of and answers from Jewish scribes informed the Magi that the coming "Ruler" (King) was predicted to be born in Bethlehem, in the territory of the tribe of Judah (Micah 5:2), not in Jerusalem.

Off they traveled, once again following the star which led them to Bethlehem and which dropped right down over the "house" where Jesus was. By this time, Jesus probably would have been anywhere between six and eighteen months old.

Why this conclusion, coupled with the so-called "poor" offering at the Temple presentation of Jesus some forty days after His birth? Several reasons: After King Herod asked the Wise Men *when* they first saw the star, he then calculated the current age of baby Jesus. On this basis, he later ordered the killing of all the babies in the surrounding area of Bethlehem, babies "up to two years old" (Matthew 2:16).

In addition, tradition, as previously stated, says that Jesus was born in a *cave*. However, the Wise Men found Jesus in a "house"—not a stable containing a cattle-feeding manger. This means the magi were not present on Christmas Day; they arrived sometime later.

Three items call for further attention.

First, assuming it took the Magi some time to prepare for a long trip, it is probable that their journey was somewhat delayed after they first saw the star. Let's say the star appeared to these Wise Men from the eastern countries of Iraq (Babylon) and Iran (Persia) on the night of the Savior's birth. They would first have had to plan and group, then travel north, and then south around the Fertile Crescent to reach the Holy Land. That preparation and journey would have taken months.

Second, and even more intriguing in this investigation, is the question of who these Wise Men were. Some of them must have been descended from those who are called magi or magicians in the book of Daniel (2:48).

There seem to have been two types of magi over which Daniel, statesman and prophet, had been placed as high overseer in Babylon and then Persia. One type would be astrologers who studied the stars in terms of "mapping out the skies" (cp. Isaiah 47:13), as in horoscopes, while the other group would be classified as more scientific—astronomers. This latter type would nicely fit with a Daniel group of followers whose descendants—over a period of some 500 years—had waited for a signal that Daniel's coming "Messiah" had been born (see Daniel 9:24–27; cp. Numbers 24:17).

Third, some have explained the star that led the Wise Men as planets coming into conjunction with one another. This theory is doubtful since the star that led the Magi eventually indicated the *exact* "house" where Jesus was. To do so, the star could not have remained high in the sky.

> **A test:** Look at a bright star right over your head, then walk a mile or kilometer down the road. That same star will *still* be right over your head. A star high in the sky would hardly have been an absolute indicator.

Consider this suggestion: Holy angels in the Bible take all types of forms, including people, chariots, and horses (e.g., Psalm 68:17). Why could such an angel not have taken the form of a *star* and have been a star-messenger sent by God to lead the Magi? Then that angel could have visibly come right down over the very "house" where Jesus was.

> For years, I have endorsed the angel-star concept in my public teaching as being biblical. Only as I was in the final stages of editing this book did I read that Saint John Chrysostom, the "golden-tongued" preacher, and also Pope Gregory the Great both thought the star of Bethlehem was an angel (cited in H, *JW,* pp. 115–117).

The phenomenon of the gifts bestowed by the Wise Men is also important. At first glance, the fact that the text identifies *three* gifts suggests only *three* Wise Men. Not definitive; never is a number stated. There could have been more gifts, but only three mentioned because of their profound significance. As the Christmas carol "We Three Kings of Orient Are" indicates, the gift of *gold* was very appropriate for the One who would become a king. The gift of *frankincense* was meaningful because it was used along with Old Testament sacrifices and would fit Jesus's future priestly role. (Ephesians 5:2 states that Priest Jesus became our "incense" when He was sacrificed on Calvary's cross.) The third gift of *myrrh* represented a time of burying, a reminder of one of the elements later used to embalm Jesus in His tomb (John 19:38–40).

In agreement with the Bible's Christmas account, how can we better design our manger scenes at Christmas? Simply place the Wise Men outside the display, a little distance away since Scriptural data indicates they arrived later.

Further, if the Wise Men had arrived on the exact night of Jesus's birth, along with that command from an angel to Joseph to flee to Egypt with the baby Jesus on that same Christmas night (cp. Matthew 2:13), well, that action could have endangered the human life of the *newly* born Christ. An older baby Jesus would better fit a journey to Egypt.

All Scriptural clues indicate a later arrival of the kings from the east (Matthew 2:1).

The Flight into Egypt

Investigative question: *Why did the heavenly Father need to send His Son to Egypt?* The answer is something way beyond the idea of mere protection for the Child Jesus. God could easily have hidden Him right in Bethlehem, just as He had hidden Moses in Egypt when Pharaoh was ruling (Exodus 2:1–10) or as He hid Elijah in Zarephath, right "under the nose" of his enemy, Queen Jezebel (1 Kings 17:8–9).

Matthew 2:15 provides the answer: "Out of Egypt I have called My Son." The context provides the clue. After Jesus's family was in Egypt for a while, Herod the Great died—making it now safe to return to the Holy Land. An angel informed Joseph to move back. Matthew interprets the purpose of that return journey via the fulfillment of a prophecy. Hosea 11:1 is assumed to be the reference to which Matthew refers—and the charge is leveled that Matthew is misapplying a passage. *Hosea*'s "Out of Egypt I have called My son" must be a reference to the ancient children

With all this heavy detective work, it's time to interject some humor; after all, serious sleuths also need to laugh!

of Israel being summoned by God to leave Egypt and follow Moses to the Promised Land. Right?

Maybe Hosea 11:1 better serves as a *secondary* thought on Matthew's rabbinic mind, but we primarily need to remember the prophecy in Isaiah 49:3, where God the Father calls His Son "Israel."

Did you catch that?

Conclusion: Just as God first called the children of Israel out of Egypt—and they failed Him (see Numbers 11–14), so Jesus, the new "Israel," is called out of Egypt to succeed. Clever.

But there is more, as the late, self-taught Christian lay-theologian Charles D. Provan (1955 to 2007) concluded. He alerted readers to the fact that Matthew was referring to the prophecy of Christ at Numbers 24:8–9: "When God led Him [Jesus] out of Egypt, He had the strength of a wild bull. He will devour nations who are His enemies [cp. Psalm 2:7–9], crushing their bones and piercing them with His arrows. He [Christ]

Today we would call the present section of our study: *The Escape into Egypt.* In past days, before increased travel by air, the *commanded* escape of Joseph, Mary, and Jesus from Bethlehem (Matthew 2:13) was called a "flight." During the transition of terms, this little story emerged. Children were asked to draw a picture of Jesus's "flight" into Egypt. One little boy drew an airplane. The teacher viewed the picture and identified Mary, Joseph, Jesus, shepherds, and Wise Men in various windows, but the figure in the front window remained a mystery until the teacher inquired. The little artist responded, "That's Pontius the pilot."

You were warned, silly it was! At least you sense Jesus's family did not go to Egypt on Delta or Kenya Airways.

crouches and lies down like a lion and like a 'full-grown' Lion—who will rouse him?"

All perceptive investigators traveling with us will notice the inseparable connection between Genesis 49:9 and the whole of the Numbers' context. One should also be alert to Jesus, referred to as "the Lion of Judah" in Revelation 5:5, as well as recall E. W. Hengstenberg's interpretation of the "great [full-grown] lion" [Jesus] in Genesis 49:9. That Lion needs to be connected to Numbers 23:24 and 24:9 (H, *COT*, I, 98–103, also 63, 87).

Hengstenberg (1802 to 1869), a well-recognized German exegete, wrote four lengthy volumes on Christology in the Old Testament. A monumental work.

There you have it! The Child "Israel" is called back "out of Egypt" to serve God in the capacity of His earthly ministry. Jesus remained sinless. In that same wilderness, the Old Testament people of Israel had not!

Weeping in Ramah for All Those Dead Bethlehem Infants

King Herod the Great was not a nice guy, even though he was a brilliant military strategist, clever politician, and magnificent builder who could pour cement under water and harden it! However, for all his cleverness and brilliance, he was a failure at family relationships; he chose power over mending family feuds, had several of his own sons killed for suspected treason, and also had his favorite wife put to death. It was his fear of losing his throne to someone else that was behind it all. So it's no surprise that he was fearful of that newborn child whom the Magi described as "King of the Jews."

Upon hearing the news of the birth of Jesus, Herod immediately went into "fear" and "protective" mode: ". . . find Him, report to me so that I too may go and bow down before Him" (Matthew 2:8). The Wise Men were warned in a dream about Herod's true intentions concerning the Christ Child; so, after visiting the young Jesus, the Wise Men chose a different route home (Matthew 2:12).

When Herod realized that he had been tricked by his eastern visitors, he ordered the slaughter of all baby boys in and around Bethlehem under two years of age. This murder rampage was not one of Herod's worst. Since he designated an isolated geographic area, possibly as few as twenty (20) babies may have been killed (taught in a classroom lecture by Dr. Siegbert W. Becker, one of my two most influential theological professors; also see H, *JW*, p. 137; there Scott Hahn—religious Roman Catholic author of numerous books—numbers the deaths at "six" or less); nonetheless, the crying coming from the mouths of parents and relatives could be heard for quite a distance.

> A hidden typological parallel can be tied into Jesus's escape from death; namely, Moses also being saved within the boundaries of Egypt, even though other Jewish babies were slaughtered in his day (Exodus 1:22–2:10).

Matthew, who quotes another prophecy as being fulfilled by this terrible event, is once again accused of taking poetic, rabbinic license; namely, falsely applying a prophecy. How could Matthew quote Jeremiah 31:15 and say it was fulfilled some 575 years later by Herod's actions? Matthew 2:18 quotes *Jeremiah*:

A cry is heard in Rama.

Weeping and loud wailing:
> Rachel crying over her children
> and refusing to be comforted,
> because they are gone.

Genesis 35:16–19 indicates that Rachel, favorite wife of Jacob (a.k.a., "Israel"), died in childbirth and was buried "some distance from" Bethlehem. Nothing is said of the city of "Ramah," which was located five miles north of Jerusalem and eleven miles from Bethlehem-Ephrathah (the latter term distinguishing it from other towns named Bethlehem).

The interpretations of the original meaning of the Jeremiah 31 reference, as well as Matthew's application, are multiple. Question: If one assumes that Rachel was buried in Ramah—that is, on the way to Bethlehem, how could *the weeping in Bethlehem* be heard as far away as Ramah? Laetsch notes that the whole surrounding context of Jeremiah 31 is *messianic*. A significant clue!

Of greatest significance in solving the overall problem is the fact that "The Masoretic [Hebrew] text points 'in Ramah,' not as a *proper* noun but as a *common* noun, 'on the height.'" Laetsch points out that many ancient translations avoid "Ramah" and go with "on the height." Thus, the sound of weeping went up from Bethlehem and could be heard on the heights or tops of the surrounding hills. As to Rachel "crying," some of her descendants now occupied the areas around Bethlehem. They would have found themselves in the path of Herod's swords, and losing babies, they surely would have wailed loudly.

With this slaughter, little babies became innocent martyrs for the Christian cause.

> See L, *J*, pp. 248–251 for the fuller argumentation and verification for Matthew's use of Jeremiah 31. And do not forget that God gave Matthew the interpretation (cp. 1 Corinthians 2:13; 2 Timothy 3:16; 1 Peter 1:12).

Let's now finish the story of the return of Jesus from Egypt.

No to Bethlehem, Yes to Nazareth

Upon returning from Egypt, Jesus's parents intended to make Bethlehem their permanent home. However, Joseph was warned in a dream not to settle in Bethlehem since Herod's son Archelaus (the apple does not fall far from the tree) was now ruler over that territory (Matthew

2:19–22). Matthew continues to give more crucial data in verse 23: "He [Joseph] came and made his home in a town by the name of Nazareth [in the northern territory called Galilee]. What the prophets had predicted was now fulfilled: 'He [Jesus] will be called a *Nazarene.*'"

Search for the clue that guided Matthew to say the Old Testament had predicted the name of the boyhood town where Jesus was to grow up. It does not seem to be there. The prophet Micah (5:2) had foretold the city of His birth, but where is one to find any prophecy about Jesus growing up in a city called Nazareth?

Isaiah 11:1 and Zechariah 3:8 will do the job. In both places, the coming One is given the title or name "Branch," a reference to that Descendant who was to generate from the "root" or family of Jesse. Jesse was the father of King David and thereby a most *significant* Judean ancestor of Jesus.

Intense investigation into the meaning of the term *branch* becomes crucial at this point.

As to the compelling evidence for Matthew's "Nazareth," its conclusion can be spied-out in the Hebrew term meaning "branch"—*nētzer.* "Nazareth" would then be considered a *wordplay* on that Hebrew term.

Is your biblical, detective mind catching on? Analyze! Just as the term *Bethlehem* meant "House of Bread" and Jesus the "Bread of Life" was born there, so our Savior—the "Branch"—grew up in "Branch Town" (review Isaiah 11:1 and Zechariah 3:8).

There! God did it again! Another theological clue and surprise that solves a mystery!

> Dedicated readers of Scripture have often been inquisitive as to what happened to Jesus during his childhood and teen years. Fictional stories generated by fanciful minds have filled in the gaps, and surely all types of speculations have been believed as fact. For example, Sunday school materials have pictured Jesus playing in a sand pile, forming birds, and then flipping them into the air where they began to fly to the thrill of His playmates! Really? You will not find that in the Bible.

The Young Jesus

Between Jesus's arrival from Egypt into Nazareth and the beginning of His adult ministry at about thirty years old (Luke 3:23), there is only one event revealed to us in the Bible. It concerns Jesus returning to the Jerusalem Temple at age twelve to become a *bar mitzvah*, that is, "a son of the commandment" (Luke 2:42). Through this ceremony, Jesus, a young Jewish boy, would now be considered a man and an adult responsible for keeping Moses's recorded Laws: morally, ceremonially, and politically.

One biblical clue concerns Jesus confounding the theological doctors of His day with His great Old Testament knowledge, both in the form of answers and questions (Luke 2:46–47). Verse 40 of that cited context had already informed the reader that Jesus had grown, "being filled with wisdom; and God's favor was with Him."

Does this mean that by osmosis God the Father filtered knowledge into Jesus? Or did Jesus need to study like other human students? Hebrews 4:15 and 5:8 answers those questions: "For we do not have a High Priest who is unable to sympathize with our weaknesses. He was tempted in every way just as we are—yet He remained without sin" and "Although Jesus was the Son, He learned obedience from the things which He suffered." Yup, He suffered just like any other school kid with tough assignments, hard tests, and the temptation to loaf and cheat—though He never did (1 Peter 2:22).

Jesus had predicted those coming boyhood challenges on the pages of the Old Testament. He had said, "The Lord GOD gives Me the speech of the learned, so that I know how to talk to encourage the weary. Morning after morning He wakes Me to hear, so I will listen like a learner" (Isaiah 50:4). And He did; and that is why He was ready to take on the doctors when He visited the Temple at the young age of twelve.

Yet another Old Testament *clue* provided to solve a New Testament *mystery*.

Evidence room conclusion: Prophecy after prophecy and instruction after instruction from the OT were fulfilled through the actions of Jesus and His family during His early childhood. Clue after clue from the pages of the OT open up meaningful insights that unlock NT mysteries.

ADDENDUM: David Limbaugh adds a necessary observation when he summarizes Michael P. Barrett (L, *EC,* p. 126; note p. 367 also): "As the New Testament writers taught, Christ is the key that unlocks all the mysteries of the Old Testament."

CHAPTER 8

THE ROLE OF JESUS AS A PROPHET

Examining Clues in the Evidence Room

*How do the four gospels move their readers
into and through the earliest days of Jesus's ministry?*

Jesus, Our Prophet via Words and Actions

Previously, we cited the importance of Acts 10:43: "All the prophets testify about Him [Jesus] . . . ." This forms the most crucial presupposition for our total investigative probe—that all of Scripture is Christ-centered; that is, Christ is humankind's "everything" (Colossians 3:11; 1:17–18; 2:10; Ephesians 1:23). So, you can expect to find Him everywhere: the Old Testament prophets did, the New Testament writers do, and we will too!

Note that OT prophets functioned both as *forth*tellers and *fore*tellers. They proclaimed both "Law and Gospel" as they recalled God's word spoken in the "past" and applied it to their "present" listeners. Thus, they spoke *forth* the words of the LORD.

At other times OT prophets spoke both of the "near future" as well as the "remote future." These spoken or acted out predictions *fore* told future events that often pertained to the coming Savior or Messiah. Spelled out in detail in G, *FOTP* (268 pages).

Beyond Acts 10:43, there is another crucial foundation that aids New Testament detectives. It pertains to the fact that Jesus's prophetic ministry was two-pronged: He was a Prophet both in word and in action—both in what He said and in what He did. The "said" part includes His preaching and storytelling through parables, while the "did" part comprises His action ministry where He performed various types of miracles. John 8:31–32 enforces the word part where Jesus states, "If you continue to [live] in My word, you will know the truth, and the truth will set you free." The *action* part is solidified in Peter's Pentecost sermon (Acts 2:22) where he says, "Men of Israel, listen to what I have to say: When Jesus from Nazareth was among you, He was a Man whom God commended to you—as you well know—by the *miracles, wonderful proofs,* and *miraculous signs* which God worked through Him."

> "Men of Israel": See Appendix 14, the section entitled, "Scripture's Usage of *Gender.*"

Recall that late Easter afternoon teaching event. Two of Jesus's disciples were traveling toward the city of Emmaus. The risen Jesus joins them without revealing His identity. These disciples express their total disappointment that their Leader had been crucified. Saddened, they spoke of Jesus as a Prophet "mighty in what He did [the *actions* He took] and said [the *words* He spoke]" (Luke 24:19).

Jesus, the "Word" Prophet

Most have heard of Jesus preaching the "word" in His Sermon on the Mount in Matthew 5–7. The same is true regarding Matthew 13, which contains the most parables to be found in any *single* Bible chapter, seven in number, known as the Kingdom parables. These were "pictures" put to words!

> *Parable*: "An earthly story with a heavenly meaning." —Edward Koehler.

Jesus, the "Action" Prophet

Most have also heard of the miracles Jesus performed, including His turning water into wine, making the deaf hear, the blind see, and raising dead people to life. These *actions* were powerful deeds, sometimes accompanied with words, sometimes not.

Jesus, Our Prophet in "Word" and "Action"

Matthew's Gospel masterfully interweaves the words preached and the miracles acted out by Jesus. Dr. Robert Hoerber, a late professor of Greek, editor of the Concordia Self-Study Bible—NIV, as well as one of the three lead editors of the NET Bible and member of the revision team of the NKJV, reveals this clue in his *Reading the New Testament for Understanding*—one of the most profound and yet reader-friendly books on the subject. One particular section is pertinent to our inquiry. It deals with the outline of Matthew and offers a magnificent arrangement that was really designed long ago by the Holy Spirit. In the out-of-print New Testament known as *God's Word to the Nations; New Evangelical Translation* (NET), 1990, Hoerber's outline is built-in and expanded at the proper places within Matthew, introducing the reader to

> Copies of *God's Word to the Nations; New Evangelical Translation* (NET), 1990 are still available through Amazon.

the literary genius of the Holy Spirit who guided Matthew's pen. Let's repeat it in its original outline form—with the exception that the word *deeds* has been changed to *actions* (see H, *RNTU*, pp. 24–25).

A. Jesus's Genealogy and Infancy (1:1–2:23)

B. Five Booklets: a Parallel to Moses's *Fivefold* Torah (3:1–25:46)
  1. First booklet (3:1–7:29)
     a. Narrative and actions: Galilean ministry begins (3:1–4:25)
     b. Words: Sermon on the Mount (5:1–7:29)

  2. Second booklet (8:1–11:2)
     a. Narrative and actions: Ten Messianic miracles of power (8:1–9:35)
     b. Words: Mission discourse (9:36–11:1)

  3. Third booklet (11:2–13:53)
     a. Narrative and actions (11:2–12:50)
     b. Words: Seven Kingdom parables (13:1–53)

  4. Fourth booklet (13:54–18:35)
     a. Narrative and actions (13:54–17:27)
     b. Words: Rules for the new Church (people of God) [*ekklēsia*] (18:1–35)

5. Fifth booklet (19:1–25:46)

   a. Narrative and actions: Judean ministry (19:1–22:46)

   b. Words: Seven woes and "last things" [eschatology]
   (23:1–25:46)

   c. Fulfillment Realized: Jesus's Passion, Death, and Resurrection
   (26:1–28:20)

C. Fulfillment Realized: Jesus's Passion, Death, and Resurrection
   (26:1–28:20)

What great symmetry! (Do yourself a favor and purchase Hoerber's book. It's worth its price in gold.)

Sharp Old Testament detectives will immediately notice that the main body of Matthew's Gospel is divided into *five* parts. Why is this significant? Matthew directed the words of his Gospel to a *Jewish* audience; he wanted to convince Jews that Jesus was their arrived Messiah. Jews were highly religious people who held their prophet Moses in the highest esteem, especially the *five* books ascribed to him. These books are known as the Torah (Hebrew: Law or Instruction) or Pentateuch (Latin: the Five).

> The Torah's five books:
> - Genesis
> - Exodus
> - Leviticus
> - Numbers
> - Deuteronomy

How do we decipher Matthew's seeming mystery? Clue: Matthew is telling his hearers that Jesus's words and actions are their *new* Torah or Pentateuch. The Apostle Paul chimes in with that same conclusion in 2 Corinthians 5:17: "So if anyone is in Christ, he is a new creation. The old things have passed away; they have become new."

Yes, for Matthew and the other New Testament writers, a new day had dawned with the coming of Christ. Moses was now superseded by Jesus (Hebrews 3:3). A new *fivefold* Torah had come. Moses and his prediction of the coming Christ had been fulfilled; after all, Moses truly had spoken of Jesus some 1,400 years before (John 5:46), foretelling that Jesus the prophet would come and that "whoever" would not listen to Him would be punished (Deuteronomy 18:18–19; see whole context of verses 15–22; cp. John 3:16).

Jesus's Baptism and Its Later Time Factors

As we continue to seek biblical truth by identifying clues from the Old Testament to help solve New Testament mysteries, we explore Jesus's public ministry—the beginning of which is His baptism. The legitimacy of that ministry of Jesus had to be verified. That was God the Father's job; namely, to bless the Lord Jesus and His work by substantiating the fact Jesus was His sent and chosen One.

Data to be noted: Only Matthew, Mark, and Luke report the actual baptism of Jesus, but it is John who later recaps that baptism. In so doing, John relates a Jordan River event that took place forty days *after* the actual baptism of Jesus; he also provides additional details surrounding Jesus's earlier baptism.

You may have read that right after Jesus was baptized, the Holy Spirit—in the form of a *dove*—landed on Jesus. At the same time, God the Father called down from heaven. Question: Did the people around John the Baptizer see this and hear those words? No! The first three gospels do not say this, but it is only the Gospel of *John* that reports that John the Baptizer did see the dove and that it was the heavenly Father who had informed John the Baptizer that Jesus was His chosen One (1:32–33).

Also, it is frequently assumed that Jesus the Messiah was known to John the Baptizer—by revelation—*prior* to the first appearance of Jesus at the Jordan River when Jesus came to be baptized. The above reference indicates that this was *not* the case. Real investigative work is needed to detect this truth. True, John knew his cousin Jesus from youth, but he did not know Him as Messiah until it was revealed to him from above at Christ's baptism.

Houston! The Dove Has Landed

The occasion when John the Baptizer called out, "Look! The Lamb of God who carries away the sin of the world!" occurred forty days *after* Jesus's baptism and *after* Jesus's forty-day temptation in the wilderness (E, *LTJM*, I, 299). While the John 1:29–35 account is simply a further explanation and

> Don't overlook the parallel fact that a dove hovered over the post-flood waters! This is especially noteworthy since 1 Peter 3:19b ties the flood waters to the concept of baptism.

affirmation of the original events, surprising data is found throughout John's whole context.

The Gospel of John begins with the same phrase that starts the book of *Genesis*: "In the beginning"—meaning: Creation alert! Jesus the Creator, as a human, had now come to be baptized! Besides, the Spirit of God, who "hovered" like a bird "over the waters" in Genesis 1:2, now hovered and landed as a dove on Jesus. "*Evidence Just Too Coincidental to Be Accidental!!!*"

Perusal of John's Gospel also identifies another clue that is often overlooked: The dove "stayed" or "remained" on Jesus *after* His baptism. Crucial! The Spirit of God stayed with Jesus throughout His entire ministry, and He was still with Him at Calvary's cross, as we will later see.

Evidence room conclusion: OT connectives will enhance our investigative quest as we learn more and more about Jesus, His ministry, and especially His role as God's ultimate Prophet via His *preaching and teaching* of the "word" as well as His *miracle ministry* of "action."

CHAPTER 9

SPLITTING THE "ADAMS"

Examining Clues in the Evidence Room
Why did Jesus do what He did to begin His ministry?

Analyzing the Fingerprints Left Behind in Romans 5

Science often references the splitting of the atom. Theologically, we will now explore the splitting of two *Adams*: the First Adam, the first created human; and the Second Adam, Jesus. This whole concept is introduced for inspection at Romans 5:14b: "Adam was a type [a picture or prefigurement] of Him [Jesus] who was to come." There you have it! We are back to that *type* stuff we considered in the Abraham saga. Some twenty parallels, both similar and dissimilar, will be interspersed over and over on many of the pages to come. You will be shaking your head in astonishment when you come to understand the various eye-openers between the two Adams.

To start, the basic essence of the Romans 5 section needs to be explained. In verses 12, 18, and 19 Paul writes:

> So then, just as sin came into the world through one man [the First Adam], and death through sin, so death also spread to all people, since all sinned.
>
> So therefore, as through the failure of one man [the First Adam], condemnation came to all people, so also through the righteous act of One Man [the Second Adam] justification [acquittal]—which brings life—came to all people. For in the same way, as through the disobedience of one man,

multitudes were proclaimed to be sinful, so also through the obedience of the One Man, multitudes will be proclaimed righteous.

Now that's deep theology!

The First Adam passed blame for his sin onto both his wife *and* God (Genesis 3:12); the Second Adam, however, takes our blame and washes us clean with His blood (1 John 1:7). Jesus takes our place on the cross. His death frees us from the First Adam's original failure and also from humankind's many failures to follow.

As we analyze, there are other parallels between the two Adams that jump off the pages of Scripture. One of them concerns the "timing" of Jesus's wilderness temptation.

Why Initial Confrontation with the Devil?

Think of the devil in the beginning. He was created holy, but rebelled against his Creator, along with other power-hungry angels (Jude 6a). He always wanted to be #1 and enticed others to desire the same (Genesis 3:5). To accomplish his goal, the devil was eager to turn God's whole creation topsy-turvy. Compare the following:

God's Designated Line of Authority	*Satan's Designed Reverse Order*
1. God	**1.** animal (a snake, used for evil purposes)
2. man (Adam at the beginning)	**2.** woman (Eve)
3. woman (Eve to start)	**3.** man (Adam)
4. animals	**4.** God

We humans still live in that distorted, rebellious society yet today. Think of it: Save the endangered animal species, but abort human babies!

The devil made his first move against the animal world and humankind in the

> You can read the entire account about the devil in the Garden of Eden in Genesis 3:1–24.

Garden of Eden. The snake granted Satan permission to invade and visualize himself for his appearance to the first woman and man. We know the snake okayed the devil's inward presence since later the snake also came under God's curse (v. 14), along with the devil and the two fallen humans (vv. 15–24).

Further affirmation of who was inside the snake is shared in Revelation 12:9 by identifying that tempter as "the old serpent, called Devil and Satan." He was the *first* to cause the woman and the man to sin. That is why Jesus—the recapitulating antitype of the First Adam— had to confront the devil as His *first* act immediately after He was baptized and before He could go on with His earthly ministry. For this reason, "the Spirit led Jesus into the wilderness to be tempted by the devil," right after Jesus was baptized.

God knew *timing* was everything to "fulfill all righteousness" (Matthew 3:15). Matthew 4:11 makes it crystal clear: Jesus defeated the devil who had to retreat.

> The concept of recapitulating or repeating in Romans 5 was expressed by the Early Church father Irenaeus. While one day searching the name "Irenaeus" ("I,"*ODCC*, pp. 713–714; "R,"*ODCC*, p. 1162), the term *recapitulation* came up. Later, when preparing to teach *Romans* in Africa, the recapitulation concept found its way in front of me again, and became personally cemented into my teaching of Romans 5. As Appendix 6 relates, it developed over the next years into finding *multi*-comparisons between Adam and Jesus. In line with this, Bible investigators will want to apply 2 Corinthians 5:17–21. Bird notes that Johann Gerhard also saw many parallels between Romans 5 and the life of Jesus (B, *ROTNC*, Part II, 36).

The First Adam had not won such a victory; the Second Adam did. Of course, Jesus was the God-Man, whereas the First Adam was not. The devil had now met his match. Christ was starting to put "God's Designated Line of Authority" back in place; "God" was demanding to be back on top, #1.

The devil had started the mess; Jesus, as the Second Adam, began His ministry by first confronting that original initiator of evil.

> The first man, later named Adam (Genesis 5:1), received the *primary* human blame because he did not carry out his responsibility to protect his wife Eve (Genesis 3:17).

Mystery solved as to why Jesus had to start His ministry in the way He did.

The 12 Disciples of Jesus

A complete list of the 12 disciples of Jesus can be found at Matthew 10:1–4; Mark 3:13–19; and Luke 6:13–16.

Question: Would it have been okay for Jesus to have picked nine or fifteen main disciples? No! The mystery of "why the twelve" is found in its parallel to the Old Testament twelve tribes of Israel. Jesus's twelve disciples now became representative of the Kingdom of believers in the dawning era of the "new covenant" (Jeremiah 31:31); thus, the necessity for His *twelve* disciples (analyze Revelation 4:4; 5:8; 19:4—"24" represents the two groups of "12" each).

A further unveiling of the *symbolic* use of "12" pops up at Revelation 7:4, indicating the total count of those who will eventually be in heaven: 144,000.

When one views 144,000 as 12 x 12 x 10 x 10 x 10, the mystery can be solved, remembering that "12" is the Scriptures' representative number for the "Church," while "10" represents "completion." (As to the latter: The *Ten* Commandments, the *complete* "will" of God, The *Ten* Plagues of Egypt, the *complete* "destruction" of God.)

If the list in Revelation 7:5–8 is meant only to include *OT* believers, then the interpreter has a big problem. The tribe of Dan is missing. What, nobody from Dan went to heaven? In contrast, the mighty Danite Samson is placed among those of faith who did go there. See Hebrews 11:32. Another explanation is demanded!

Now the solution: 12 (Old Testament believers) x 12 (New Testament believers) x 10 x 10 x 10 (the complete, complete, complete number of believers, making it very *complete* via the threefold saving action of the Trinity) = the totality of souls who will be saved for eternity.

There you have it: 144,000 saved persons!

This is Scripture's way of communicating truth in *symbolic* code by way of clues. Besides, you now understand why Jesus picked twelve (12) main disciples; they are representative of all who come to believe in Christ in *New Testament* times.

A "Fishy" Clue

At least five of Jesus's twelve disciples were fishermen before they were chosen for ministry. It was to be so, even beyond the statement of Christ: "I will make you fishers of men" (Matthew 4:19). Jeremiah 16:14–21 proves this. Verse 16 focuses in on a special fact; it prophesies, "'I am going to send for many fishermen,' says the LORD, 'to catch them. After that I will send for many hunters to hunt for them on every mountain and hill and in the clefts of the rocks.'"

Jeremiah's surrounding context speaks of God bringing His people—and the generations to follow—back from the seventy-year Babylonian Captivity, as foretold by Jeremiah about 600 years before Christ came (25:11–12). God initiated this action in the days of Jewish heroes—Zerubbabel, Joshua the high priest, Haggai, Zechariah, Ezra, Nehemiah, and Malachi—who returned to the Holy Land; however, it jumped into full swing at the first Pentecost in Acts 2:5–11. There, in Acts 2, Peter, the *fisherman*-now-turned-preacher, witnesses three thousand converts being baptized into the Christian faith (v. 41). People were fished out of the waters of unbelief.

What about the "hunters" of the Jeremiah 16 passage? They refer to all those who have followed Christ through the centuries after Pentecost. Through evangelism and foreign mission work, these followers *hunt* down those who will listen to the message of Christianity.

What an interesting passage from the pen of Jeremiah!

Evidence room conclusion: The early days of Jesus's ministry are better understood by viewing OT clues that unravel the meanings of *why Jesus did what He did.*

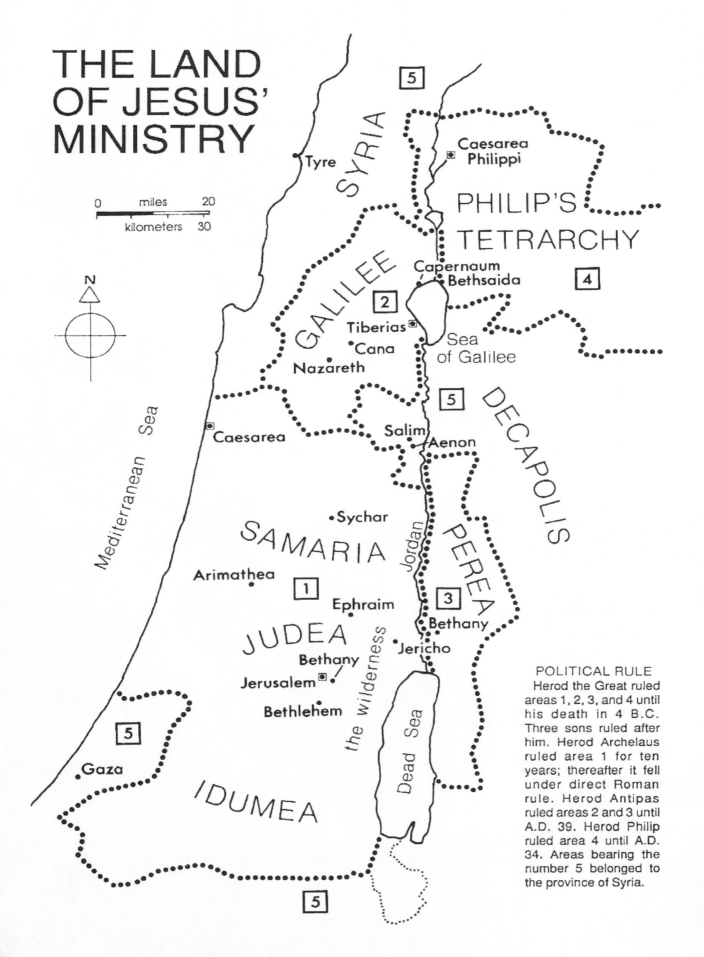

THE LAND OF JESUS' MINISTRY

0 miles 20
kilometers 30

N

Mediterranean Sea

SYRIA

Tyre

Caesarea Philippi

5

PHILIP'S TETRARCHY

4

GALILEE

2

Capernaum
Bethsaida

Tiberias

Cana

Nazareth

Sea of Galilee

DECAPOLIS

Caesarea

Salim

Aenon

5

Sychar

SAMARIA

Jordan

PEREA

Arimathea

1

Ephraim

JUDEA

Bethany

Jerusalem

Bethlehem

the wilderness

3

Bethany

Jericho

Dead Sea

5

Gaza

IDUMEA

5

POLITICAL RULE
Herod the Great ruled areas 1, 2, 3, and 4 until his death in 4 B.C. Three sons ruled after him. Herod Archelaus ruled area 1 for ten years; thereafter it fell under direct Roman rule. Herod Antipas ruled areas 2 and 3 until A.D. 39. Herod Philip ruled area 4 until A.D. 34. Areas bearing the number 5 belonged to the province of Syria.

PART III

SURPRISES, SURPRISES, AND MORE SURPRISES

CHAPTER 10

DETECTIVES, LET'S FAST-FORWARD TO THE WEDDING AT CANA!

Examining Clues in the Evidence Room
What was the first *miracle of Jesus?*

By Way of Introduction

After Christ chose His first disciples (John 1:35–51), He headed north from the Jordan River, toward Galilee—the territory where He had grown up as a boy. He and His disciples were invited to a wedding near His boyhood town of Nazareth. The wedding was to be held in the nearby city of Cana. Mary, the mother of Jesus, was also invited. While at the wedding, Mary became aware of a problem; she told Jesus. (Before I relate those wedding events in detail, maybe you will want to review them ahead of time in John 2:5–11.)

Turning Water into Wine

Before He performed any of His other miracles, Jesus *initially* had to turn water into wine. The wedding festivities at Cana had run out of wine. Jesus solved the problem. The original Creator of the world was present in human flesh; He could change things (John 2:6–11).

At the wedding, Jesus had noticed six stone water jars that were filled with dirty water. These vessels had been used by Jewish wedding guests to wash their dusty hands and feet on the way into the reception. When full, each of the six vessels held eighteen to twenty-seven gallons (v. 6). Christ told the wine servers, now standing idle, to add water to the six vessels; they filled the containers to the top (v. 7). After this, Jesus told those servants to take various samples [my interpretation, based on verse 9b] of the new contents to the manager (*maître d'*) of the wedding. They did (v. 8). *Voilà!* The dirty, diluted water had turned to wine (John 2:6–11).

Who would be dumb enough (or faith-filled enough) to believe *that?* Well, the manager who tasted the wine was (vv. 9–10), as well as the servants who knew from where the contents had come (v. 9b)! The disciples of Jesus also believed the water had become wine (v. 11c). The manager was shocked. Why would the groom serve wine of lesser vintage first—and a better vintage later? The opposite should have been the case: the good wine first; then, when the taste buds were dulled, the not-so-good substitutes (v. 10).

The wedding reception crisis was solved; Jesus, the difference maker, had saved the day.

There is so much more to the story, however.

John the disciple was there. He believed. He writes that the turning of water into wine was a "miraculous sign"—one of *three* types of miracles Jesus performed during His ministry. This *sēmeiōn*-type miracle implies Old Testament significance, even a previous foretelling.

> Greek: *sēmeiōn* ("sign"). This type of miracle assumes a repeat by Jesus of some parallel miracle done by an Old Testament prophet. And Jesus had to do it "better."

We go to my very favorite extended Old Testament prophecy; it's in Genesis 49:8–12:

> **8** Judah, your brothers will praise you;
> > your hand will be on the necks of your enemies;
> > your father's sons will bow down before you.
>
> **9** Judah is a young lion;
> > you have come up from eating the prey, my son;
> > > he crouches and stretches out like a lion;
> > > > as a mature lion, who will rouse Him?
>
> **10** The scepter will not pass away from Judah
> > or a ruler from between his feet
> > > until SHILOH [Man of Rest or Peace] comes,
> > > whom the nations will obey.

11 He *or* he will tie His *or* his donkey to a vine;

His *or* his donkey's colt to the choice vine.

He *or* he will wash his clothes in wine;

His *or* his garment in the blood of grapes.

12 His *or* his eyes are dark from wine;

His *or* his teeth white from milk.

Hengstenberg, mentioned in a former chapter and well-known for his unbelievable thoroughness, calls verses 8–10 the "fountainhead" of all Old Testament prophecy (H, *COT*, I, 78). The messianic prophecies that precede this predictive section in Genesis 3; 9; 12, and 22 are more *single*-pointed. With the coming of Genesis 49:8–12, several old and new concepts and their expansions come bubbling out of this marvelous prophecy. It contains several main items that demand fulfillment if Jesus really is *who* He claimed to be. As we will see, this prophecy predicts that an expected "SHILOH" will come from the tribe of "Judah," will be a king, and will turn water into wine (even *much* wine); in addition, it not only predicts four major events that eventually took place in the latter part of Jesus's earthly ministry, but it also predictively hints at the fact that Jesus's *first* miracle will parallel Moses's first *public* miracle.

Insightful biblical observers need to spot these many details in Genesis 49:8–12. Let's explore them!

The context of this prophecy is stated in Genesis 49:1: "Jacob called for his sons. 'Come together,' he said, 'and I will tell you what will happen to you in the future.'" Jacob, whose name was changed to Israel, is now the father of twelve sons (Genesis 46:8–27). He finds himself in Egypt where his son Joseph serves as prime minister. Israel, the grandson of Abraham to whom the promise of a world-saving Descendant had been made (Genesis 12:3; 22:18), was near the end of his life. He called for his twelve sons who, at the end of his prophecies in Genesis 49:28, are named "the Twelve Tribes of Israel."

One by one, from oldest to youngest, the sons pass before their father to hear his last words. The fourth son, Judah, receives the main *spiritual* promise—the Messiah-to-come will generate through his family line. Genesis 49:8 predicts that all of Jacob's other eleven sons will "bow down" to Judah; this is verified by 1 Chronicles 5:2: "Judah grew strong among his brothers and the chief prince was to come from him . . . ." It is also supported by the fact that Jesus was later born in "Bethlehem—in the land of *Judah*" (cp. Micah 5:2 with Matthew 2:1 and Luke 2:4–6).

Genesis 49:9 presents a fascinating history lesson pertaining to Judah and his descendants. This is accomplished by way of "lion" imagery—anticipating Jesus to be the future "Lion from the tribe of Judah" (cp. Revelation 5:5). This is the meaning of the words "Judah is a young lion" (v. 9a): the young lion tribe of Judah will grow in population.

> The poetic indentations in verse 9 represent historical *progression* throughout OT Jewish history—and even forward into Christ's time.

"You have come up from eating the prey" (v. 9b): King David of Judah, like a lion, chews up the Philistines and other enemies, winning many victories.

"He crouches and stretches out like a lion" (v. 9c): King Solomon of Judah, son of David, can now be a king of *peace* and *rest*, because David had ended war for the time being.

> The translation "lion" (male)—though feminine for "lioness" in the Hebrew—is to be preferred for "poetical" reasons (H, COT, I, 63).

But what about the poetic line, "As a mature lion, who will rouse Him" (v. 9d)? No one messes with a "mature" or "full-grown" (H, *COT*, I, 57) lion, especially when the lion is resting after a hearty meal!

What a picture of the ultimate Lion of Judah—Jesus! He will prove to be the "mature lion" of the fourth line of verse 9. Not even Satan will be able to challenge Him successfully *after* His Good Friday victory—a victory solidified by His Easter resurrection. Remember that Calvary featured the "battle of the lions": Satan, who "like a roaring lion, prowls around, looking for someone to devour" (1 Peter 5:8), and Jesus, "the Lion of Judah" (Revelation 5:5). Genesis 49 predicts that battle of Calvary and its outcome—our salvation.

Verse 10 of Genesis 49 is the heart and core of the prophecy. Judah's "scepter" will not pass away. It is secured forever through the victory of Christ, the King of kings (Revelation 19:16). He is the ultimate *Ruler*, born "from between his [Judah's] feet," as were His other Judean ancestors.

> The "scepter" refers to *kingship*.

> The translation "ruler" is supported by Isaiah 33:22, rather than "ruler's staff" (see H, *COT*, I, 67-68).

This phrase is a euphemism for "conception," in line with a child being conceived "from between" a father's legs via the father's sexual organ that impregnates the child's mother. The underlying concept imports the idea that the genealogy of Jesus would not be interrupted—"scepter will not pass away . . . until SHILOH comes" (v. 10).

One day, SHILOH would definitely come.

> It is crucial to remember that Jacob spoke his prophecy in Egypt—the land of the sphinx.
>
> What was a sphinx? It was an Egyptian statue that had the head of a *ram* (male lamb) and the body of a *lion*. Between the front paws and under the chin stood an image of the Pharaoh, king of Egypt.

Have you caught it, fellow detectives?

Look at Revelation 5:5–6. There John views the "Lion from the tribe of Judah." But when he looks up, the lion looks like a lamb. It's the risen King Jesus. Fitting imagery for God to use during Jacob's *Egyptian*-spoken deathbed prophecy. Jesus came from between the feet of human Judean lions. They had composed His continuous genealogy.

> Recall that a "lion" is called "the king of beasts."

Now for a discussion of the most important word in this prophecy: *SHILŌH* – and concerning this Hebrew term, many are the interpretations offered by various non-Christian and Christian interpreters. Seemingly, the soundest contextual meanings of the word *shilōh* revolve around the Hebrew words *shālōm* ("peace"), *shālah* ("stretch out" or "rest"), or possibly the interpretive *wordplay*

> The Hebrew term *SHILŌH* is known as a *hapax legomenon*, a word used only *one* time in Scripture.

of Ezekiel 21:27: "until he comes to whom it rightfully belongs" (NIV); "until He comes whose right it is" (NASB); "until the rightful ruler comes" (JNTP); "until the Righteous One comes" (AAT).

The Ezekiel wordplay represents a further revelation beyond Genesis 49:10 via a reconstruction of the Hebrew: "until the 'rightful' or 'worthy' One comes." This

> Some ancient Jews viewed the Hebrew term "*shilōh*" as a reference to the promised One. This is testified to by the Jewish Targum, a paraphrase-like Old Testament translation expansion, known as Onkelos, where "*shilōh*" is translated "Messiah" (H, *COT*, I, 95).

nicely aligns with Revelation 5 where "worthy" is used three times, showing that Christ the slain, yet the now victorious One, is "worthy" to open the seven seals on the Book of Life to reveal the names of the chosen ones—those who will enter heaven.

As to Genesis 49:10 itself, I translate *shilōh* with the phrase "Man of Rest" since the context has the full-grown lion lying at *rest* after defeating all His enemies. This is right in sync with the words of Jesus in Matthew 11:28: "Come to Me all you who work hard, and I will give you *rest*."

Verse 10 ends by declaring that the "nations" will come to give the "obedience" of *faith* and service to *SHILŌH*.

In verses 11 and 12, the mysteries maximize.

> The "nations" indicates *peoples* from all over the world.

> The better you know the text of Genesis 49:11–12, the more you will appreciate the barrage of quotation marks in the following argumentation—and even throughout the rest of this chapter as to the many words directly quoted from other parts of Scripture. Everything in *quotation marks* are words taken directly from the Bible. Thorough detective work requires tedious alertness.

Let's discover how easy it is to break the Old Testament codes of Genesis 49:11–12 in order to solve some New Testament mysteries! Carefully note these words of Jacob: "donkey" and "donkey's colt"; "wine" and "blood of grapes"; "eyes dark" and "teeth white"!

Now give me church festivals that come to mind if you are a Bible enthusiast.

"Donkey"; "donkey's colt." Yes, Palm Sunday, the day Jesus rode into Jerusalem on a "donkey's colt" at the beginning of what is called Holy Week.

> As we will later learn, Jesus using wine at the Last Supper and shedding His blood both happened on the same day—on a Jewish Friday, not on *two* different days.

"Wine"; "blood of grapes." How about Jesus using "wine" at the Last Supper and shedding His "blood" on the same day?

"Eyes dark"; "teeth white." This is tough one, though able to be understood if you keep traveling on through Holy Week to Easter, the day when Jesus resurrected, "eyes" and "teeth" looking very healthy.

That's all there in verses 11 and 12—and much more!

Besides the Palm Sunday prediction in verse 11a–b, which is further developed in Zechariah 9:9–12, there comes the hint of the water-into-wine miracle at the wedding at Cana. Derek Kidner, a well-respected exegete, agrees (K, *G*, p. 219). The phrase "*blood* of grapes" would foretell

> Somewhat beyond the scope of our investigation are the three small "he's" of verses 11 and 12. Therefore, their explanation has been relegated to Appendix 7.

the changing of water into "red" wine, in addition to Jesus obviously bleeding "red" blood. The "dark eyes" and "white teeth" express good health—and the risen Savior was very healthy and alive forever on Easter morning.

> An exhaustive treatment of SHILOH and the whole of Genesis 49:8–12 is set forth in G, *SJL-K* (153 pages).

Explaining the *Q-Q-1-D* Code of John 2:1–11

Now, let's tie the Genesis 49 clues together with the John 2 mystery.

The Lion of Genesis 49:9d was on the prowl at the wedding, taking total charge. He was Jesus, the Creator of the world come in flesh (John 1:14). He had created water and grapes in the beginning. Now He speeds up a Napa Valley process. He skips the *seed-* and *growing-time-* factors and goes immediately from *water* that helps vines grow, and even beyond the existence of *grapes* and *grape juice*, right to the final product: *wine.*

Nice wedding gift to the bride and groom during what could have been a time of party embarrassment.

Q: And what a gift it was: Not only wine, but also lots of wine, an overabundance of wine, and the best of wine at that (John 2:6, 10)! There was so much wine that a donkey and its colt could chomp away at the central part of the grape arbor (the "choice" section), and still the supply would not be hindered. **Q = quantity** (Genesis 49:11b; John 2:10).

No way did the manager of the reception underestimate the ordering of wine by some 140 gallons within those six stone jar vessels! Think and calculate, Bible detectives.

Q: In addition, there would have been lots of "good" wine left over after the wedding, many gallons that hypothetically could be used the next day for "wash" water (Genesis 49:11c). And its great quality (John 2:10b) would have been able to dye clothes with *one* washing (Genesis 49:11d). That's what Jesus's blood did at Calvary. His *one-time* death (Hebrews 9:27–28) covered the whole stain of the whole world's sin forever (1 John 1:7: "The blood of Jesus His Son washes us clean from every sin"; Isaiah 1:18b: "Though your sins have become like scarlet cloth, they will turn white as snow"). **Q = quality** (Genesis 49:11b; John 2:6).

1: John reports that the Cana phenomenon was the "first" public miracle Jesus performed. No, not the first one among others in Cana but *the* first

> Was Moses really the greatest prophet of the OT? Did Jesus think so? See Appendix 8 for an enlightening discussion of this important question as it also relates to every follower of Jesus.

one—period. It had to be that way to copy Moses, the greatest prophet of the Old Testament, and "better" him. As *Hebrews* says, Christ became "greater" than Moses (3:3).

What, then, was Moses's first *public* miracle? His "leprous-hand" and his "rod-into-a-snake" episodes were events done *privately*, both executed before God alone at the Burning Bush and also later before a limited number of the elders of Israel (cp. Exodus 4:1–7, 29–31). However, Moses's first *public* miracles—"leprous hand," "rod to snake," and "water to blood" (cp. 4:9)—were done *publicly* before numerous "believing" Jews in Egypt (4:30–31). The latter miracle—water being turned into blood—was later done *publicly* before all the population of Egypt when God's miracle through Moses turned the Nile River into blood. This *first* of Ten Plagues [destructive miracles] parallels Jesus doing His *first* miracle *publicly* before a crowd of "believing" disciples and Jews in Cana.

At first glance, you may *not* see the parallel—*water to blood* and *water to wine*. Let's say it this way: water to "red," water to "red" ("*blood* of grapes"—Genesis 49:11d). Certainly, the first *public* miracle of Moses before the *unbelieving* population of Egypt (turning the Nile River blood-"red") was a *curse*; all the fish in that region of the Nile died. With Jesus, however, His "red" wine miracle was a *blessing*. Now there's a prominent Bible motif: "curse" and "blessing"! Last word of the Old Testament: "curse" or "destruction"; last thing in the New Testament, a statement of *blessing* (Revelation 22:21). Check it out! **1 = 1ˢᵗ** ["first"] (cp. John 2:11a)!

D: Finally, the *belief* factor concerning the disciples of Jesus. John reports that "His *disciples* believed in Him." In parallel, Exodus 4 reports that the "people believed" Moses when he repeated God's miracles in front of them, *publicly* (v. 31). Moses had turned water into "red" blood *in public*; Jesus turned water into "red" wine *in public*.

The bottom line is that the Cana miracle had a target audience. Jesus performed this first miracle to gain the trust of His disciples. He succeeded! His disciples "believed." **D = disciples** (Exodus 4:31; John 2:11c)!

Thus, *Q-Q-1-D* illuminates the Cana miracle. Its "letters" summarize clues that solve the water-to-wine mystery: *Q*uantity, *Q*uality, *1* ("first"), *D*isciples!

Evidence room conclusion: The "first" miracle of Jesus was a real *tone setter*, based on the multi-pronged Genesis 49:8–12 prophecy. That prediction—full of clues—makes a multitude of NT mysteries come to life in amazing ways.

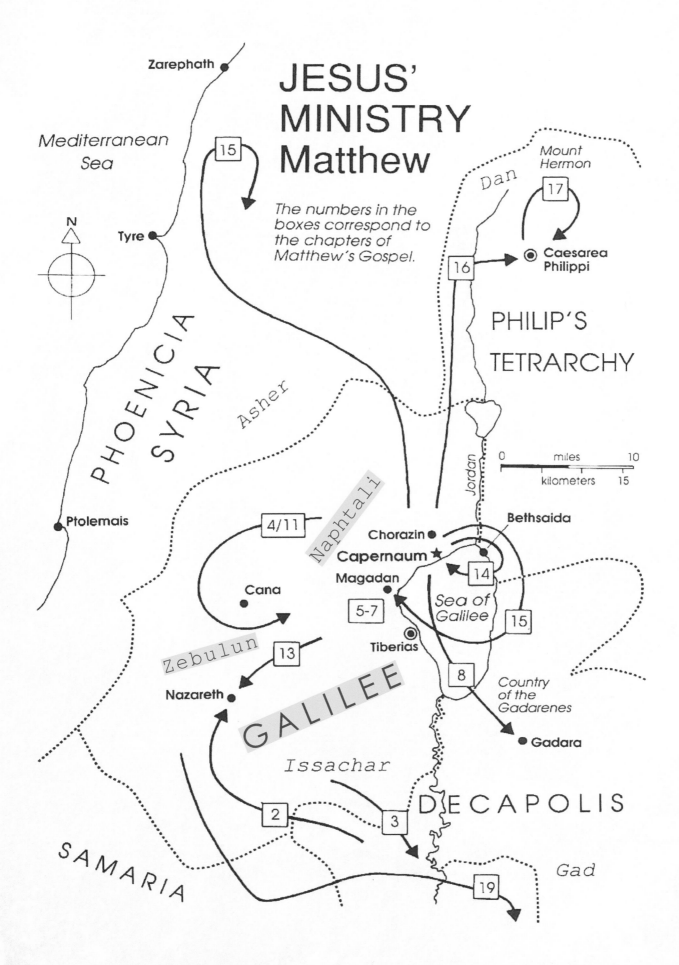

JESUS' MINISTRY Matthew

The numbers in the boxes correspond to the chapters of Matthew's Gospel.

Zarephath

Mediterranean Sea

N

Tyre

PHOENICIA

SYRIA

Asher

Ptolemais

Naphtali

15

Mount Hermon

17

Dan

16 Caesarea Philippi

PHILIP'S TETRARCHY

Jordan

0 miles 10

kilometers 15

4/11

Chorazin

Capernaum

Bethsaida

Cana

Magadan

14

Zebulun

5-7

Sea of Galilee

15

13

Tiberias

Nazareth

GALILEE

8

Country of the Gadarenes

Issachar

Gadara

2

3

DECAPOLIS

SAMARIA

Gad

19

CHAPTER 11

THERE'S A NEW EQUALIZER [JUDGE] IN TOWN!

Examining Clues in the Evidence Room

*Why does Matthew force his readers to review
their Old Testament geography?*

Appreciating the Importance of Biblical Geography

In the Old Testament, that "new 'equalizer' in town" would be called a *judge*. The book of Judges tells us about several of them. One of them, a gal by the name of Deborah, was a judge in the legal sense of the word; she heard court cases (4:4–5). Others like Othniel, Ehud, Barak, Gideon, Jephthah, and Samson were warriors, dishing out God's justice on enemies of His people.

There is one overriding clue in these accounts that ties in with Matthew's strange mention of territories called "Zebulun and Naphtali" (4:13). Jesus left his hometown Nazareth and was making the city of Capernaum His stomping grounds. This was in the New Testament territory of "Galilee," better known formerly as the assigned region given by Joshua to the tribes of Zebulun and Naphtali, sons of Jacob. This territory lay west of the Sea of Galilee, and both areas witnessed many wars on its battlefields. For this reason, Matthew chooses to quote Isaiah 9:1–2 and tie it to the healing ministry of the Savior.

Let's analyze that quote from Matthew 4:15-16:

> Land of Zebulun and land of Naphtali,
> the way to the sea, across the Jordan, Galilee of the Gentiles!
> The people sitting in darkness have seen a great Light;
> for those sitting in the land of the shadow of death,
> a Light has risen.

Into this formerly war-torn territory, Jesus came teaching His good news of the "Kingdom" (Matthew 4:17). As He ministered, people from all around brought their sick who had every kind of disease and malady imaginable. Matthew reports that Jesus healed "every kind of disease and sickness" (4:23). Verse 24 names all these ailments and shares that Jesus "made them well."

Healing every kind of sickness? None that Jesus could not heal? Certainly not at all like modern faith healers who see most sick participants return home after evangelistic gatherings—"unhealed"!

Matthew's message conveys Christ as the One who could conquer every disease!

Strange? Maybe not.

The Old Testament book of *Judges* provides clues that relate to the total effectiveness of Jesus's healing ministry as reported in Matthew 4:23–24. Note them well, detectives!

Judge Ehud's victory was so complete over his Old Testament enemies that "not one escaped" (Judges 3:29). Next, Judge Barak commanded Israelite troops from Zebulun and Naphtali. His defeat of a Canaanite army was so great that "not a single man was left"—in fact, even Sisera, the leading general of that Canaanite army, was executed by a woman named Jael. She was an Israelite spy, a double agent (Judges 4:16, 21). Following this, Judge Gideon, with an army of a mere 300, seems to have had identical results against a Midianite army of well over 120,000 troops (Judges 8:10–12). Finally, Judge Samson singlehandedly overcame his Philistine foes so mightily that when he pushed the pillars down in the temple of their god Dagan, well, every high governmental dignitary, political official, army leader, and high societal person of so-called importance died—simultaneously (Judges 16:29–30).

Now think! Have you ever heard war results where every enemy combatant was killed? Skeptics would claim it is Jewish "fake news," media embellishment of the Scriptures—or, is it true? Were those results worked out by God? Were they meant to serve as *types* that prophetically connected the various Old Testament judges to the coming ultimate, victorious Judge Jesus?

Bible interpreters often fall short. They forget that what God permitted His Old Testament heroes to accomplish on an *earthly* level, Jesus accomplished on a *spiritual* level, sometimes with positive *earthly* ramifications too. Remember, all physical ailments common to humankind came because of God's curse on sinners (cp. Genesis 2:17; 3:17–19), and then Satan got into the act, moving human minds to blame God for all the evil and misery in the world (cp. James 1:12-14; Revelation 12:12b, c, 17–18).

But now there was a new Judge in town who could conquer all evil, right down to the last three most power enemies—sin, death, and the power of the devil. His was—and is—the most complete victory of all.

Let's read Revelation 20:11–15:

> And I saw a great white throne
> and the One sitting on it from whose presence the earth
> and the sky fled away,
> and ˌI saw thatˌ no place was found for them [for the earth and sky].
> And I saw the dead, great and small, standing before the throne.
> And books were opened,
> and another book was opened—the Book of Life.
> And the dead were judged on the basis of the things
> > written in the books according to what they had done.
> And the sea gave up the dead who were in it,
> and death and hades gave up the dead who were in them,
> and each one was judged according to what he had done.
> And death and hades were thrown into the fiery lake.
> > The fiery lake is the second death.
> And if anyone was not found written in the Book of Life,
> > he was thrown into the fiery lake.

There you have it! Fascinating clues from the text of Judges, unravelling the mystery of Matthew's mention of "Zebulun" and "Naphtali"! They were there for consumption by alert Jewish readers in Matthew's day and are still there for interested observers in our day.

Evidence room conclusion: NT truths often spring to life when readers comprehend OT geography. At times, this geography holds clues that open a vast gateway into the halls of NT mysteries. Like the judges of old, Jesus came into the OT territories of Zebulun and Naphtali [the NT area named Galilee]. There He did battle against disease, healing every type of physical ailment. Later, at Calvary, He would defeat the greatest physical and spiritual malady—death. This was verified on Easter morning when He rose from the dead and exited His tomb. As we shall see, *death* could not hold Him.

CHAPTER 12

WAS JESUS THE AUTHENTIC MESSIAH OR JUST ANOTHER FRAUD?

Examining Clues in the Evidence Room

What three events in the teaching and miracle ministry of Jesus further seek to prove His Messianic validity?

Learning to Love John 7:31

Surely, inquiring minds want to know the vital answer to the Jesus question of whether He was the authentic Messiah or just another fraud. The crowds of Jesus's day yearned to know. John 1:19–28 and Matthew 11:2–3 certainly show that expectations for the *imminent* appearance of the Messiah ran high during the days when Jesus walked the earth.

John 7 best expresses this truth.

A big argument broke out. Was He or was He not the Messiah? One group concluded that Jesus was a fraud; He was demon-possessed (vv. 14–27). Others in the crowd disagreed. They asked, "When the Christ [Messiah] comes, will He work ˌevenˌ more miraculous signs than this One has worked" (v. 31)?

These latter observers expected a miracle-working Messiah, one who would outdo the great prophets of the Old Testament. Their conclusion was this: If this miracle worker was *not* the expected One, then a later Messiah would have to do *more* miracles than this Jesus of Nazareth.

Not likely, they concluded; this Nazarene had already done so much—much more than any of the prior prophets (cp. John 21:25).

How could and why would any future personage do more?

I cannot overemphasize the wisdom of this group of Jews who carefully examined the evidence and correctly concluded that Jesus of Nazareth truly was the Messiah, that is, the Christ sent by God!

Back to Acts 2:22

I now return to the crucial Acts 2:22, as Peter proclaims, "Men of Israel, listen to what I have to say: When Jesus from Nazareth was among you, He was a Man whom God commended to you—as you well know—by the *miracles, wonderful proofs,* and *miraculous signs* which God worked through Him." Our clue-searching will put much emphasis on those actions called "miraculous signs."

An Acts 2:22 assumption: Those who experienced the ministry of Jesus should have known He *was* the promised Messiah, just by witnessing His many miracles. The John 7 believers did. They also should have recognized that Jesus was a Prophet *both* in word and action, that is, via His speaking *and* His miracles (Matthew 4:23). Why? His actions were surrounded with His words—with His preaching and teaching.

Notice how John 7 tells of unbelievers rejecting *both* His words and miracles.

To reach solid evidence, our investigation of clues and mysteries will put emphasis on both of these aspects of Jesus's ministry, showing that He was anything other than a fraud. Both His *word* ministry and His *action* ministry verify this.

Further Foundational Leads

John the Baptizer sent his disciples to Jesus, asking: "Are you the One who is coming, or should we look for someone else?" It was the question of the day, and it needs to be our burning question also! We continue with a related question of significance: Why were the people of Jesus's time looking for the coming of a great miracle worker?

Well, personalities and prophets like Jacob and Isaiah had predicted the coming of such a person. That person proved to be Jesus, who on that occasion said, "Go, tell John what you have seen and heard: 'Blind people see and those who were lame are walking; lepers are made clean and deaf people hear; those who were dead are raised and poor people hear the 'gospel' . . .'" (Genesis 49:11; Isaiah 35:5–6; Luke 7:22).

At this point, another foundational lead kicks in. It also comes from the lips of Jesus. In Matthew 12:41-42, Jesus claims to be "greater" than both the prophet Jonah and King Solomon. That's quite a claim! It goes right along with Jesus proclaiming, "I am the Way, the Truth, and the Life. No one comes to the Father, *except by Me*" (John 14:6).

Either Jesus was the biggest nut and egotist ever, or He was right.

> For decades I taught this fact, but just recently I was told that the famous C. S. Lewis had also expressed this same conclusion in different words.

Hang on! You'll stand in wonderment as the "words and actions" of Jesus are presented in additional and surprising ways!

Jesus, the Great "Word" Prophet

We start with *three* narratives that best illustrate Jesus as the great word Prophet: Nathanael and the "ladder" into heaven, the Canaanite woman, and a lesson Jesus taught concerning forgiveness.

Narrative 1: The Appeal of Riding Jesus, the Ladder, to Heaven

John 1:45–51 introduces us to Nathanael, likely Bartholomew, a disciple known by that name in the first three gospels. He was told by the disciple Philip that the One promised by Moses in the Torah had arrived, and that His name was Jesus from Nazareth. Of course, Nathanael did not realize that Jesus had really come from Bethlehem, the location the Old Testament had designated (Micah 5:2). Therefore, Nathanael showed his skepticism by saying to Philip, "Nazareth—can anything good come from there?" How could the Messiah be from Nazareth? He was to come from Bethlehem.

Philip the disciple replied, "Come and see!"

Jesus saw Nathanael coming and already knew him to be a full-practicing Jew per Old Testament guidelines. Jesus had an answer ready for Nathanael's question, "Where did You get to know me" (John 1:48a)? The answer Jesus gave surely blew Nathanael's sandals off! Jesus replied, ". . . when you were under the fig tree, I saw you" (John 1:48b). That statement brought Nathanael to faith. He replied, "You are the Son of God! You are the King of Israel" (John 1:49)!

What just happened? Did we readers miss something?

Clue time!

Nathanael did not live near the place where Jesus was presently located. Yet, Jesus knew that Nathanael was sitting under a fig tree at home when Philip found him. How could Jesus see Nathanael when he was in one place and Jesus in another? Nathanael reasoned, "He must be omniscient; Jesus must be the true Son of God." But the continuing dialog must have shocked Nathanael even more.

> To have your own fig tree meant you owned property and you made your home there. Hence, Jesus saw Nathanael sitting out in his yard under his fig tree.

To paraphrase, Jesus said something like: If you were impressed with that fig-tree thing, you will really be impressed by what you are going to see if you become My disciple (cp. John 1:50b). Be on your toes, detectives!

Jesus continued, "I tell you the absolute truth, you will see heaven opened and the angels of God going up and coming down on the Son of Man" (John 1:51).

Readers must stay sharp on two fronts. First, there is an Old Testament clue that relates to Genesis 28:10–19! It's the story of Jacob or Israel dreaming and seeing a "ladder" connecting heaven to earth. Going up and coming down on it were God's angels.

Second, Jesus relates that Nathanael would be the new Jacob. If he joined Team Jesus, he would also see a ladder with heavenly angels descending and ascending on it.

However, do not miss this most important, new revelation!

Those angels would be "going up and down *on* Jesus, the Son of Man" (John 1:51).

That should blow your socks off! Chad Bird, previous identified, concurs (B, *ROTNC*, Part I, 4–5).

The new ladder that connects heaven to earth is Jesus Himself. He is the "Way" to get to heaven (John 14:6). 1 Timothy 2:5 verifies Jesus's claim, "There is one God. There is also one Mediator between God and humankind, the Man Christ Jesus."

> *mediator*: intercessor; go-between

The "word" Prophet had spoken to Nathanael, and He still speaks to believers today. They also ride the Jesus ladder [that is, the Jesus escalator] to heaven by faith (Ephesians 2:8–9).

Narrative 2: The Canaanite Woman

Check out Matthew 15:21–29 and Mark 7:24–30. The "word" Prophet was at it again, and most important to the following discussion is the fact that Matthew notes that the lady to be discussed below was "a *Canaanite* woman."

Mark identifies the woman as to her *geographical* local: she "was a Greek, a Phoenician from Syria by birth." However, Matthew, writing to Jews, identifies the woman in terms of her *cultural* roots; she was of "Canaanite" lineage, generating from Noah's son Ham and Ham's son Canaan.

This Canaanite connection drives us back to a great messianic prophecy in Genesis 9:24–27, an often misinterpreted passage of Scripture. Background: The flood was over; Noah was now a farmer, growing grapes and making wine. Noah drinks too much; he is laying asleep in his tent, drunk and naked. His son Ham goes into Noah's tent, sees his father's nakedness, goes out and mocks his father in front of his two brothers, Shem and Japheth. Those two brothers enter the tent *backward*, not viewing their father's nakedness, and they cover him with a blanket. Noah wakes and realizes someone has been in his tent. The truth comes out, and then God has Noah prophesy these words: "'Cursed be Canaan [the fourth oldest son of Ham]; he will be the lowest slave to his brothers.' And he added: 'Blessed be the LORD, the God of Shem. Canaan will be his slave. May God make room for Japheth ["enlarge Japheth"], and may he [Japheth] live in the tents of Shem; and let Canaan be his slave.'"

The prophecy is not hard to understand when we first note the Canaanite woman's theological acumen and then couple it with the great compliment Jesus paid her.

We first probe the prophecy in order to understand the reason for Christ's praise.

The interpreter needs to note the *threefold* "curse" put on Canaan, a curse *not* put on Ham's other sons. Ham's descendants were Cush [Ethiopia], Mizraim [Egypt], Put, and Canaan. Ethiopia represents "black people," those who were dispersed after the changing of languages at the Tower of Babel (Genesis 11) and who came to occupy all the territories *south* of the Blue Nile and White Nile rivers in Africa. They were *not* cursed by Noah's prophecy. Neither were the descendants who went to live in the lands of Egypt and Put; only Canaan was cursed.

Those who look down on persons of African heritage *misuse* Genesis 9 to say a curse was put on *all* dark-skinned peoples.

God was merciful when He only cursed one of Ham's sons, when Ham and his whole family should have come under a curse. As Exodus 20:5b–6 records, ". . . I the LORD your God am a jealous God. I discipline the children who hate Me for the sins of their fathers to the third and fourth generations. But to the thousandth generation, I show grace to those who love Me and keep My commandments."

Grace was shown to Cush, Mizraim, and Put, but why not Canaan? Part of the answer comes in Isaiah 55:8–9, while the part concerning the Canaanite woman is solved by the covenant plan God had in mind for Abraham and his Israelite descendants. He had promised them "land" (Genesis 12:1), and that land turned out to be "Canaan," the land later occupied by the Canaanite peoples who were the evil inhabitants listed by God in Genesis 15:19–21: "the Kenites, Kenizzites, Kadmonites, Hittites, Perizzites, Rephaites, Amorites, Canaanites, Girgashites, and Jebusites," and all the other human "termites" in the land. Joke! Lighten up, investigators.

God predicted He would give these Canaanites 400 years to repent, starting in Abraham's time (Genesis 15:16). They did not repent. Therefore, God later sent Joshua to begin their extermination. (Read about it in Joshua 6–12.) Some Canaanites escaped the swords of Joshua's army. As a result, one of their descendants (the Canaanite woman) was alive in Jesus's day to receive grace, God's undeserved love.

In Noah's prophecy, we need to understand that *Jesus* is declared to be the "blessed" coming One; He is referred to as "the LORD, the God of Shem." The Messiah would descend from the genealogical line of Shem. A blessing is also put upon Japheth. The prophecy seems to say that most of Noah's descendants would come from that son. He is to occupy the tents of Shem, who will need to get a bigger tent. In New Testament terminology, Noah promised that many of Japheth's descendants would become believers and thereby would be welcomed into Jesus's Semite Tent, the Holy Christian Church.

Remember, however, that the Canaanites would be "slaves" *in* the Tent of Shem—that Tent also occupied by Japheth. The Canaanite woman, a sharp theological detective in her own right, caught this truth.

Now to the New Testament account of that Canaanite woman. She begged mercy from Jesus, that special Descendant of Shem. But Jesus seems to rebuke her; He refers to her as a "dog" (Matthew 15:26). The disciples played right into Jesus's teaching hand. He was luring His bigoted, Jewish disciples into a trap. The text says they desired Jesus to send this nuisance-of-a-woman away, that woman who kept begging Jesus to heal her demon-possessed daughter (Matthew 15:23). Now the great Prophet could go into "action" with His educating "word"!

Jesus kept playing His curious game of insult, so uncharacteristic of Him. He said to the woman, "It is not good to take the children's bread and throw it to the dogs."

> Dogs were regarded as unclean in Bible days (cp. 2 Kings 9:36–37).

What does that mean, investigators? Christ was baiting the woman, saying that the saving bread of the Jews, the people descended from Shem, was not for Canaanites, as Genesis 9 seemed to imply.

Respectfully, the woman came right back at Jesus, saying, "You are right, Lord, but even the dogs eat some of the crumbs that drop from their master's table." Jesus was really impressed with her answer. He said to her, "O woman, you have a strong faith!" With that, this Canaanite woman received the *second* greatest compliment from Jesus on the pages of the New Testament (cp. Luke 7:9).

What did this woman say that was so impressive? She also knew the Genesis 9 passage very well. Maybe some non-bigoted Jewish rabbi had explained it to her! She realized that slaves ate leftovers in their master's tent *after* the honored guests [the people of Shem] and their other guests [the people of Japheth] had eaten. And since God above has plenty of leftovers ["plenty of redemptive" forgiveness, Psalm 130:7], even the Canaanite people could expect to receive "blessings" from "the LORD, the God of Shem"—Jesus Himself.

That woman was one sharp clue-finder who solved the mystery of Genesis 9, and, in turn, educated Jesus's disciples, who would later need to go into the whole Jewish and Roman world to spread God's love and forgiveness to the descendants of Shem, Ham, and Japheth (Matthew 28:19).

A lot for mystery-solvers to take in!

> By the way, Jesus healed the daughter. That Canaanite woman and her daughter were no longer "cursed." They were now "blessed" by the S(h)emite "Blesser" (Matthew 15:28).

Narrative 3: Way to Go, Peter!

Oh, was Peter in for a surprise when he thought he would razzle-dazzle Jesus with his generous approach to the doctrine of "forgiveness" (Matthew 18:21–35). Fascinating narrative!

Traditionally, Jews taught that a person should forgive another person a total of *three* times. Try *that* one with children—they would be out of the house by age two.

But Peter was way more loving and understanding, or so he thought. He doubled the three, added one, and expected "a pat on the back" from Jesus when saying that "seven" would be a good number of times to forgive others (v. 21). Think how that would work if our God was willing to forgive us *only seven* times—and no more.

Jesus, as usual, had a mysterious answer that needs solving via an Old Testament clue. He told Peter everyone should be willing to forgive the other guy "seventy times seven" (Matthew 18:22). No, not 490 times. You, your children, and the world would still not be safe. All of us would be out of the house by age five.

Jesus knew that the number "7," when used symbolically, stood for "perfect perfection." Thus,

He was saying that a person should forgive their neighbor a "perfect" number of times, as many times as that neighbor needs forgiveness—always, over and over.

But how forgiving are people in this world? In America, there is a saying, "First time, shame on you. Second time, shame on me." In practice, that would mean that some Americans are not as generous as the Jews of Peter's day. Those who follow this American saying are willing to forgive "one" time, but not a second. Maybe most of the world is as generous as Peter. Many are not!

To solve the mystery of the 70 x 7, we must recognize that Jesus was playing off Genesis 4:23–24. It concerns the unforgiving, evil Lamech, not to be confused with the other Lamech who was Noah's father (Genesis 5:28–29). This evil Lamech was the world's first bigamist (Genesis 4:19). (Like Adam didn't have enough trouble with *one* wife.)

This evil Lamech was the seventh generation from Adam, descending from his ancestor Cain, who had killed his brother Abel. When this first Lamech was wronged, he placed forgiveness on the *negative* side of the ledger. He was totally unforgiving; to him revenge was the name of his human game.

God had showed Cain, the world's first murderer, some mercy when Cain complained about God's punishment for his crime. God promised that if anyone killed Cain, well, that person would be "punished seven times," meaning seven times more severely than Cain.

In the Bible's first certain poetry, Lamech bragged:

> Adah and Zillah, listen to me;
> Lamech's wives, hear what I say:
>> I killed a man for wounding me
>> and a young man for bruising me.
>>> If Cain is avenged seven times,
>>> then Lamech seventy-seven (77) times.

It does sound like the world some share. Get revenge, get even!

The religious arena into which Jesus invites His followers is so different. In sports' terminology, it's like a soccer and football stadium full of forgiveness, endless forgiveness for those who are willing to repent, ask for forgiveness, and, turning to Jesus, run forward in trust, knowing they are forgiven by His shed blood. He turns no one away, no one who seeks His loving forgiveness (note that Psalm 136 endlessly repeats, "His mercy lasts forever"). No matter how terrible the iniquity, God promises, "I will forgive the wrong they did and not remember their sins anymore" (Jeremiah 31:34). Hebrews 7:25: "And so He [Jesus] can forever save those who come to God by Him, because He always lives to pray for them."

Oops, Peter had just received a significant theological readjustment.

The "word" Prophet had spoken again, and sinners should be comforted and then heed His command to show mercy toward others in the form of *forgiveness*, even if the other person continues to hate them (Matthew 5:44).

By Way of Transition

The New Testament book of Hebrews adds greatly to our preliminary findings. It testifies to the *superiority* of Christ. Again, its key superglue-word is the term *better*. Jesus, the final Messenger, the Son of God (1:1–2), is presented as "better" than the angels, Moses, ˌJoshuaˌ, and Melchizedek, in addition to being the One who has brought a "better" salvation, hope, and covenant or last will and testament, as well as being a "better" Mediator with "better" promises. And the zinger: a "better" sacrifice with eternal possessions, like a "better" land, namely, heaven, life, and an accomplished hope brought about by the shedding of His own "better" redeeming blood (Hebrews 1:4; 3:3; 4:8–9; 6:9; 7:7, 19, 22; 8:6 [2 times]; 9:23; 10:34; 11:16, 35, 40; 12:24)!

Have you figured it out yet? Answer: In part, certain "word" items of the Old Testament, as well as its miracles, had to be *interpreted* and *repeated* by Jesus—but in a much more significant and powerful ("better") way. (This aspect will be dealt with over and over in the chapters to follow.)

Evidence room conclusion: Jesus was a multifaceted Teacher, who—through words and actions—"bettered" OT historical accounts in unimaginable ways, proving Himself to be authentic and not a fraud. This must be illustrated throughout all the chapters to follow.

CHAPTER 13

EXCITING INVESTIGATIVE BREAKTHROUGHS

Examining Clues in the Evidence Room
*What are the two miracles of Jesus
that may have superior Old Testament connectives?*

Three "Bread" Surprises

Having now laid the foundation of our investigation in previous chapters, we are ready to cite multiple examples that unveil *New Testament mysteries with Old Testament clues*. We travel onward, shadowing additional "actions" of Jesus, unmasking other miracles He enacted.

We begin with two fun and clever clues. They both concern Christ Jesus feeding lots of people with just a few loaves of bread. Read on to be surprised!

What Kind of Bread Did Jesus Use to Feed the "5,000"—and Who Cares?

In John 6:9, you'll discover that Jesus chose to use "barley" bread to feed over "5,000" people. Twelve baskets of bread were left over. By this miraculous action, Christ Jesus was repeating two miracle incidents from the Old Testament—one relating to the prophet Elisha; the other to the military leader Judge Gideon.

Let's deal with Elisha first.

The Elisha "Barley" and "Leftovers" Connections

On one Old Testament occasion, Elisha the prophet fed a hundred hungry people with twenty small "barley" loaves—and there were *leftovers* (2 Kings 4:42–44).

Jesus did His "barley" miracle "better." He was given a mere five loaves and two fish. These he multiplied to feed "5,000 men" (probably around fifteen thousand, if women and children would have been counted). After everyone was fed, there were *twelve* baskets of bread left over. In John's Gospel, this miracle is called a "miraculous sign," and Jesus is proclaimed "the Prophet," in accordance with Deuteronomy 18:15, 18. You can read these facts in John 6:1–14.

Concerning "The Feeding of the Five Thousand" with bread, Matthew presents this miracle of Jesus in just nine verses, Mark in fifteen verses, and Luke in eight verses. About forty years after those first three gospels were written, the Fourth Gospel explains the same event in thirty-seven verses. Quite a difference. John's added *doctrinal* input is invaluable (see John 6:22–58). He is the only writer who reports that Jesus used "barley" bread; however, all four gospels confirm the twelve baskets of *leftovers*.

Oh, so many significant things to relate! Let's explore the "leftovers" first. To make the account fully meaningful, we need to realize that Jesus later fed "4,000" on another day, having *seven* baskets of leftovers on that occasion (Matthew 15:32–38; Mark 8:1–9).

Now the detective work.

After viewing the feeding of the two groups, the disciples climbed into a boat with Jesus. As usual, they were off target, theologically. They were upset they had forgotten to bring some of the *leftovers* along to eat. Jesus redirected their attention to more important things of the Kingdom, asking His disciples how many baskets of leftovers they had picked up after each feeding? They responded quickly: "twelve" and "seven." Jesus then asked them, "Do you still not understand" (Mark 8:21)?

And that's where the account ends in Mark 8:21.

Why does Jesus not state the significance of the *twelve* and the *seven*? Simply because He has given His people *spiritual* brains! Twelve disciples; twelve baskets of bread: The twelve disciples are to feed the masses with Jesus—the Bread of Life—spiritually!

But what about the seven baskets? They also have a *spiritual* meaning: Feed the people of the Kingdom every *seven* days in public church services, in line with the "Remember to keep the Sabbath day holy" commandment (Exodus 20:8).

The Gideon "Barley" and "King" Connections

How could Judge Gideon figure into a "barley" motif and fulfillment, being connected to Jesus's bread miracle? Hard to detect.

Understandably, Gideon was God's *reluctant* general. He was chosen to go up against a Midianite army that was 120,000 strong. God cut Gideon's army down to 300 soldiers. I think I understand Gideon's reluctance to enlist under these circumstances.

Through a series of "signs," God mustered up faith and courage within the heart of Gideon (cp. Hebrews 11:32). He eventually went into battle and won an overwhelming victory.

One of those signs of encouragement involved barley bread. On the night of the battle, God told Gideon to go down to the outskirts of the Midianite camp to observe the changing of the guard, a change that took place every four hours. Most likely, the hour was around 10:00 p.m., the time when the enemy soldiers were in their deepest sleep.

The soldier coming on duty had been sent a dream from God. He saw a loaf of "barley bread tumbling around in the camp of Midian" until it came and flattened the guard tent. He told this dream to the soldier going off duty. That soldier was given the momentary gift of interpretation. He announced that the barley loaf was none other than Gideon and the Israelite army, and that the Midianite army was doomed (Judges 7:9–14).

With this revelation, Gideon gained confidence, rallied his 300, surrounded the Midianite camp, had the battle trumpets blown and the lanterns of fire broken, and watched as the Midianite camp went into a panic. Coming out of deep sleeps and being disoriented, the enemy soldiers swung their swords widely, killing each other. Those who got away were pursued and eventually killed.

Now the neat part of the account.

When Gideon returned from battle, what did the Israelites want to do with him? Make him a king (Judges 8:22). What did the people want to do with Jesus after He fed the "5,000"? Make Him a king (John 6:15). The parallel between the two accounts is just a bit *"Too Coincidental to Be Accidental!!!* Don't you think? Another New Testament mystery solved with Old Testament clues!

But there is more to the story!

Moses was mentioned in relation to "manna" in the aftermath of Jesus's New Testament barley miracle (John 6:30–31). The Jewish opposition that followed that miracle revolves around the fact that Jesus had only fed the crowd *once* with barley bread, but Moses had daily performed the manna or bread miracle for forty years. Bad analysis; faulty deduction!

> John's added *theological* aspects highlight Jesus as the "Bread of Life come down from heaven" as "Manna." The manna aspect certainly brings the person of Moses into the picture.

Jesus set His opponents straight.

God—not Moses—had fed the people for forty years (John 6:32).

But was Moses not "better" if he was God's instrument to feed the people every day for forty years? Not so fast! Jesus had a "better" bread—Himself, meaning that to eat Jesus by faith saves souls forever, never to hunger again in heaven, physically or *spiritually* (John 6:43–58).

He Walked on What?

Yes, that is what Scripture says: Jesus walked on water. To be sure, that God of heaven always has something mysterious up His sleeve. But this time the mystery is not very difficult to solve if you know the big water miracles of the Old Testament—miracles that God worked through His various prophets.

The Moses "Dry Ground" Connection

First, there was Moses who was given the power to divide the Red or Reed Sea. And no, it was not a shallow body of water that had dried up by the time the Israelites arrived. Rather, when the fleeing Jews crossed over it, the waters stood high on both sides of them as a "wall" (Exodus 14:22). Nor was the Red or Reed Sea a marsh through which the Israelites wadded. As Josh McDowell,

Amazon sells McDowell's masterpiece, *Evidence That Demands a Verdict.*

famous Campus Crusade for Christ speaker, said publicly in the past, the whole Egyptian army did *not* drown in six (6) inches of water (cp. Exodus 14:23–28). Humor with a punch.

But something was obvious; Moses had to divide the waters to walk across on dry ground (Exodus 14:21).

The Joshua "Dry Ground" Connection

Second, Joshua, Moses's successor, crossed the Jordan River on dry land; that is, after the priests who were carrying the "Ark of the Covenant" had first stepped into the water. In his day, God caused the waters up north to dam up, and then the Israelite army and people crossed over on dry land. Once again, another prophet had to have water removed in a miraculous way to cross from one side to another.

The Elijah and Elisha "Dry Ground" Connections

Lastly, the prophets Elijah and Elisha had to divide the waters of the Jordan River to cross over (2 Kings 2:8, 13–14). They, too, crossed on dry ground by getting rid of water.

The Connecting Disconnect concerning Jesus

Yup, you guessed it; Jesus did it "better"; He crossed the Sea of Galilee without dividing the waters. He just walked on top of the water to reach His disciples who were in a boat in the middle of the sea and who were having a hard time rowing because of the fierce wind against them. Jesus got into their boat, and just like that, He made the boat reach shore "in a moment" (John 6:15–21). (John 6:15-21; see similar conclusion at L, *EC*, p. 223.)

At times, Jesus does not just outdo the former prophets by repeating their actions in extraordinary ways; He also does miracles that are totally *new* in all shapes and forms. That's the kind of Savior the world needed: unique, strong, and innovative. Drove Satan crazy, all the way into hell.

Evidence room conclusion: Bible investigators will get nowhere if they do not use OT clues to solve NT mysteries. As this chapter detected, the use of "barley" bread by Jesus to feed "5,000," as well as His walking on water, instead of *dividing* the Sea of Galilee, prove this point in a most determinate way.

CHAPTER 14

MORE MIRACLE INVESTIGATIONS

Examining Clues in the Evidence Room

*Why is it important to connect certain miracles of the Old Testament
with the New Testament miracles of Jesus
and observe the element of "fulfillment"?*

Two Comparable "Leprosy" Miracles

Our first miracle evaluation in this chapter will compare a New Testament leprosy healing done by Jesus with an Old Testament leprosy healing accomplished by Elisha the prophet.

In the seventeenth chapter of his Gospel, Luke the doctor records one of the leprosy miracles performed by Jesus: the healing of ten lepers. This miraculous healing event in the ministry of Jesus directly paralleled the healing of an Old Testament man named Naaman, a military captain, who formerly had also been cured of leprosy at the directive of Elisha the prophet (2 Kings 5:1–27).

To understand the full impact of the two accounts—their similarity and difference—you must realize that the Bible speaks of *two* types of leprosy. One of these skin diseases was *contagious*, the other not. Naaman must have had the *non-contagious* kind. Since he was an army captain, he would not have been able to be in close contact with fellow soldiers if his leprosy had been contagious.

The ten lepers who approached Jesus for healing stayed "at a distance" since they were *contagious* (Luke 17:12b). Obviously, the healing performed by Jesus was "better" because of the greater *severity* of the disease.

Naaman was a Gentile from Syria, not Canaan. This important clue parallels Jesus's healing of the ten lepers. Only one of those ten men came back to thank Him, "and he was a Samaritan" (Luke 17:16b), a Gentile half-Jew.

> It is conjectured by Bible scholars that Samaritans were Jews who had been forced to intermarry with Gentile foreigners after 722 BC at the command of their Assyrian conquerors. You can read about this Samaritan background in the NET, "Jews Contrasted with Samaritans," pp. 553–554.

Jesus repeated the Naaman event in a heightened way with ten lepers, not only one being healed. He was thanked by the healed "Samaritan" (Luke 17:16), as Elisha had been offered appreciation by Naaman the Gentile (2 Kings 5:15).

> We will call Jesus the "Recapitulator" or "Repeater" when we later develop the First Adam and Second Adam motif of Romans 5 in Appendix 6.

Three More Very Remarkable Miracles

The next reported miracles connect Elijah and Elisha to a special action of Jesus. Let's start with Elijah.

By direction and protection of God, Elijah was sent to the northern city of Zarephath, near Sidon in Phoenicia. There he performed another bread miracle which relates to Jesus "Feeding of the 4,000" (Matthew 15:32–38; Mark 8:1–9; 1 Kings 17:10–24.) 1 Kings 17 tells us that God sent Elijah to stay with a widow and her son during a time of famine. Eventually the son died. Elijah resurrected the boy by laying on him three times—nose to nose, shoulder to shoulder, knees to knees. After the third time, the boy came back to life.

> Rev. Chad L. Bird, former professor of exegetical theology, Concordia Theological Seminary, Fort Wayne, IN, reveals that some of the Greek of the LXX concerning the raising of the boy of Zaraphath and Jesus raising the boy of Nain in *Luke* is identical (B, *ROTNC*, Part II, 27; cp. LXX: 3 Kings 17:23c; Luke 7:15b).

Elisha did the same for a mother and father of the city of Shunem when their son died. This time, however, the prophet Elisha laid on the boy *once*—nose to nose, shoulder to shoulder, knees to knees. Then when he got off the boy, the boy remained dead. Following this, Elisha just leaned over the boy and the boy came alive.

Do you detect the meaning?

How many times did Elisha approach the boy? One-and-a-half times.

Elisha had *doubled* the power of Elijah. Why? Well, that's what Elisha had asked for before his teacher Elijah was taken to heaven alive in a chariot of fire. It was granted: "a double portion of Elijah's spirit" or accomplishments (2 Kings 2:9–12).

Elijah performed *eight* miracles during his ministry; Elisha *sixteen*. Elisha's miracles doubled those of Elijah. Just coincidental? Doubtful! Author Rob Schwartz has penned an entire book that treats all *twenty-four* miracles of Elijah and Elisha from 1 Kings 17–2 Kings 13, noting the significance of the eight and its doubling—sixteen (see S, *MMP*, pp. v–vii; also H, *EE*, pp. 50–51).

Now onward to the third miracle: a resurrection event in the ministry of Jesus the Savior. He entered the city of Nain, Luke tells us (7:11–17). It was a sad scene Jesus encountered, a situation that only a caring doctor like Luke could report with such empathy. A dead boy was being carried out of the city for burial; he was the only son of his mother, and she was a widow. What a buildup of pathos in Luke's compassionate telling of the surrounding circumstances! Jesus felt the same kind of compassion for the grieving mother. Time for Him to take merciful action!

Jesus went up to the open coffin and touched it, commanding the young man to wake up. The boy rose.

Have you sleuths caught it? Jesus raises the boy without even touching him. He possessed more power than both Elijah and Elisha put together. *Better* is the word! Just bow in awe! Most interesting!

Let's now tackle a very strange miracle mystery.

Paralleling Miracles: Not an Easy Task!

Elisha made an ax head float in the Jordan River. When did Jesus ever do something like that to "better" Elisha? He did; let's investigate.

2 Kings 6:1–7 relates this story. A student in Elisha's seminary was helping build a dormitory. He was chopping down a tree to get wood for the structure. His borrowed ax head flew off and landed in the

> Elisha's seminary = "the school of the prophets"

muddy Jordan. Trouble! He would have to quit school to get a job to pay for the lost ax head. Elisha saved the day; he made the ax head float; it was retrieved; the man could stay in Elisha's seminary.

Where can anyone find a miracle of Jesus that parallels that of Elisha? Inspectors must parallel objects of like substances. Compare: metal to metal.

That's it! Now it's crystal clear!

Jesus did it in Matthew 17:24–27. The context: It was tax time. Jesus told Peter, the fisherman, to go to the Sea of Galilee, throw out a fishing line and hook, take the first fish caught, open its mouth, and take out the coin that would be inside, and then go and pay the Temple tax that was owed by Jesus and Peter.

Bet Matthew, the former tax collector, liked that miracle!

Surely you clue-searchers catch the connection! The coin was metal like the ax head. When Peter paid the Temple tax, he could stay in Jesus's seminary (like the borrower of that ax head was able to stay in Elisha's seminary), and Jesus could continue as seminary president of His class of disciples. Besides, Jesus remained *sinless* by fulfilling His tax obligation (Matthew 22:21).

The "better" part? Elisha asked the student where the ax head had entered the water. Jesus asked no information; He knew where Peter should go to catch the fish that had the coin in its mouth. Jesus, the God-Man, was omniscient!

> **Evidence room conclusion:** True mystery lovers should be tantalized by the interaction between OT clues and NT mysteries. This interrelated phenomenon is most intriguing, but beyond that, it is crucial to the overall impact that screams "F U L F I L L M E N T" on the pages of the NT.

CHAPTER 15

BY WAY OF TRANSITION

Examining Clues in the Evidence Room
*How did several seemingly disconnected accounts
in the New Testament
relate to Christ's imminent death?*

Two Major Interjections

It's time to wrap up our study of the action or miracle ministry of Jesus as we prepare for the following chapters that will critique His suffering, death, resurrection, and ascension. We begin with two interjections.

The first will note the importance of comparing King David, the great Old Testament warrior, to Jesus, the ultimate Warrior of Mount Calvary. The second interjection will treat three *transitional* episodes that took place quite near the time when Christ's ministry entered its violent stage.

The King David Interjection

We begin our paralleling of the warriors David and Jesus by asking multiple number-related questions: Why "five" stones when David fought Goliath the giant (1 Samuel 17:40), and why "five" porches at Bethesda when Christ healed a desperately sick man on a Sabbath day (John

5:2, 8), and why "five" brothers in the episode of "The Rich Man & Lazarus," as told by Jesus (Luke 16:28)? Once again, thorough detectives want to know.

Did you notice the clues hinted at above by the number "five"? *Symbolically*, "5" is the number that expresses "human experience" in terms of "suffering, fear, courage, sadness, joy, tears, laughter, hope," in short, "the full experience of human senses and emotions."

> You can read all about the number "5" and other Bible numbers in a book by G. M. "Jack" Cascione. In addition to analyzing the meaning of various Bible subjects appearing in numeric sets according to subject matter, this book reveals the meanings of the numbers "1" through "7," as well as well as "10" and "12"— even compounds of these Bible numbers. See C, *SBO*, pp. 71–84 concerning the number "5" and its meanings.

When David picks up five stones to fight Goliath, this is the Bible's way of expressing David's "fear and courage," both at the same time. The "five porches" at Bethesda bring "suffering and hope" to mind, while the situation of the rich man and his "five brothers," who are headed to hell, spells "agony and despair."

For the moment, we center on one aspect of the David and Goliath narrative. David the warrior must be viewed as a "type" of Jesus the warrior. As David faced Goliath the giant, so Jesus went to war against Satan, the giant of hell. With His victory, Jesus "undid the works of the devil" (1 John 3:8). The latter was a "miracle of miracles," one far superior to that of David.

> Appendix 14, the section on "The Real Meaning of the 'David and Goliath' Account" addresses the whole David and Goliath episode in detail.

A Threefold Interjection

We now head toward three events that seal Jesus's fate. These episodes may seem unrelated, but they are not. The first deals with a miracle that spells certain death for the Messiah, namely, an action that leads to His crucifixion. The other two accounts compliment the first, as they also guide the reader's attention to the cross of Calvary. In harmony, all three accounts help us transition to the area of Jerusalem where the Savior dies and then physically resurrects three days later.

"Lazarus, Come Out!"

Minus the Passion saga of Jesus, most would call the raising of Lazarus from the dead the most pivotal event in the ministry of Jesus. Read the account in John 11:1-57. It was mind-shattering and caused Jesus's popularity to skyrocket (v. 45). In contrast, it angered the Jewish religious authorities so much that from this time on these Temple leaders determined Jesus must be arrested and killed (vv. 46–50, 57).

Jesus was not in Bethany when his dear friend Lazarus, brother of Mary and Martha, became deathly sick. With theological purpose, Jesus intentionally dilly-dallied around when He got the news and delayed His departure to Bethany. He did not arrive there until Lazarus was already dead four days, and Lazarus's body was already decaying (vv. 38–39).

Tough restoration to perform! But Jesus was Jesus, and He could overcome anything.

After Lazarus's sepulchral stone was moved away, Jesus *spoke* to perform His resurrection miracle. It's a good thing He said, "Lazarus, come out!" If He would have withheld the name "Lazarus," all the graves in the world could have opened, as they will when He speaks on the Last Day, so the Scriptures say (John 5:28–29).

Lazarus walked out, in full command of all his mental and physical capacities.

There had been a few resurrections performed in biblical days of old, but none compared to this one; none was a pure parallel to the resurrection of Lazarus.

Just as Jesus had spoken at Creation ("Let there be light," and the light hopped into existence), so His words on this occasion once again sounded forth, and Lazarus jumped back to life. Yes, the voice of Jesus carried power.

Yet sometimes, in accordance with His human nature in His state of humiliation, Jesus the Savior needed a "word" to strengthen Him for the task ahead. We now consider such a need.

The Mount of Transfiguration: Its Mystery Revealed

Jesus and His inner circle of disciples—Peter, James, and John—are on a "high" mountain, possibly Mount Hermon, far, far north of southern Jerusalem. Suddenly, the two most prominent Old Testament prophets appear from heaven: Moses and Elijah. They are considered the most important in that Moses represented the "Law" (Torah) and Elijah "the order of the prophets." Jesus's human figure is momentarily glorified; it is

You'll find the full account of Jesus's Transfiguration in Matthew 17:1–9; Mark 9:2–13; and Luke 9:28–36.

transfigured; it is drastically changed.

But wait a second. How can Moses be present and alive? God buried him on Mount Nebo (Deuteronomy 34:5–6). Sherlock Holmes time! Jude 9 solves the dilemma. New Testament readers are brought up to date by this passage. Here's the lowdown.

After Moses's death, the devil asked for Moses's dead body. *So* sneaky! Why would he want Moses's body, except to make an ancient Islamic-type Medina? Satan would have loved to set up a shrine for the Israelites to make a hajji out into the desert to worship Moses. How devilish!

Think about it. There are two ways for a pastor to become real popular: take a call to another congregation or die. While Moses was alive, many Israelites despised him and caused him continual grief. Satan, who well understands the human condition, knew Moses would become very popular *after* death. The people of Israel might even come to worship him through the centuries—if given the opportunity—and they would then forsake the God whom Moses served. Just compare Jesus's day: The Jewish leaders hated Jesus, but they loved to quote Moses in opposition to Him. Go figure! People are people, and the devil counted on it.

This time, however, Satan was up against his Creator, Michael the Archangel (Jude 9). Indeed, "Michael" surely is none other than Christ Himself! Here are four clues that lead to this realization: First, the name Michael means "Who is like God." No one is more like God than Jesus Himself.

> Read the *"Michael the Archangel"* appendix of the NET, pp. 555–557, an argument in defense of the belief that Michael the Archangel is Jesus.

Next, *archangel* means "high angel." Remembering that the term *angel* means "messenger," we quote Hebrews 1:1–2: "At many times and in various ways, God—who long ago *spoke* to our fathers by the prophets—has in these last days *spoken* to us by His Son, whom He made the Heir of everything and by whom He also made the world." There it is; Jesus is the final Messenger Angel and the "highest" heaven-sent Messenger at that.

Third, Michael is mentioned in *Daniel* but never in any context in the whole Bible where the "Angel of the LORD" or "Jesus" Himself is present. Why? Because all three are the same Person. It is only after Jesus ascends back into heaven that Michael is again mentioned in *Jude* and *Revelation*.

Finally, you are challenged to find anyone in the sixty-six Bible books, except Michael, who is ever called *archangel*. Roman Catholicism claims "seven" archangels but needs extra-religious writings to try to substantiate this claim (see 1 Enoch xx. 1–7).

Now back to Jude 9.

In this New Testament passage, it is reported that Michael—*after* the death of Moses in the Old Testament—had asked God the Father to rebuke the devil's request for the dead body of Moses. As an astute investigator, you might wonder why Michael, if He is Jesus, would not have denied Satan's request Himself.

Quite simple!

Jesus had *not* yet appeared on earth, died, and conquered Satan. Jesus's redemptive act was yet to come; He had not yet proved Himself superior to the devil.

The Jude 9 text implies that the heavenly Father did not grant Satan's request. As a result, a solid assumption can be made. God had secretly removed the body of Moses, resurrected it, and had taken Moses to heaven alive. That's how Moses comes to be alive on the Mount of Transfiguration, along with Elijah, who had gone to heaven *alive* in a chariot of fire.

What did Jesus and Moses and Elijah talk about on the mountain when Jesus had His figure transformed into a most glorious form? They talked about Jesus's "departure" from this world; they talked about His coming death (Luke 9:31). Pastor Robert Green of Bethlehem Lutheran Church, Parma, Ohio, USA, insightfully broke the code in one of his brilliant sermons. He concluded that Moses and Elijah appeared in order to strengthen Jesus in preparation for His coming suffering and death.

Makes great sense!

Hebrews 2:28 reports: "He Himself [Jesus] experienced testing when He suffered." That meant Jesus Himself would also need encouragement. Moses and Elijah brought it from heaven. Both Old Testament prophets had been through exceedingly difficult ministries. They understood Jesus's coming dilemma, empathized, and brought that needed encouragement. They were now able to offer Jesus comfort and words of support for His journey to Calvary. Jesus, who spoke and gave so much support to others through His word and miracle ministry, now received such encouragement for the struggles ahead of Him.

Strengthened, He was now off to Jerusalem to suffer and die (Matthew 16:21).

Way Out of the Way

After three-and-a-half years of ministry (inferred by Luke 4:25–30; cp. Daniel 9:27b), Jesus started His trek to Jerusalem to die; however, he went way out of His way to get there. Why did He do this when He could have gone straight down south from Galilee, through Samaria, up to Jerusalem? Clues appear as we evaluate Matthew 19:1: "When Jesus finished these sayings, He left Galilee and went to the territory of Judea on the other side of the Jordan."

For the route of Jesus's trip to Jerusalem, see map below.

If Jesus had gone straight down from Galilee, He would have stayed west of the Jordan;

instead, He went to the *eastern* side. Why? Jesus wanted to emulate the journeys of two previous prophets, Joshua and Elisha. Both of these Old Testament prophets had entered the Holy Land from the *eastern* side of the Jordan to start the main parts of their ministries.

Joshua, the man after whom Jesus was named, crossed the Jordan River, marched his army to "Jericho," and then continued marching around the city every day for a week until its walls "fell down" (Joshua 6:20). From there, Joshua went on to accomplish his main task: dividing the land among the twelve tribes of Israel (Joshua 10–22).

After Elijah's chariot-of-fire ascension, his successor Elisha also journeyed westward across the Jordan to "Jericho," where he healed waters that were causing miscarriages for pregnant mothers (2 Kings 2:18–22). From there, Elisha went on to accomplish his main tasks (many actions of Elisha are recorded in 2 Kings 2–13, along with other data).

After Jesus crossed the Jordan from the *eastern* side, He also passed through "Jericho" where He healed two blind men (Matthew 20:29–34), one was named Bartimaeus (Mark 10:46–52). From there, Jesus went on to accomplish His main task of suffering, dying, and rising again (see Matthew 20:18).

A journey containing *"Evidence Just Too Coincidental to Be Accidental!!!"*

Evidence room conclusion: Even NT accounts that seem very unrelated on the surface prove to be unified when OT clues are used to delve into NT mysteries. Those cited above aid our upcoming research into the particulars of Christ's suffering and death.

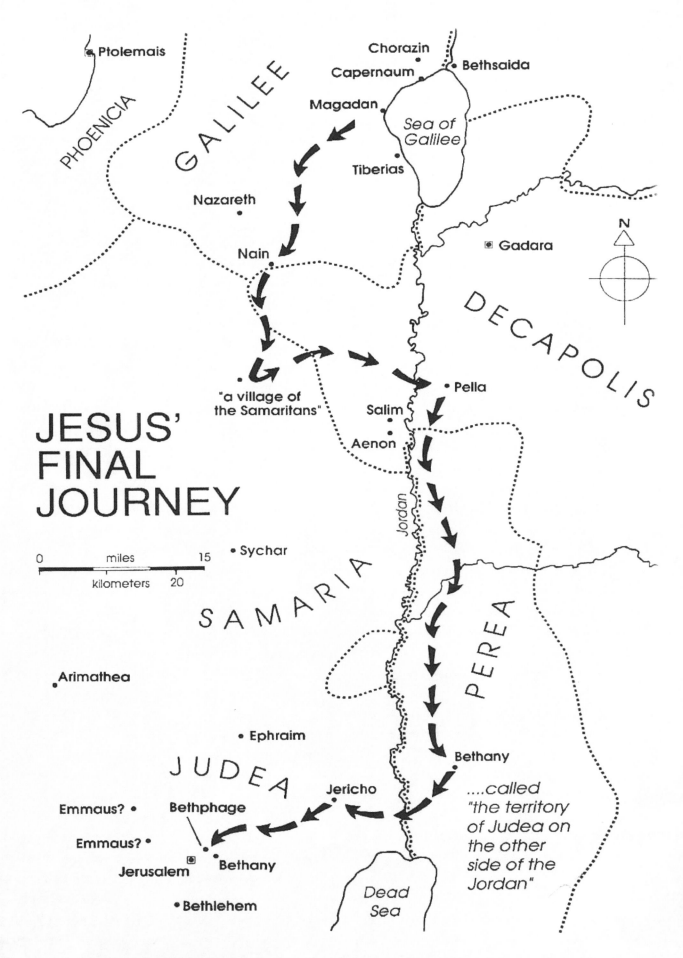

Ptolemais

PHOENICIA

GALILEE

Chorazin

Capernaum · Bethsaida

Magadan

Sea of Galilee

Tiberias

Nazareth

Nain

DECAPOLIS

Gadara

"a village of the Samaritans"

Pella

Salim

Aenon

Jordan

JESUS' FINAL JOURNEY

0   miles   15

kilometers   20

Sychar

SAMARIA

PEREA

Arimathea

Ephraim

JUDEA

Jericho

Bethany

Emmaus? ·

Bethphage

....called "the territory of Judea on the other side of the Jordan"

Emmaus? ·

Jerusalem   Bethany

Bethlehem

Dead Sea

N

109

Jewish and Roman *time* designations: For modern clarity, I have used English a.m. and p.m. indicators. The four canonical Gospels, being written in a period before clocks and wristwatches, denotes *time* via the word *hour* (cp. "sixth hour" and "ninth hour"). A comparison of Matthew 27:45–46; Mark 15:25, 33–34; and Luke 23:44 with John 19:14 will show that the first three gospels use the Jewish method of telling *time*, while John employs the Roman system.

The " . . . biblical hours cannot be translated exactly into modern clock-hours" since the Jews measured "hours" from "sunset to sunrise" and "sunrise to sunset" (B, *NBD*, p. 543)—and that measurement varied from season to season. The Romans reckoned *time* from 12 a.m. (midnight) to 12 p.m. (noon) and then completed the 24-hour cycle with another 12-hour period.

Two Greek words—both translated "about" in John 19:14 and Matthew 27:46—stand in contexts that indicate hours or times. As such, the word *about* leaves minutes for things to be accomplished right before Jesus becomes the world's vicarious "morning," "evening," and "Passover" Sacrifice—right on schedule with the daily and yearly bloody sacrifices that were an OT foreshadowing of the final NT actions of Christ. Awesome *"Evidence Just Too Coincidental to Be Accidental!!!"*

PART IV

FORWARD TO CALVARY'S CROSS,
THE RESURRECTION,
AND THE ASCENSION

CHAPTER 16

GOOD FRIDAY: 6:00 P.M.–6:00 A.M.

Examining Clues in the Evidence Room

*What are the many events of the first twelve hours of Passover Day
that led up to Jesus's crucifixion?*

The Setting

Our clue-finding journey through the Old Testament is proving to be enlightening and exciting. Its New Testament mysteries continue to be unraveled before our very eyes.

With that said, we now enter a true crime scene where sterile gloves are needed to handle delicate clues of prime significance. Evidence lurks everywhere inside the yellow tape of this crime-filled "passion" location.

passion: suffering

All four gospels report this coming travesty, but leave many mysteries to be solved. As a precursor to it all, before He was arrested to be put on trial, Jesus the Victim had said, "This is your time when darkness rules." What did that mean? Jesus was declaring that the "ruler" of this world, Satan himself (John 12:31), was now ready to make his last stand, make his last-ditch effort to dethrone his greatest opponent: God Himself.

Fellow investigators, on the pages to come we will witness worldly justice sinking to its lowest ebb. The Jewish system of fairness will wain (cp. Deuteronomy 17:6); justice within the Roman courts will disappear when one of its top representatives repeatedly says, "I do not find this Man guilty of anything," and then turns right around and has Jesus whipped and ultimately crucified (John 18:38; Luke 23:22; Mark 15:15). This lack of justice had been thoroughly predicted in Isaiah 59:9–20 some 700 years before.

Consider pausing here to read Isaiah 59:9–20 to better understand the predicaments Jesus would face throughout His many trials before the Jewish and Roman courts.

The lead-in setting: Jesus had arrived in Jerusalem to be everyone's substitute, receiving "in His body" the pangs and wounds of punishment that He now deserved because of the disobediences of humankind that His heavenly Father had placed upon Him (1 Peter 2:24).

Grasping the *Time* Factors

The time has arrived for us detectives to put on our best brain caps. Tough areas of comprehension now follow.

To have a solid grasp of the full meaning of the biblical account of the suffering, death, and resurrection of Christ, it is critical to learn how Jews of Jesus's day kept time. It was not like westerners of today who start new days at twelve midnight. No, Jews began a new day around what would be comparable to our 6:00 p.m., the start of evening time. Thus, what Christians call Maundy Thursday, the time when Jesus celebrated the Passover or the first Lord's Supper, was *already* a Jewish Friday, the true beginning of what Christians call Good Friday.

With that in mind, I quote my favorite Bible passage: Zechariah 3:9d. There God promised, "I will remove the sin of that land in *one* day"—in *one* twenty-four-hour (24-hour) period.

Astounding prediction!

Just as the First Adam brought sin into the world in *one* day, so Jesus would take it out in *one* day—*one* twenty-four-hour period. And He did.

Observe the original Good Friday timetable.

The new day had started around 6:00 p.m. on that first "Good Friday"—*good* for us, and in another way, yet *not so good* for Jesus when we consider what He was about to go through. For Jesus Christ, it was a "Bad Friday," physically and mentally—though at the same time also a Good Friday for Him since it would complete the main part of His earthly purposes. It was both bad and good!

In the first hours of that 6:00 p.m.–6:00 a.m. Jewish Friday framework (about seven hours initially), the Savior instituted the Lord's Supper with His disciples in the

John Mark was the later writer of the Gospel of *Mark*.

"upper room" in the house of John Mark's mother. That Passover Supper lasted until maybe around 9:30 p.m. Adding another half-hour to journey eastward away from the Jerusalem Temple area and down through the Kidron Valley, Jesus and His disciples would have reached Gethsemane up on the Mount of Olives around 10:00 p.m.

Gethsemane was a place where Jesus often went to pray. On this night, He repeated the *same* hour-long prayer *three* times. This would move the clock to around 1:00 a.m. Now it was time for Jesus to be betrayed by Judas, the money-hungry mole within His group of disciples.

Judas had left the Supper *before* it ended to lay plans with leading Jewish priests to help lead them to Jesus in Gethsemane. Judas, along with many soldiers, Jewish religious leaders, and others, arrived where Jesus was. This group of enemies was intent on arresting Jesus; their large number was meant to make it impossible for Jesus to escape physically (Matthew 26:47).

Christ was arrested after Judas identified Him in the torch-lit night by giving Him a kiss of welcome which turned out to be a kiss of betrayal (cp. Psalm 2:12). In answer to Jesus's former prayer, His other eleven disciples escaped capture (John 17:9–12; 18:8–9; Matthew 26:56b).

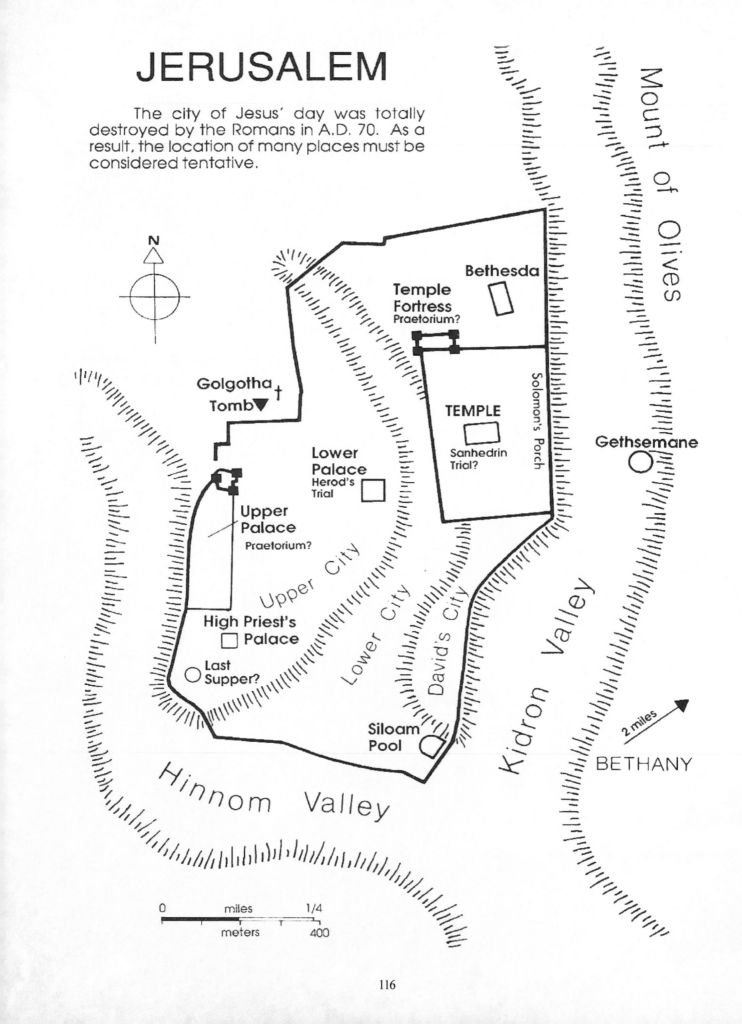

JERUSALEM

The city of Jesus' day was totally destroyed by the Romans in A.D. 70. As a result, the location of many places must be considered tentative.

N

Mount of Olives

Bethesda

Temple
Fortress
Praetorium?

Golgotha †
Tomb ▼

Solomon's Porch

TEMPLE

Sanhedrin
Trial?

Gethsemane

Lower
Palace
Herod's
Trial

Upper
Palace
Praetorium?

Upper City

Lower City

David's City

Kidron Valley

High Priest's
Palace

Last
Supper?

Siloam
Pool

2 miles

BETHANY

Hinnom Valley

0   miles   1/4

meters   400

Now continued that long night when the weakened Jesus, enjoying no sleep, was hauled off to trial. He was first brought before the former high priest Annas and a little later was sent to the high priest Caiaphas. After Christ was twice charged "guilty," the Jews handed Him over to the Gentile governor, Pontius Pilate. The hours of agony dragged on. Pilate tried to hand Jesus's trial off to King Herod Antipas. This Herod was in Jerusalem at Passover time, along with his soldiers, to prevent any riots that might break out with so many people in town for this big festival. Herod, however, sent Christ back to Pilate; Pilate was now stuck with the dirty work of judging Jesus.

Following many accusations brought forward by the vindictive Jewish leaders, as well as several interrogations by Pilate and beatings by Roman soldiers, Jesus was sentenced to death by crucifixion around 6:00 a.m. on Friday morning (John 19:13–16a), the time of the "morning sacrifice."

Grasping the *Time* Factors *beyond* the Parameters of This Chapter

Comprehensively, passion detectives need to grasp the absolute need for Jesus to complete His work of redemption within a twenty-four-hour time frame—in line with Zechariah 3:9d, quoted above. Permit me to complete the gamut in an uninterrupted way, covering the rest of the Passover or Good Friday hours. (Remember that we have just covered a 6:00 p.m.–6:00 a.m. time period which, for Jews, was all part of a "Friday" time frame. The Jewish "Thursday" had already ended at 6:00 p.m. the night before. Hard for a modern western mind to grasp.)

For the next three hours, namely, Friday 6:00 a.m.–9:00 a.m., Jesus was mistreated, mocked by Roman guards, cleaned up and redressed in His regular clothes, forced to carry His cross toward a hill *outside* the city of Jerusalem, and it was "there" He was crucified at 9:00 a.m. (Mark 15:16–25; Matthew 27:27–36; Luke 23:26–33; John 19:16b–18).

Following this, during the next three morning hours of Good Friday (9:00 a.m.–12 noon), the Lord Jesus spoke the first three of His seven statements from the cross.

Then at 12 noon on that first Good Friday, a three-hour-long darkness covered the whole earth. Near the end of that period, the crucified One spoke His last four statements in rapid succession. He then died at 3:00 p.m., the time when the "evening sacrifice" was being offered (John 19:25–30; Mark 15:27–37; Luke 23:39–45a; Matthew 27:38–50).

Over the next three Good Friday hours of 3:00 p.m.–6:00 p.m., the body of Christ was taken down from the cross, placed in a tomb, and embalmed. Finally, the entrance to the tomb was closed off by rolling a large stone over it (John 19:31–42). This was all completed by 6:00 p.m., which marked the beginning of a new day—Saturday, a special Sabbath day of rest (John 19:31).

Zechariah 3:9d came to be fulfilled. In one twenty-four-hour (24-hour) period on Passover,

God's Son, the world's Passover Lamb, had "removed" all the sin of the world. Surely we should be awestruck! The suffering-and-death components of God's grand plan had been accomplished with perfection.

There you have it! The Good Friday *time* factors that enable us to grasp what happened on that greatest day in human history!

We now move back to examine certain mysteries and clues pertinent to the initial hours of Passover, which on the biblical timetable ran from 6:00 p.m.–6:00 a.m., a period already regarded as Friday (not Thursday) in the Jewish culture.

The Gethsemane Connection

There is a significant clue concerning the Gethsemane connection and why Jesus had to *begin* His most intense suffering in that location. Gethsemane was called a "garden" when Peter, after the arrest of Jesus, was down in the courtyard below the place where Jesus was on trial. Here Peter was accused of having been with Jesus in the "garden" (John 18:26; see also v. 1).

This is the key to unlock the mystery. The First Adam lived in the Garden of Eden when he first sinned; the Second Adam now began the events of His final suffering in a *garden*, the Garden of Gethsemane (also recognized by Johann Gerhard, as referenced in B, *ROTNC*, Part II, 36). This again agrees with Romans 5:14b: "Adam was a type [picture] of Him who was to come."

Of course, there *is* more! That night in the garden, Jesus was under extreme stress, so much so that He began to sweat blood right through His pores. Luke, being the doctor that he was, was especially interested in this phenomenon and shares it with his

> There are medical reports of others who have experienced the same when under extreme stress.

readers. He reports that Jesus was "struggling inwardly," and not just outwardly in a *physical* way (Luke 22:44; cp. Matthew 26:36–37).

Why Three Identical Prayers in the Garden?

What? God the Father could not catch the meaning of Jesus's prayer the first time? Or maybe He was too busy to answer until the third time? Nonsense! Jesus's heavenly Father answered each time. Jesus just checked it out *three* times to make sure He perfectly understood what His Father wanted Him to do (Matthew 26:44). That may sound silly to us, but here's the lowdown.

Do you recall how Moses did not listen to God in a careful way when he was told to "talk" to the Rock? Instead, he hit the Rock, as he had been told to do on a former occasion (see Numbers 20:7–8, 11; Exodus 17:6). Here's the problem: Moses had put the pre-incarnate Jesus in a predicament. Jesus could have made a fool of Moses by providing no water, but then all the Israelites would have died in the wilderness, and Jesus's genealogy would have come to an end; also, *world salvation* would have come to a screeching halt. Jesus could not permit that. So, He permitted drinkable water to "gush out." Nonetheless, Moses was *not* out of trouble. God accused him of "unbelief" (Numbers 20:12) and informed him that

> Notice how the term *Rock* is capitalized. 1 Corinthians 10:4 seems to tell us that the Rock Moses struck was Jesus Himself. That should not surprise us. He who claimed to be the Bread of Life and the Light of the World (John 6:48; 8:12) was also the Water of Life. For when Moses struck the Jesus-Rock, water came out, and the people were saved from dying of thirst.

his sin would prevent him from entering the Promised Land of Canaan—not, however, the *promised land* of heaven.

Now comes Jesus; He cannot afford to make a similar mistake. He cannot afford to fall into the unbelief and sin of Moses by not listening to His heavenly Father—carefully. Therefore, the Lord Jesus checks signals three times to make sure He understands His Father perfectly.

The Judas "Kiss-Off"

Judas's kiss of betrayal is tied to Psalm 2:12: "Kiss the Son or He will get angry and you will perish on your way, because His anger can blaze quickly." To be sure, Judas approached Jesus with the ordinary Middle Eastern form of greeting: a kiss; however, this was a kiss of betrayal, and the anger of Jesus did "blaze" (Mark 14:21).

A New Balaam

The high priest Caiaphas is one of the most despicable characters on the pages of the whole Bible. From Jesus's comment in John 19:11b, a reference to Caiaphas, not Judas, it is fair to say that Caiaphas is burning deeper in hell than Judas.

It was Caiaphas who was willing to sacrifice an innocent Jesus to save his own "hide" and position of power, like most modern politicians; in addition, he tried to rescue the power base of his fellow unbelieving Jewish clergy, as well as save the unbelieving Jewish citizens of Jerusalem.

119

When meeting to plot the arrest and death of Jesus, Caiaphas said, ". . . it is better for you that one Man [Jesus] should die for the people . . ." (John 11:49–50).

Caiaphas did not know how true his statement was *in a different sense.*

Following Jesus's raising of Lazarus at Bethany, the followers of Christ increased bigtime (John 11:45). This threatened the religious Jewish hierarchy; Jesus was becoming too popular. If Jesus were to declare Himself "Messiah," a title others had claimed for themselves on former occasions, a riot could break out at Passover time. This was Caiaphas's reasoning. A riot was the last thing he desired! That could mean the Romans would come, blame Caiaphas and his dictatorial group of Sadducees, and replace them, maybe even destroy the Temple and banish all Jews from their homeland (John 11:48).

Caiaphas had a plan: Get rid of Messiah Jesus and protect the people. If this Man Jesus died, the other Jews would be saved. It would spell a one-man death in place of all the other people. It was good political strategy from a human viewpoint, but it was an even greater idea on a higher God-level. It was best for all humankind to go free by having a one-Man substitute take the place of all people, of all time, on a designated cross, designed long before by the gracious, loving God of the universe (Ephesians 1:3–14; 3:2–13). Caiaphas did not know the brilliance of his statement on a *spiritual* level. By giving Caiaphas's declaration a higher meaning, God declared Caiaphas the "Balaam" of the New Testament.

Who was Balaam? Balaam was a world-renowned prophet residing in Mesopotamia, today's Iraq (c. 1400 BC). King Balak of Moab was well over five hundred miles away, around the Fertile Crescent, on the eastern side of the Dead or Salt Sea. During the time of Balaam and Balak, Moses and the Israelites were making their way

> You can read about Balaam in Numbers 22–24. It's a cliffhanger!

northward from Egypt and Mount Horeb, a part of the Sinai mountain range. As Moses and his people came closer to the Promised Land, certain nations would not permit them passage. Wars followed during which God gave His people overwhelming victories over King Sihon of the Amorites and King Og of Bashan.

These victories struck fear in the heart of King Balak. To remedy the problem, Balak sent for Balaam to come and place a "curse" on the traveling nation of Israel. Balaam was promised a rich reward if he would use his "magical curses" against God's people. On three occasions, God turned Balaam's

> There is much more to the story. See Numbers 25 and 31 where the latter reference reports Balaam's God-directed death; Balaam had previously enticed the Israelites to commit idolatry, fornication, and adultery with Moabite women.

words around in his mouth, and Balaam's *curses* became *blessings*. When King Balak became furious, Balaam departed.

Of parallel interest is the statement of Caiaphas. In similar manner, God took this high priest's evilly intended words and turned them into a *blessing* for His people of all times. Yes, it was "better" that one Man [Jesus] die as substitute, in place of all the people of the whole world.

The Proverbs 26:4 and 26:5 Man

Throughout the Passion narrative of the Lord Jesus, there are many little twists and turns that can easily be missed. One of them pertains to the "silent" Jesus, while another explains the *responding* Jesus. Isaiah 53:7 predicted Jesus would remain "silent" before His accusers. He did; He knew Proverbs 26:4: "Do not answer a fool according to his foolishness, or you too will be like him." There were a lot of fools opening their lying mouths at Jesus's trial. Jesus kept His mouth shut (Mark 14:61). If a person on trial remains silent, he cannot incriminate himself.

Caiaphas was in a predicament. No two agreeing witnesses could be found to make charges stand up against Jesus (cp. Deuteronomy 17:6). In desperation, and with human cleverness, the high priest found a way to break Jesus's silence (Mark 14:55–62). He called for the "Oath of the Testimony," notes Frank Morison (M, *WMS*, p.28). The high priest asked Jesus whether He was "the Messiah, the Son of God," which meant, "Are You God?" (Matthew 26:63b). Jesus was now obliged to answer according to Proverbs 26:5: "Answer a fool according to his foolishness, or he will think he is wise."

Did you catch that?

Two passages from King Solomon's wise *Proverbs* stand side by side and make opposite demands. Can they be reconciled; did Solomon know what he was talking about? Yes, they apply to different situations. There's a time to remain silent—and a time to talk. Jesus applied these two seemingly contradictory passages perfectly—in both cases while He was standing before the same "fool" Caiaphas. In the first circumstance, Jesus remained silent and did not make a fool of Himself. In the second case, Jesus spoke the truth ["I am He"] and made a fool of Caiaphas.

Funny, if not so sad!

With Jesus's claim that He was "the Son of God," namely God Himself, the Jewish court, called the Sanhedrin, felt obligated to condemn Him. Jesus was then handed over to Pontius Pilate, the Roman governor, for trial and execution.

> See Pitre's expanded discussion of why Jesus was condemned by the Jewish Sanhedrin. It is both thorough and excellent (P, *CJ*, pp. 156–168).

Our "Buddy Barabbas"

Surely, one of the most intriguing parts of the Good Friday story concerns a man named Barabbas. This time we take a different path to do our clue-finding. It leads us to the Aramaic language that Jews had come to speak 600 years before when they were captives in Babylon. All four gospels have something to say about the vital storyline of Barabbas. You can read the details in Matthew 27:15–26; Mark 15:6–15; Luke 23:17–25; John 18:38b–40. By counting all those verses, we

> Some of the OT is written in Aramaic, one of the languages Jesus spoke.

moderns would say, "Barabbas sure got a lot of print" on the pages of the New Testament for being a seemingly *minor* character.

The above passages note that Barabbas was a murderous criminal who came to have his sentence dismissed by Governor Pontius Pilate. Barabbas went free, while Jesus ended up on the cross.

Barabbas was a bad dude, a revolutionary or terrorist in terms of today's tumultuous world. He was well-known and a favorite of certain Jews. Most likely, he was a Zealot who seems to have favored killing Romans in order to restore Jewish rule.

> Recall that Jesus chose a member of the Zealot Party to be one of His disciples (Matthew 10:4)—Simon the Zealot (not to be confused with Simon Peter). Zealots believed in the violent overthrow of the Roman government. Simon the Zealot must have given up his endorsement of terrorism and his worldly sword, so he could use the "sword of the Spirit" to help change the world for the better (Ephesians 6:17b).

Pilate tried to get the Passover crowd "off Jesus's case" in several different ways. He knew Jesus was innocent of the bogus charges being brought against Him (John 18:38b); he realized that is was the Jewish leaders, not the ordinary Jewish people, who had handed Jesus over because these church authorities were "jealous" of Him (Matthew 27:18). The presence of Barabbas offered Pilate an opportunity to free Jesus, so he thought.

The governor was reminded it was a "custom" to free one criminal each Passover (John 18:39). Therefore, he gave the Jewish mob a choice: Barabbas or Christ. To Pilate's surprise, the crowd yelled for Pilate to free Barabbas and crucify Jesus, but Pilate really wanted to "let Jesus go" (Luke 23:20), so he offered the crowd a Passover bonus, two prisoners to be set free—Barabbas *and* Jesus (Matthew 27:22). The accusers did not buy into Pilate's scheme. They were hungry for the crucifixion of Jesus.

> For fascinating data concerning the Good Friday mob that wanted Jesus crucified, and in particular, who some of the accusing agitators may have been, see Appendix 9. You will be quite surprised.

All along, these accusing Jewish religious leaders were concerned about their own job security (cp. Matthew 27:18); Pilate now joined them in worrying about his also, especially when the Jewish leaders implied they would send a delegation to Rome to inform Caesar that Pilate was permitting Jesus of Nazareth to claim kingship over the Jews (Luke 23:3; John 18:37; 19:12). Treason!

Under these circumstances, Pilate saw only one course of action. He caved, freed Barabbas, and sentenced Jesus to crucifixion (Mark 15:15).

With this historic backdrop, we can now dissect the name *Bar-abbas*. The latter part, *abba*, means "father" in Aramaic; see Romans 8:15 to note its usage by the Apostle Paul. Aramaic is closely associated with Hebrew; in that language "father" is spelled *'ab* and is the first part of the name "*Ab*raham," meaning "*father* of many peoples." The word *bar* is the Jewish way of saying, "son." When a Jewish boy becomes twelve years of age, he becomes a *bar-mitzvah*, "a son of the commandment" (cp. Luke 2:42).

Thus, *Bar-abbas* means "son of the father." Jesus is also "Son of the Father."

Let's parallel both for theological impact.

Barabbas,
the son of the father
went free when

JESUS,
the Son of the Father
went to the cross.

Very ingenious!

It was not just coincidence that a man named Barabbas was before Pilate at the same time as Jesus. If a man of a different name had been there with Him, the parallel would be absent.

> Once you have a better understanding of the secret of Barabbas's *name*, you will view him as your buddy and brother.

It had to be a man named "Bar-abbas." He *represents* you and me; the Bible calls both males and females "sons of God" (Romans 8:14: "For all who are moved by God's Spirit are God's sons," sons of the heavenly Father).

When our representative Barabbas went free, that was all people going free, while the Savior went to the cross for Barabbas and all of us at the same time (2 Corinthians 5:15). We do not like to hear it, but all people are murderers, like Barabbas. 1 John 3:15 says, "Everyone who hates his brother is a murderer, and you know no murderer has everlasting life awaiting him."

Who of us has not hated someone at one time or another? But the great news is that Jesus has already washed us clean with His blood when He went to the cross in the place of Barabbas—and in place of each one of us (1 John 1:7). We are free.

Neat stuff, huh? God had that Good Friday plan well calculated to keep us shaking our heads in amazement.

How Much He Loved Us!

In the middle of the whole trial, including the Barabbas episode, Jesus was whipped several times, slapped, mocked, and spit upon. Before Pilate brought Him out before the angry crowd for a final time, the soldiers had placed a royal robe on Him, as well as a "crown of thorns" (Matthew 27:29). This should ring a bell in our minds immediately. The First Adam had been cursed with the promise that "thorns" growing in the ground would make his farming most difficult (Genesis 3:18); later, it is reported that Noah's father, Lamech, was looking for the coming of a "Comforter," who would ease farming by removing the curse of thorns (Genesis 5:29). That thorn-remover was now present, carrying that curse on His own head so all people could become "curse" free (cp. Deuteronomy 22:22–23).

I am certain I am not alone as I stand here in awe of how Jesus loved all of us so much that He was willing to let "thorns" be driven into His head so we would not be forced to suffer such pain in hell.

Well, Was It "Scarlet" or "Purple"? Make Up Your Minds!

Some Scriptural mysteries can be solved right at the headquarters of our desks, just by reading our Bibles, as the next puzzle answer will prove.

> I never grasped the human part of this account until I visited Jerusalem back in 1965, while in seminary. During a tour of the ancient dungeon of Pontius Pilate's Roman prison, the biblical account of the robe, the stick in Jesus's hand, and the crown of thorns were explained.

During the mistreatment of the Lord Jesus, one eye-grabbing event stands out. The soldiers placed a robe on Him, so they could torment Him. Jesus had claimed to be a king. The soldiers capitalize on this by making fun of their prisoner. They played "The Game of the King" with Him. They dressed Jesus up like a king, threw dice, and soldiers who won throws were permitted to inflict various types of pain on Christ.

But once again, like Balaam and Caiaphas, they did not realize what God was communicating through their actions. God allowed the soldiers to dress His Son in a certain way, but the meaning of the event was totally different in the mind of God.

Would you like to learn its meaning?

Matthew 27:28 tells us soldiers placed a "scarlet" robe on Christ. However, Mark 15:17 and John 19:2 report it was "purple." Certain colors represent "sin" in Isaiah 1:18:

> Oh, come, let us reason with one another, says the LORD.
>> Though your sins have become like scarlet cloth,
>>> they will turn white as snow.
>> Though they are red like crimson,
>>> they will become like white wool.

The Hebrew and Greek words translated "scarlet, crimson, blue, purple" are closely related colors. Exodus 26:1 uses them in a threefold combination. God ordered Moses: "Make the Tabernacle of ten curtains of fine twisted linen . . . *violet, purple, and scarlet* material with angels worked into it by a skillful artist."

That solves the "scarlet" and "purple" mystery of the robe put on Jesus. It was *multicolored*, like the Tabernacle and Temple veils or curtains, the one that tore when Jesus died (Mark 15:37). Though purplish colors represent royalty and kingship in our world, they represent sin in God's arena. When those colors were put on Jesus, they indicated He was carrying the *sins* of the whole world.

The varying colors in the four canonical Gospels look like a contradiction at first glance, but not after some good Old Testament detective work! Conclusion: We learn that the God of the Bible is clever and most communicative when we just take time to follow His clues!

Jesus, Our "Morning Sacrifice"

It's more *"Evidence Just Too Coincidental to Be Accidental!!!"* when we hear that Pilate condemned Christ around 6:00 a.m. The importance of the *times* when things took place on that first Good Friday is paramount to a full understanding of the events of that day.

This cannot be overemphasized!

Our investigation has already summarized some of those hours on the Jewish clock when decisions were enacted that affected Christ and impacted the eternal plan of God. However, we have hardly touched the surface in explaining the *theological* implications surrounding these *time* factors. We begin that process at this moment, and along the way we will additionally interject other explanations to enliven the storyline of the events that took place on that initial Good Friday.

Passover day had started at 6:00 p.m. on the very day when God began to "remove the sin" of the world. This means that twelve hours had now passed by the time Governor Pilate announced his approval to crucify Jesus. The clock now ticked nearly 6:00 a.m. (John 19:14, 16). Why was this important? Our search for clues takes us to Exodus 29:38–39 and 30:7.

God ordered Moses,

> This is what you should offer on the altar: two yearling [one-year-old] lambs regularly every day. Sacrifice the one in the *morning*, the other in the *evening*.
> Aaron should burn fragrant incense on it every morning when he gets the lamps ready. Also, when Aaron sets up the lamps in the evening, there must be burning of *incense* regularly before the LORD in the coming ages.

Every day a lamb was sacrificed around 6:00 a.m. It was called the "morning sacrifice." Jesus was as good as dead when Pilate condemned Him at that same time; nothing would reverse the governor's verdict. Jesus now became the world's "morning Sacrifice."

Along with the morning sacrifice, "incense" was to be burned. It symbolized a sweet odor going upward into the nostrils of God so He would *not* smell the stench of

> Alert investigators on our journey can really appreciate the predictive gift of "frank*incense*" given to the Christ Child by the Magi.

sin. Jesus became "incense" for all peoples of the world on that first Good Friday. As Ephesians 5:2 says: ". . . Christ also loved us and gave Himself for us as a *fragrant offering* and sacrifice to God."

With clarity, we clue-seekers now understand why it was necessary for Jesus to be sentenced to death around 6:00 a.m.

Evidence room conclusion: Bible detectives can become overwhelmed by all the clues (both in the OT and NT) that have to be applied by true investigators. This is why Bible study is an ongoing venture, as Jesus said, "If you continue [live or remain] in My word, you are really My disciples, and you will know the truth, and the truth will set you free" (John 8:31–32). A major sleuth question: Do you desire to be *spiritually* free?

CHAPTER 17

GOOD FRIDAY: 6:00 A.M.–9:00 A.M.

Examining Clues in the Evidence Room
*Are the three hours between Pilate's crucifixion edict
and the time the nails were driven into Christ's flesh
of any significance?*

Investigating the 6:00 a.m.–9:00 a.m. Good Friday Time Frame

The Bible does not tell us very much about the three hours from the time Jesus was sentenced ("about six in the morning"—John 19:14a) to the time when He was actually crucified (9:00 a.m.—Mark 15:25). We do know that following His sentencing, and after being tortured via a crown of thorns being pounded into his head with a wooden "stick" (Mark 15:16–19), Jesus was redressed in His regular clothes. Mark 15:20a reads: "After they had made fun of Him, the soldiers took off the purple robe and put His own clothes on Him." Christ was then forced to carry His cross toward a hill *outside* the city of Jerusalem (Matthew 27:31, 33; John 19:16b–17a; Hebrews 13:12). It was "there," very "near" Jerusalem, that He was crucified (Luke 23:33; John 19:18, 42).

A few details warrant extra special attention.

Following Governor Pilate's edict of crucifixion and several acts of military torture,

> Jesus was very popular in most places outside Jerusalem among the people who were not so brainwashed by the Temple clergy.

Jesus was marched out to appear before the public. Now He was in the midst of a larger Passover crowd. This crowd was more diverse than the one that had yelled, "Crucify Him!" Additional people were now on their way into Jerusalem. Many of them had slept *outside* the city overnight.

With this additional crowd to consider, the Roman rulers were wise enough not to agitate it unnecessarily on Passover day and start a riot (cp. Matthew 27:24). Therefore, the Romans would not have wanted to take a Jewish prisoner like Christ out into public all bloodied up and give the masses opportunity to yell, "Police brutality." This is why I believe Jesus was bathed before He was led out to be crucified. This conclusion

> In our next chapter, another reason will be added to prove that the soldiers had applied some type of *styptic* to stop any bleeding before Christ appeared in public.

can be evaluated in light of the fact that certain Jewish women bemoaned the very existence of *crucifixion* as they saw Jesus on His way to Calvary (Luke 23:27).

At this point, I add what may shock old-time Christians. It is my belief that Jesus's crown of thorns was removed *before* He was taken out into public to be crucified. In other words, Jesus was not wearing a crown of thorns when He later was hanging on the cross.

No, not heresy. Though Jesus is regularly viewed on church crucifixes with a crown of thorns on His head, nowhere is that stated in the Calvary crucifixion account. Think about it!

More Data as the Hours between 6:00 a.m.–9:00 a.m. Are Contemplated

> The name Simon was a popular name that came from the OT name "Simeon," the second son of Jacob or Israel.

Many Jews in the New Testament days were named Simon. We meet a man by this name when Jesus was carrying His cross to Calvary. He was from the city of Cyrene in Africa, and the Bible refers to him as Simon of Cyrene. Simon, like all Jewish men over the age of twelve, was required to appear in Jerusalem *three* times yearly—on Passover, Pentecost, and Tabernacles (Leviticus 23:1-44, especially vv. 37–38).

Just think of that! Since Simon lived very far from Jerusalem, he would no more than get home to Africa from a Passover festival, and it would almost be time to turn around and head back for Pentecost. (Sure hope Simon was a traveling salesman, so he could make money along the way, or had an employer who gave him plenty of "personal days.")

But why would God make such stringent laws? Paul educates us in Galatians 3:19: "Why then was the Law given? It was added to point out trespasses until the Descendant [Jesus] would come . . . ." In other words, multiple laws, impossible to keep, were "added" so people would learn they could *not* be saved by their own human works (see D, *G*, p. 359, sec. 5). Rather, they could only be saved by the perfect works of the Descendant who would come and keep the Law for everyone and wash away all the transgressions of all the peoples of the world, peoples who had violated the Law (cp. Ephesians 2:8–9). *What a God!*

And so, this Simon was present for Passover. Little did he know his life would be changed forever by the events of that first Good Friday.

Jesus was carrying His cross on His way to Calvary; He was totally exhausted from His lack of sleep and the whippings He had endured. Finally, He could no longer carry His cross. Roman guards grabbed Simon, the passerby from the crowd and forced him to carry the Savior's cross (Matthew 27:32).

Now think, observing detectives! Put yourself into Simon's sandals! Simon carried Jesus's cross and possibly stayed at Calvary to watch Him die. Then three days later he would have heard that this crucified One had risen from the dead. Yes, I suspect that if you had been Simon, you would have investigated the truth or falsehood of that "resurrection" thing very carefully. Right?

I think Simon did dig into the facts. I think he became one of several post-resurrection detectives, similar to modern-day inquirers.

Following his AD 30 Passover activities, as stated above, Simon would have returned home to Africa but would have been back for the next Jewish festival fifty days later on Pentecost. Maybe he heard Peter's sermon on that occasion and was baptized with the three thousand converts that day (Acts 2:41).

But one thing is for sure. Mark 15:21 records the names of Simon's two sons, Alexander and Rufus. Does that sound superfluous? Consider this: If Simon became a Christian, he certainly would have taught his two sons

> Peter is said to have influenced Mark's Gospel.

about the crucified and risen One. Mark may have met this Simon or one of his sons; that would be how Peter or Mark could have learned the names of Simon's two sons, as recorded in Mark's Gospel.

Then comes Romans 16:13! Paul writes, "Greet Rufus . . . ." If this Rufus is the son of Simon of Cyrene, then it is safe to deduct that this Rufus had become a well-known leader in the Roman congregation to which Paul wrote. Also, if this Rufus truly was the son of Simon of Cyrene, then it all makes sense that Simon did investigate "*Who*" the crucified One was.

The surprises just go on and on.

Jesus's Arrival at Mount Calvary Shortly before 9:00 a.m.

The crucifixion procession finally arrived at the "Place of the Skull," which in Aramaic is called "Golgotha" (John 19:17) and in Latin "Calvary."

"There" they crucified Jesus (John 19:18; Luke 23:33). Where was "there"—that place which is known as Calvary? A long, long string of clues are needed to solve this mystery.

We start way back in Genesis when God told Abraham to go to the Mount Moriah range to sacrifice his son Isaac (22:2). From there we travel to 2 Samuel 24 and 1 Chronicles 21 to the time of King David—around one thousand (1,000) years later. It is then that we encounter a key episode in David's life!

After many years of faithfulness to God, also with some serious sinful bumps along his road of life, King David again seriously sinned when he ordered a comprehensive census of his whole nation in order to bolster his own ego. Joab, King David's lead army captain and appointed overseer of the census, knew this was a bad, bad idea. Or, to put it in the words of David's son and successor, King Solomon, "Pride goes before destruction" (Proverbs 16:18).

Joab's objections were "overruled" and the census was taken with "Satan's" approval (1 Chronicles 21:1). God became angry and divine consequences followed, even though King David confessed his wrong. The "LORD" sent the prophet Gad to David to give him *three* choices for appropriate punishment.

What were King David's three choices? (Pray you never have to choose your punishments; God is a better Chooser, because He works "all" things out for *good* for those who love Him. See Romans 8:28. "All" in that passage also includes evil and sinful things. God is a merciful God, as King David found out.)

> The whole context of the "David census episode" is spelled out in great detail in 2 Samuel 24 and 1 Chronicles 21.
>
> Superb chapters to read.

The first choice for punishment had no appeal to David: "seven years of famine." Not good at all. Israel was already in the middle of a three-year drought; another four would devastate the kingdom, making it very vulnerable to enemy armies.

The second option was even worse for King David, personally, and for the nation in the long run: "three months" of David running for his life as his enemies pursued him. In his younger days, David had fled from King Saul and others for years (1 Samuel 18–30). Now David the king was old and not fast on his feet anymore. Besides, during the absence of their fleeing king, Israel would be at the mercy of invading troops.

Let's hear the third choice; it certainly must be better! Yeah, right!

God promised "a three-day," seventy-two hour (72-hour) plague throughout the whole land from the northernmost town, called Dan, down to the southernmost town of Beersheba.

What should, what would, King David choose?

King David was already repentant. His God-based values made the impossible decision possible. Throw yourself upon the *mercy* of God. The first two choices would put David at the mercy of man. (And you who live in this world made evil by humans know how that would work out!)

Yes, King David took the third option—the one that left him totally at the mercy of God. Good choice, even though it didn't look so good in the early hours of the plague. Horsemen from all over the kingdom came galloping in to report the early tally of victims—seventy thousand dead.

King David raced out of Jerusalem; he was on his way to pray in Gibeon where the Tabernacle was then located six miles away (cp. 2 Chronicles 1:3).

As David passed over the threshing floor of "Ornan the Jebusite" (1 Chronicles 21:15), God opened David's eyes. David saw an angel of plague holding an outstretched sword in his hand and standing over Jerusalem, ready to strike.

> Ornan is named "Araunah" in 2 Samuel 24:16d.

Do you catch the potential tragedy of the situation, biblical observers? The ancestors of Jesus were housed in Jerusalem; if they died, there would be no Savior born in Bethlehem or nailed to the cross. Salvation hung in the balance. It was then that God called from heaven and told the angel to "stop." Maybe it was Jesus, the Angel of the LORD, who held the sword (cp. 1 Chronicles 21:15). David, terrified by the whole scene, immediately confessed his sin and pleaded for his people.

King David was under the false impression that his people were innocent and that he was the only guilty party. Not so; God does not think as we do (Isaiah 55:8–9). The people were also plenty guilty (2 Samuel 24:1). On a previous occasion, these people of Israel had sided in rebellion with David's throne-usurping son Absalom against David himself. God had not forgotten; often He delays punishment to give people a chance to repent. Probably many had not! Obviously, at this moment in Israelite history, God killed "two birds with one plague."

Following the end of the plague, Gad returned to David and relayed God's instructions to buy Ornan's threshing floor, a place where wheat was separated from chaff. This was the location where the plague had ceased. David purchased it.

Later, King Solomon built the Temple on this very spot; it was the same place where Abraham had most likely taken Isaac for sacrifice and where David had been shown mercy. 2 Chronicles 3:1 reads: "Solomon began to build the LORD's Temple in Jerusalem, on Mount

Moriah, where the LORD appeared to his father David and where David had prepared the site, on the threshing floor of Ornan the Jebusite."

"There," on that Moriah threshing floor, Old Testament Temple sacrifices were then offered for years by Jewish priests, *symbolically* offering mercy and forgiveness for sin.

Where Was "There"?

I warned you that the location of the "*there* they crucified Him" involved a long string of clues. You need to recall the "there" of Abraham's sacrifice of a ram instead of Isaac and the "there" of King David's purchase of the Jerusalem Moriah Temple site. Both locations served as places of blood sacrifice in the Old Testament (Genesis 22:2, 13; 1 Kings 8:63).

But where was the "there" where Jesus shed His blood; it would have to be at the same place to parallel the Abraham and David events. Correct?

Not quite so! More investigative data is needed—and the Holy Spirit has given us spiritually enlightened reasoning to follow further trails of evidential facts.

So let's travel on to learn that the "there" of the Temple site was *not* the same "there" of Calvary—though it was a God-designed parallel location. The fact is that both locations were on the same Moriah mountain range. However, Christ's cross had to be placed on another Moriah hill.

Why?

Jesus had another prophecy to fulfill on Good Friday. He needed to become the final Scapegoat, the One typified in Leviticus 16:20–22. Jesus needed to take the rap for all wrongdoers of all of history.

How then can Bible investigators identify the "there" of the Calvary location? Difficult, but not impossible! John 19:20

> The Leviticus 16 scapegoat was ceremonially led "outside" the camp to carry away sin; the high priest was instructed to lay transgressions, symbolically, on the head of the scapegoat before it was led away.

tells us Jesus was crucified "near" the city of Jerusalem, which makes it "outside the city gate" (Hebrews 13:12), but, as stated above, still on the Mount Moriah range.

More Insight into King David's "Plague" Choice

One unsolved mystery remains concerning King David's "plague" episode. In part, it concerns the deaths of those seventy-thousand plague victims. That factor still needs deciphering. Hang on; another big surprise to follow!

Originally, the LORD's plague was to last for seventy-two hours (72-hours), but when David received the "70,000" assessment, the plague had only lasted "from the morning until the appointed time" (2 Samuel 24:15). What does that mean? You more-seasoned detectives will understand the text if it is paraphrased this way: "from the time of the morning sacrifice until the time of the evening sacrifice." That's correct, "from 6:00 a.m. until 3:00 p.m." A total of seventy thousand had died in just *nine* hours. How many would have died if God had *not* stopped the angel and had stayed with His original time frame, namely, three days or seventy-two hours of plague, instead of just nine hours?

Suddenly, two things should be illuminated for our minds: (1) God had shown mercy, and (2) David had made the correct choice. He had put the situation totally into the hands of his God. This second realization is way beyond man's imagination. God halted the plague after just *nine* hours. Do you see the parallel?

An Old Testament Clue That Unravels a Vital Time Factor

Though this chapter has been all about what related to Jesus in the *three* morning hours of 6:00 a.m. to 9:00 a.m., yet, another time element, a *nine*-hour Good Friday phenomenon, should be added to make sure I do not forget to make mention of it.

Carefully note this: It was nine hours from the time Pilate sentenced Jesus at 6:00 a.m. until Christ died at 3:00 p.m.—and after those nine hours the "plague of sin" stopped on a dime. "It is finished," Jesus exclaimed (John 19:30).

God had done it again. Just as He stopped the plague after nine hours in David's day, so He also stopped the ultimate plague of sin after just nine hours of condemnation on Good Friday. Too much! Is that God of Scriptural mystery not just the greatest with the meaningful parallels He lays out in the Bible?

What a connection between the Old and New Testaments—a connection that parallels God's plan of redemption in greatest detail!

Evidence room conclusion: Sometimes biblical data can seem so helter-skelter, but competent Sherlocks stick with related clues until the various mysteries make sense. As this chapter revealed, investigative endurance proved worthwhile. Many points of significance were uncovered pertaining to the three hours between Christ's sentencing and His crucifixion.

CHAPTER 18

GOOD FRIDAY: 9:00 A.M.–12:00 NOON

Examining Clues in the Evidence Room

What is the crucial meaning of the fact
that Jesus's crucifixion took place at 9:00 a.m.
and what is the clue-filled content
of His three morning statements from the cross?

Data, Data, and More Data

Scriptural investigators, ready yourselves to examine numerous pieces of evidence that relate to Christ's crucifixion on Good Friday between the hours of 9:00 a.m.–12 noon!

Data 1: Before they drove the nails through Jesus's wrists and feet, they offered Him a *sedative* to numb the pain—"wine mixed with myrrh and gall" (Matthew 27:34; Mark 15:23). Jesus refused to drink. Why? He had to endure *full* pain in our place to pay the price for the punishment that we deserved for our iniquities. And out of love, our Savior was willing to do this for us!

Myrrh: a "gum" or "resin"; *gall*: an "herb."

The pictures of crucified victims being tied with ropes to crosses seems fictional, created by artist-type renditions.

Data 2: Above, you may have noticed the statement that nails were driven through Jesus's *wrists*. Most say, "His hands."

Scripture does not say either way. However, based on Exodus 12:46 ("Do not break any of its [the Passover lamb's] bones"), and then making an interpretive application of this in the light of the John 19:36 reference to Exodus 12:46 in connection to Christ's crucified body ("None of His [Christ's] bones shall be broken"), well, it seems wise to opt for nails *through the wrists* for three reasons.

First, the *weight* of Jesus's body on nails in His hands, most likely, would have made the nails pull through the skin and on the way through would have broken bones in His hands. Second, driving nails though hands would tend to break bones more easily than finding an open passage through wrists. (Wrist bones would also be way more supportive of weight than fine and fragile hand bones.) Finally, biblical languages do not contain words that distinguish between the hand and the wrist. You decide.

Data 3: John 19:18 states, ". . . they crucified Him with two others, one on each side and Jesus in the *middle*." How appropriate! It is contended that Romans always put the *worst* criminal in the middle. That is where Jesus belonged. All the wrongdoings of all time had been laid on Him, our Passover Lamb. In that sense, He truly was the worst.

> Jesus being crucified with two transgressors fulfilled both Psalm 22:18 and Isaiah 53:9, 12.

Data 4: Some of the most important data in our crucifixion narrative pertains to the *time* when Jesus was crucified. Mark 15:25 says, "It was *nine* in the morning [9:00 a.m.] when they crucified Him." Again, how significant that Bible detectives interpret Bible mysteries correctly!

If Jesus is nailed to the cross at 9:00 a.m. and dies, as we will observe, at 3:00 p.m., that indicates Jesus suffered on the cross *six* hours. How interesting. God created the world in *six* days. The first man, Adam, was created on the *sixth* day, a Friday. As a consequence, Adam's sin negatively affected the *whole* creation (cp. Romans 8:19–22). Centuries later at Calvary, Jesus fixes up the *whole* sinful mess in *six* hours on Friday, the *sixth* day of the week, via His redemptive act. Wow!

Data 5a: One other action should catch our attention, namely, the dividing of Jesus's clothes between the Roman soldiers who crucified Him.

The basic wardrobe of a Jew consisted of five pieces. There were four Roman guards in charge of Jesus at the cross, and in fulfillment of Psalm 22:18, they divided the first four pieces among them. When they evaluated the fifth piece, Christ's valuable, seamless tunic, they decided *not* to divide it but rather to throw "dice" to see which soldier would get it (John 19:23–24). Another fulfillment of an additional prophetic *clue* that falls into the category of proving *Who* Jesus really was, the predicted Messiah.

Data 5b: Two more valuable clues accompany this dividing of the clothes! First, if the clothes had been all blood-soaked, of what value would they have been? Therefore, I conclude that the soldiers had very likely bathed Jesus and applied some type of *styptic* to His body to stop any massive amount of blood from getting on His clothes.

The second clue is dynamite!

If all Jesus's clothes were divided up, this means He was "naked" when crucified. (A loincloth on Jesus on church crucifixes exemplifies modesty.) But Romans crucified their victims naked; victims were displayed in a non-dignified way.

How apropos! The First Adam was "naked" when he brought sin into the world (cp. Genesis 3:7); now the Second Adam is "naked" when He takes sin out.

The evidence just gets better and better. So awesome!

Those Good Friday "Morning" Hours of 9:00 a.m.–12 noon

Our Savior spoke *three* times from 9:00 a.m.–12 noon while on His cross—and *four* times in the afternoon hours of 12 noon–3:00 p.m. The total number of His statements is significant. By speaking *seven* times, Jesus utilized the most-used *symbolic* number of Scripture—seven! This number stands for *perfection*. Therefore, Christ spoke a "perfect" number of times on the cross. By means of His *seven* statements, He verbalized everything that needed to be said to fulfill several more goals of His earthly ministry.

Those three morning statements uttered by Jesus are quite majestic. The first is so merciful, the second is insightful beyond words, and the third is unbelievably brilliant!

The Savior's First Statement from the Cross

Jesus spoke for a first time while on His cross: "Father, forgive them, for they do not know what they are doing" (Luke 23:34). One aspect of these words jump off the page; the other not so much so!

Jesus must be God, merciful to the nth degree! Who do you know who would pray for others who had so brutally beaten and mocked them, mocked them in the same way the Messiah was mistreated? Jesus practiced what He taught; He loved His "enemies" (Matthew 5:44; cp. Psalm 109:4). And He was right; those enemies did not realize what they were doing when they crucified the Son of God.

The second item that demands attention concerns the fact that the *first* and *seventh* statements of Jesus from the cross both start with the word "Father." Do you know why? More on this when we consider Jesus's seventh saying.

The Savior's Second Statement from the Cross

Christ spoke a second time from the cross. To one of the two criminals crucified with Him, Jesus said: "I tell you the truth, today you will be with Me in Paradise" (Luke 23:43).

Most do not realize that the repentant thief, the one who evoked the above response from Christ, had *also* been mocking Jesus in the early minutes after crucifixion, right along with the other thief (Matthew 27:44).

Here is how I see the story developing.

The repentant robber eventually shut his mouth as he hanged on his cross; he began to do some serious *spiritual* thinking. The Holy Spirit who had "stayed" on Jesus from His baptism forward (John 1:33) was certainly at Calvary too. He now penetrated the heart of this meditating sufferer (cp. 1 Corinthians 12:3). The Spirit must have moved the now-thoughtful thief to remember his old "Saturday school" lessons from synagogue days, those days prior to his choosing a career of crime. Recalling those lessons about the coming One, the Spirit caused this robber to recognize Jesus as that saving Messiah who had now come. As this thief continued to look at Jesus, he suddenly thought, "That's the Guy!" He turned to Jesus and begged, "Jesus, remember me when You come into Your Kingdom" (Luke 23:42).

What faith! The suffering Jesus certainly did not look like a "king" while hanging on the cross. It only looked like He was going to enter a kingdom called "death"! But the thief saw beyond death and put his trust in Jesus, the One who would prove to be "the Resurrection and the Life" (John 11:25), as well as "King of kings" and "Lord of lords."

Then that response from Jesus, "I tell you the truth, today you will be with Me in Paradise." The statement is loaded with *doctrinal* content. There would be no purgatory for this man. Right that same day, after death, he would be right with Jesus the King in the bliss of "Paradise." This is the second time a *garden* ["paradise"] is mentioned in the passion story of Jesus. (It was first used in connection with the "Garden" of Gethsemane. A third occurrence awaits our later investigation of Easter morning in Chapter 21 of our book.)

Jesus usage of the term *paradise* is startling when Bible examiners think about it! It should remind them of the Garden of Eden in Genesis 3. In other words, Jesus had just told the dying thief that he would be back in the "garden" that very day, a garden in eternity. So incredible.

The Greek word for *paradise* in Luke 23:43 is of Persian origin (*AGAGNT*, p. 279). It means "garden." The LXX, a translation of the Hebrew Old Testament into Greek, uses this word in translating "Garden of Eden" in Genesis 3:23. Did that refer to the *original* Garden of Eden? No, that garden had most likely perished in the flood of Noah's time. Instead, it may refer to the garden pictured in Revelation 22:2: *heaven*, or, it may refer to the place of total rest where Christians, and only Christians, go between death and their eventual resurrection on Judgment Day. (See Appendix 10 and its section entitled, "From Here to Eternity" for an extensive discussion on the possible meaning of "Paradise.")

In any event, Jesus certainly chose that "garden" word very carefully.

Many endorse a place called *purgatory* where occupants face "purging and purifying punishments" (one Roman Catholic view), or, as the place where a "process of transformation" takes place (proposed by Cardinal Ratzinger, who later became Pope Benedict XVI)—in either case, a place of *second chances* (see S, *E*, p. 56, plus fn. 17).

In diametric opposition, Hebrews 9:27 teaches: ". . . people are appointed to die once and after that comes judgment." This passage is in total agreement with the Lord Jesus when He emphatically told the repentant thief who had confessed faith in Him as King and Savior that right that very day ("today") he would be "in Paradise." Detective-like question: If that terrible thief got to go to heaven right away, without a stay in purgatory, why would others not get the same privilege since the heavenly Father is a God who does not show "partiality" (Romans 2:11)? Should make one think hard and long!

This long interjection is presented here, and not relegated to an appendix, because of its importance in bringing comfort to the souls of those grieving over the loss of loved ones and in providing the certainty of immediate deliverance into the arms of Jesus at time of death to all those who believe the promises of Scripture (John 3:16)—no exceptions!

Another important factor must be connected to the repentance of the "Paradise"-bound thief. In Christian churches, *faith* is spoken of as generating good works (Ephesians 2:8–10). It's like a horse and cart. The horse (faith) comes *before* the cart (works). Some people put the cart before the horse and conclude that additional human "works"—beyond those provided by Jesus—are needed to get them into heaven. If so, why did Jesus waste His time by saying, "It is finished," when people themselves need to finish Christ's work to get God's approval to enter heaven?

Something serious to think about!

Rather, "faith" automatically produces "good works," and that explains why the repentant robber, as soon as he came to *faith*, told the other crucified robber to shut his mouth, as that second thief continued to curse Jesus (Luke 23:40–41; cp. James 2:26).

The Savior's Third Statement from the Cross

Speaking to His mother, Jesus said, "Woman, there is your son," and to John His disciple, "There is your mother" (John 19:26–27). The examination of these two sentences from the Savior's lips demands many words of explanation in view of a particular Old Testament prophecy, but that is what makes Scriptural investigation so rewarding.

Around 500 years before Christ's crucifixion, it had been predicted that Jesus's mother Mary would be present at Calvary—but Joseph her husband would not. No way, Jose! Yes, in Zechariah 12:10–14, the pre-incarnate Jesus Himself had prophesied this fact—and many more details also. He promised:

> I will pour out on David's family and those living in Jerusalem the Spirit of grace and of prayer. They will look at Me whom they have pierced. They will mourn over Him as parents mourn for their only son and weep bitterly as they weep over their firstborn. On that day the mourning in Jerusalem will be great, like the mourning at Hadad-rimmon in the valley of Megiddo. The country will mourn, each family by itself, the family of David by itself and their wives by themselves; the family of Nathan by itself and their wives by themselves; the family of Levi by itself and their wives by themselves; the family of Shimei by itself and their wives by themselves. All the families that are left, each by itself, and their wives by themselves.

What a prophecy!

The context specifies individuals from King David's genealogy (David, Nathan, plus some unnamed wives), as well as some from Levi's family (Levi, Shimei, plus some more unnamed wives). Jesus Himself is certainly indicated by the words, "They will look at Me whom they have pierced" (cp. John 19:37). "Weeping" is the main *human* theme of the prophecy. It is compared to the sorrow that accompanied the news that faithful King Josiah of Judah had been killed in battle at the city of Hadad-Rimmon in the valley of Megiddo (c. 609 BC), a memorable Old Testament occasion.

Mysteries and Clues #s 1–3: (1) The combining of David with his son Nathan should immediately remind one of Mary, the mother of Jesus, and of genealogical references in

Matthew 1:16 and Luke 3:23b, 31. (2) The combination of Levi and Shimei reminds us of the Levitical priesthood. (3) The great "mourning" causes one to think of the extreme sadness of the three women, all named "Mary," who were watching Jesus suffer on the cross (John 19:25).

One of those named Mary, as stated above, refers to the mother of Jesus. She had descended from David through his son Nathan. Note this fact carefully by recalling its discussion in Appendix 4 of our book. It will let you catch the impact concerning the "wives" who descended from David through Nathan; also note the "wives" who descended from Levi through Shimei (Numbers 3:17–18). In both cases, the *absence* of the mention of "husbands" should be viewed as very significant.

It is also crucial to remember what Simeon had told mother Mary on her former visit to the Temple with her over-forty-day-old Son: "a sword will pierce your own soul too" (Luke 2:35b). It did when she watched her Son Jesus suffering on the cross.

> Scripture does *not* record the many appearances of Mary that were portrayed in Mel Gibson's movie, *The Passion of the Christ*. People are surprised to hear that the *last* time Mary speaks on the pages of the NT is at the Wedding of Cana, way back at the beginning of Jesus's ministry. Shocked? But what a "curtain call" Mary had made. She "signed off" with the words, "Do anything He [Jesus] tells you" (John 2:5). What a great world we would have if everybody followed that advice!

Because of the multifaceted complexity of the Zechariah 12 prophecy, I feel it necessary to repeat it here:

> I will pour out on David's family and those living in Jerusalem the Spirit of grace and of prayer. They will look at Me whom they have pierced. They will mourn over Him as parents mourn for their only son and weep bitterly as they weep over their firstborn. On that day the mourning in Jerusalem will be great, like the mourning at Hadad-rimmon in the valley of Megiddo. The country will mourn, each family by itself, the family of David by itself and their wives by themselves; the family of Nathan by itself and their wives by themselves; the family of Levi by itself and their wives by themselves; the family of Shimei by itself and their wives by themselves. All the families that are left, each by itself, and their wives by themselves.

Mystery and Clue #4: Mary was one of the Nathan-generated wives who wept *by herself*, as others wept or would weep "by themselves" because of Jesus's death or the effect His death would have upon their daily lives.

Mary, the former virgin, was probably a widow by this time or Jesus would *not* have needed to put John in a mother-son relationship with His third words from the cross.

Some say Mary never had sexual relations, even after the birth of Jesus. Doubtful; Joseph and Mary had a normal marriage after Jesus was born. This is definitely implied by Matthew when he writes that Joseph ". . . did not have ˌsexualˌ relations with her [Mary] *until* she had a son" (Matthew 1:25).

Scott Hahn, a famous and current Roman Catholic author, is one who *vehemently* holds that Joseph and Mary never had sexual relations; thus, no biological children. He writes: "They [Joseph and Mary] were truly husband and wife, but their relationship was not sexually consummated" (H, *JW*, pp. 77–81). His main argument concerning the meaning of "until" in Matthew 1:25 is a most one-sided viewpoint. Dr. William F. Arndt gives argumentation from all points of view (A, *GL*, pp. 233–235). He concludes the opposite of Hahn. (Hahn's presentation over this matter, contrary to his usual careful and open-minded scholarship, is curious. In this case of whether Mary and Joseph had children after the birth of Jesus, Hahn selectively limits all data that is contrary to his own personal viewpoint.)

Warning: Never underestimate the importance of the Gospel of Mark. It is often taught that extreme amounts of Mark are repeated in Matthew and Luke. True, but the portions that are unique to Mark are so valuable. Years ago, Pastor Michael Hageman of Zion Lutheran Church in Cleveland, Ohio, USA, and now at Trinity Lutheran Church in Garden City, Kansas, USA, told me his favorite Gospel was Mark. I thought that strange. Who would pick Mark? There is so much more great info in the other gospels? However, my research has turned me on a dime. As the second sentence in the paragraph below shows, as an example, Mark is invaluable for the additional data that it supplies from time to time.

The comment in Matthew that Joseph and Mary did not have sexual intercourse "until" or *before* Jesus was born has moved many theological investigators to conclude that James and Jude, writers of the two New Testament epistles bearing their names, were *half-brothers* of Jesus, not cousins. In addition, Mark 6:3 gives strong evidence that Mary and Joseph had four sons and also some daughters *after* Jesus was born.

This generates a serious question: If Jesus had four half-brothers, then why did Jesus not assign "son" duties to one of these brothers? Answer: None of them were *believers* at the time of the Calvary event (John 7:5; E, "J,"*NLBC*, p. 1314, v. 3). For example, James only became convinced of Jesus's Lordship when his resurrected half-Brother Jesus appeared to him after Easter (1 Corinthians 15:7). Besides, we can surmise Jesus knew that two of them, James and Jude, would die before His disciple John, and thus Mary would have John the apostle as family right up to the time of her death.

So, John and Mary both accepted the responsibility Jesus demanded from the cross. John, presumably the youngest of Jesus's twelve main disciples, became a son Mary looked after like a mother; John conscientiously took responsibility to watch over Mary like a good son would, as he himself reports, "From that time on this disciple [John] took her [Mary] into his own home" (John 19:27b). This statement may imply that Mary was *not* at the cross during the afternoon hours, that she did not see the death of her Son. Why? She is not mentioned as being with the other women during the *post-death* events concerning Jesus. However, John—after he presumably took Mary away from the cross and to his home—was again back at Golgotha in the midafternoon of Good Friday. His Gospel reports events he witnessed *firsthand*. (We will note those events later in Chapter 20.)

Students of Acts conclude that as Mary aged, she must have moved around with John. From Luke's introductory comment in his Gospel (1:3), we suspect that Luke may have received boyhood info about Jesus from Mary at Caesarea, where he probably wrote his Gospel while his traveling companion Paul was under arrest (see Acts 23:12–26:32). Later tradition says Mary's grave is in Ephesus, a place where John is said to have resided before he was exiled to the nearby island of Patmos (Revelation 1:9; cp. 1:10; 2:1).

Mystery and Clue #5: Now for a final comment regarding *general* "Mary" data: Marriage in Mary's day is still very much the same in Palestine and Israel today. Soon after girls begin menstruating, they are most often married off to older men. When traveling through Palestine in 1965, our travel group was taken by its guide to his home to meet his wife; she was about twenty-eight and he was forty-five. This would very likely be true of Mary and Joseph; she was probably between thirteen to fifteen years of age when the Holy Spirit impregnated her, and she was already engaged to the likely thirty-plus-year-old Joseph. This would explain why Joseph may have died by the time the thirty-three-year-old Jesus was crucified. (Calculate this data with the help of Luke 3:23, noting that Jesus had a three-and-a-half-year ministry. That would have made Joseph over sixty by that time, and with life expectancy being much lower than it is today, he could likely have died prior to the crucifixion of Jesus.)

Mystery and Clue #6: As we continue our clue connections between Zechariah 12 and Jesus's third statement from the cross, another aspect of the Zechariah 12 prophecy very nicely ties into the death account of Jesus. It concerns Zechariah's mention of the priestly line of "Levi" and one of its descendants, Shimei.

Bible students need to realize that Israel's priests came from the tribe of Levi. Shimei is named as one of its descending priests in 1 Chronicles 6:17. Tracing his lineage backward, he is noted to have come from Levi's oldest son, named Gershon. We learn the duties of the Gershon line of priests in Numbers 3:17–26. These duties pertained to the overall *structure* of the Tabernacle and its *protection*; this is very applicable to the distant future when some of the priestly descendants of Gershon and Shimei converted to Christianity (see below).

Mystery and Clue #7: Another mystery is now raised by the Zechariah 12 prophecy: Why are the descended "wives" of Levi and Shimei all *weeping and mourning* "by themselves"—in addition to Mary and some of Jesus's close friends? Why are they sad? The answer is complex.

With the death of Jesus, the need for further sacrifice ended (Hebrews 9:12). Meaningless sacrifice continued to be carried on after Jesus's death by the Jewish priesthood for forty more years, that is, until its Jerusalem Temple was flattened by the Roman army in AD 70. That spelled the "end" of Jewish animal sacrifice, the absence of which has continued right down to this very day—no continuing sacrifices being offered over the centuries, contrary to the directives of *Leviticus*.

Daniel prophesied this in Chapter 9 of his book. Referring to the redemptive work of Jesus the Messiah, verse 27 reads: "He [Jesus] will make a strong covenant with many for one week. In the *middle of the week*, He will *stop the sacrifices* and food offerings . . . ."

In Luke 4:25, Jesus strongly implied that the time of His ministry would last three-and-a-half years, parallel to the famine in Elijah's day that also lasted three-and-a-half years. Thus Jesus's ministry, a ministry *starting* in the latter half of AD 26, and then ending three-and-a-half years later, would take one to the early part of AD 30 when Jesus was crucified. This could possibly fulfill the Daniel prophecy, if Daniel's prediction is meant to be taken in terms of the "*Literal* Traditional Messianic Viewpoint" of interpretation. In the overall context of the Daniel prophecy (9:24–27), "weeks," *literally* "*sevens*," is most often taken in terms of "years," not "weeks." Therefore, if literal, the interpreter is taken

Josephus the historian makes an astounding comment about Daniel's predictions concerning the "time" of future happenings, saying that " . . . he [Daniel] did not only prophesy of future events, as did the other prophets, but he also determined the *time* [my emphasis] of their accomplishments" (J, *WJ, Antiq.*, 10.11.7 [267]).

directly to Daniel's "middle of the week," splitting the "seven" years right down the "middle," then having *two* three-and-a-half-year periods. Right then and there, the sacrifice of God's Son would immediately "stop" the necessity for all further sacrifices, right after His three-and-one-half years of ministry.

A possible parallel example of such "exactness" might be found at Exodus 12:40–41 concerning the first-ever Passover day: "The Israelites had been living in Egypt for 430 years. At the end of 430 years, *on that very day*, all the people of the LORD marched out [made an exodus out] of Egypt"—"free at last," as the world-famous Dr. Martin Luther King put it.

That's a lot to take in, detectives. Maybe a coffee break back at your headquarters will provide time to think these things through. Consider: As God the Father sent His Son to earth at just

> A thought concerning parallel Passovers, possibly a clue, just popped into my mind: Because of that "very day" when Jesus died (also on a "Passover" day, as was that original Passover day mentioned in Exodus 12), all humans can now "march" out of Satan's bondage, and via Jesus's blood forgiveness, they can make an exodus out of sin and journey forward into the land of heaven—and truly be free at last of sin.

the right or exact "time" (Galatians 4:4), so one could also expect Him to have designed the absolute "appointed time" for His Son to die (cp. 2 Samuel 24:15).

Mystery and Clue #8: Considering that "stoppage" of sacrifice and returning to the thoughts of the Zechariah 12 context in terms of the weeping Levitical wives, we come to an obscure and usually overlooked passage at Acts 6:7:

> The word of God kept on spreading, and the number of disciples in Jerusalem was growing very large. Even a large number of *priests* came to believe and obey the word.

What a verse to help us interpret one of the *weeping* aspects of the Zechariah prophecy!

Those weeping priestly wives are *symbolically* "mourning" over their loss of income caused by Jesus's death. Fulfillment: Their husbands did lose their Jerusalem jobs when they converted to Christianity or later when the Temple was destroyed in AD 70; all forms of sacrifice and food offering could no longer be made. What would priestly families now eat? What would Shimei's priests do without jobs? What could Shimei's husbands now watch over according to their Gershon instructions?

God the Holy Spirit had a plan. Convert the priests to Christian service (both before and after the destruction of the Jerusalem Temple); let them watch over the "structure" of Christ's new tabernacle, His Church, and they could "protect" it by preaching the word in all its truth and purity. These ex-priests—who formerly "protected" the Old Testament Tabernacle—would be a great addition to early Christianity; they had been priests, trained to teach in synagogues throughout the Holy Land, and now they could teach new Christians the fuller word of God and "protect" that word from false teaching.

But what about those wives married to priests descended from Shimei? Well, just as Mary's tears of weeping turned to smiles of joy when her Son rose from the dead, so the priestly wives would go from tears to smiles when their newly employed husbands came home with their first Christian paychecks—in the form of the meat of lambs, bagels, and lox. (Roll with modern humor, detectives! We know God has a sense of humor; He created us and puts up with us. There's humor, if ever!)

Bet you did not know all that was connected to the truth of Mary being at the cross, as foretold by the Zechariah 12 prophecy! God does like to lay out mysteries, the meanings of which He reveals by sending His Spirit into Bible-investigating minds. Glad Jesus spoke to His mother from the cross and permitted us to know she was there. Opened up a lot of secret doors of worthwhile info.

"There Is Nobody to Help Me"

Calvary was a most lonely place for the Savior. Though many people—friend and foe—physically surrounded the cross, Jesus was still very much alone. He Himself had foretold this coming reality over 700 years before. Yes, the pre-incarnate Christ saw it all in advance. He now was experiencing it firsthand. He had predicted, "I have tramped alone in the winepress" and "I look, but there is nobody to help Me. I shudder, but there is nobody to support Me" (Isaiah 63:3a, 5a, b).

How sad!

A harmonization of the four gospels into chronological order permits one to recognize this "all alone" factor more easily than trying to find it by reading each of the four gospels separately (see *TGPGS*, pp. 16–17.) The first three gospels portray the *loneliness* of Jesus on the cross so well; all four (4) basic groups of society tortured Him with their cruel words—(1) the passer-byers who represented the *common, ordinary people,* (2) the ruling priests who represented *the religious establishment* of the church on earth, (3) the soldiers who represented *the governments of this world,* and (4) the two robbers who spoke evil in line with *the world's criminal element* (Luke 23:35–37, 39; Mark 15:29, 31; Matthew 27:40–44). Nothing kind was spoken to Jesus. He was all alone, carrying the sins of world.

We humans bemoan our days of despair and loneliness; the Savior understands; He went through it all, hundreds of times moreover (Hebrews 3:18: ". . . He Himself experienced testing when He suffered. He is able to help others when they are tested." Need more be said?

The morning words of Jesus were now complete, and 12 noon came.

Evidence room conclusion: Crucifixion clues, along with their surrounding data, drive Bible discoveries that are mounting to ever higher levels. That Triune God of ours packed so much planning into His quest to get us, His children, back into "Paradise."

CHAPTER 19

GOOD FRIDAY: 12:00 NOON–3:00 P.M.

Examining Clues in the Evidence Room
How can Bible investigators even hope
to comprehend the meanings of everything that
happened on Good Friday
between 12 noon and 3:00 p.m.?

Darkness at High Noon, and Way, Way More

"It was about noon when darkness came over the whole land—lasting until three in the afternoon, because the sun stopped shining" (Luke 23:44–45). Does this *darkness* indicate a mere eclipse (cp. *AGAGNT*, p. 279), or just a darkness over the whole "land" of Palestine or Canaan, or does the Greek (*gē*) in this instance, as in some other places (Matthew 5:18, 35), imply the whole "earth"? I opt for the latter, taking the Greek *eklipontos* ("failing" or "ending") to mean the sun "stopped shining" over the *whole earth*. This is in agreement with the NET Bible version used in this book.

Clue-seekers, get ready to get busy. This "darkness" miracle is jam-packed with two crucial Old Testament parallels!

On the surface, one might think this "darkness" was no more than an allusion to Satan, "the ruler of this world" (John 12:31). True, Scripture describes Satan as the prince or main ruler of "darkness" (cp. Ephesians 6:10–12; Acts 26:17–18); besides, Jesus had spoken of "darkness" in terms of His arrest and crucifixion to come. He said to His Jewish accusers, "This is your time when *darkness* rules" (Luke 22:53b).

But the true import of the three hours of Good Friday "darkness" is way more involved than that! There are two very significant Old Testament connectives, apart from any reference to the devil.

The first Old Testament parallel deals with General Joshua, the hero after whom Jesus was named. In Joshua 10:12–14, Joshua spoke a powerful command that had God listening and obeying a mere man for the first time in history. Would Jesus be able to *outdo* this prophet? Would He be able to do a "sun" miracle *better*? Let's read that *Joshua* account:

> Then Joshua spoke to the LORD on the day the LORD delivered the Amorites to the people of Israel. And while Israel was watching, he [Joshua] said: "Sun, stand still over Gibeon, and moon over the valley of Aijalon!"
>
> Then the sun stood still, and the moon stopped until a nation took vengeance on its enemies. Is this not written in the Book of Jasher? The sun stopped in the middle of the sky, and for about a whole day, it did not hurry to go down. Never before or after was there a day like this one, when the LORD did what a man told Him, because the LORD fought for Israel.

Did Joshua call for a miracle of "darkness" or "light"? This writer opts for *darkness*. You choose. Did Joshua want more *light* to chase the enemy, or did he want more *darkness* to lay a sneak attack on his foe? A parallel to Good Friday may call for a miracle of "darkness."

There did come another day when the LORD again listened to a Man, the God-Man Jesus, who "bettered" the first Joshua. This *new* Joshua did not stop the sun in its course to make it "stand still" over a mere section of Palestine, as Joshua had the sun affect a city like Gibeon, nor did He call for a mere eclipse; rather, Jesus made the sun "stop shining" altogether.

> How did the sun stop or "stand still" for Joshua? To cease its motion would mean that the sun would leave its orbit and wander aimlessly through space. Possibly the sun just appeared to be stopped, when, in fact, the LORD may just have bent its rays to stay shining in one area while the sun itself kept moving.

Why not? He had created the sun and moon; they were at His command (see John 1:2–3). This caused a worldwide darkness, so I teach, for if the sun totally stopped shining, then there was no light over the *entire* earth. (On the other side of the earth, the moon would also have gone dark, obviously.) Wouldn't it be great if we had "instant replays" of some of these events to fully grasp all the details? (Later argumentation will explain why Jesus had to cause this total "stoppage" of sunlight in order to "outdo" Joshua. The evidence will let you check it out and make the call.)

As to the moon, Jesus died on the day of the "full moon," which always fell in the middle of the month on the Jewish calendar. In the month of Nisan, as usual, Passover fell right in the middle of the month. Also, a "full moon" sometimes appears "blood red." I believe it appeared like that on the night Jesus was praying in Gethsemane.

Analyze Peter's comments at Pentecost. He says the prophet Joel had predicted a blood red moon in the "last days" (Acts 2:28–32; cp. Joel 2:28–32). The biblical words "last days" is a reference to the *whole* New Testament period. Many take this prediction as referring to the very last days on earth—and it can have that extended meaning. However, initially, since Peter says the Joel account refers to events at the *First* Coming of Jesus (Acts 2:14–21), its first fulfillment refers to the time of Jesus on earth.

Joel's phrase, "the sun will turn dark and the moon to blood," surely connects to Good Friday—in my estimation.

It was a great miracle from the arsenal of Joshua when executed, and a great prophecy from the pen of Joel when written (Joel 2:28–32), but it was an even greater miracle when performed by the Son of Man, the Messiah, as He was hanging on the cross.

Now to introduce *another* super important mystery clue; it is truly one of the most startling connectives between the Old and New Testaments in all the Bible. Stand ready to be amazed at God's genius.

Every Jew acquainted with the history of the Israelite *exodus* from Egypt should know why Jesus ordered "three" hours of darkness on Passover Friday. Have you caught on? Stop and think. Yes, you have it: One of the Egyptian plagues, sent by God, was a "darkness" that lasted "three" days; now Jesus parallels it with "three" hours of "darkness" at Calvary.

But that is not the main point.

The question becomes: Which of the ten plagues was the "darkness" one? Was it number two, five, eight, or one of the other numbers? The "darkness" of Exodus 10:21–23 falls into the *ninth* slot.

Now another question that demands an answer: What came after the ninth plague? For those of you into higher math, the answer: The tenth plague. (Just a joke!) And what was that plague? See Exodus 12:29–30. The tenth plague brought death to every "firstborn" son in Egypt who was in a home that did *not* have the blood of a lamb painted on its doorposts and lintels.

> Lintels: the crossbeams on top of doorframes.

The Israelites had eaten Passover lambs on the night of their exit from Egypt, and they painted their doorframes with the blood of those lambs, using a paintbrush made from "hyssop" shrubs. When the LORD went through the land of Egypt, He "passed over" all the homes protected with blood, but "death" fell on every "firstborn" who was in a home *not* protected by blood.

And so, it came to pass on that glorious Good Friday Passover that God struck down Jesus, "the *Firstborn* among many brothers" (Romans 8:29), as the substitute for all humans. However, protection still prevails to this very day for all who have the blood of Jesus painted, by faith, on the doorposts of their redeemed hearts (1 John 1:7).

So, as said, it is an Old Testament Egyptian clue that solves the "darkness" mystery of that first Good Friday. Every Jew should have made the connection between the ninth and tenth plagues, between the "three" days of darkness in Egypt and the "three" hours of darkness at Calvary and beyond, that is, between the deaths of those Egyptian firstborns and the death of Jesus the "Firstborn," who died at 3:00 p.m., the very hour when Passover lambs were being slaughtered. *"Evidence Just Too Coincidental to Be Accidental!!!"*

What a God, what a Savior, everything carried out to perfection per God's eternal plan! Think about it. On that first Good Friday, Jesus took our place as our "morning Sacrifice" (6:00 a.m.), as our "evening Sacrifice" (3:00 p.m.), as our "Passover Lamb" [on Passover Day], and as our "Scapegoat" "outside the gate" of the city of Jerusalem (Hebrews 13:12)! We went free, as He went to the cross as the "Firstborn Son" of God (Hebrews 1:6). God turned His back on His own Firstborn, so we could live with Him forever in heaven.

Need we say more as to "how" three hours of darkness was the *pre-clue* to the death of God's "Firstborn"?

The Clock Was Ticking!

As the three hours of darkness were coming to a close, things started to happen in rapid succession at Calvary:

> First, the Savior spoke all four of His final sayings shortly before 3:00 p.m.
> (Matthew 27:46 introduces this short timeframe.)

Second, Christ quickly died right at 3:00 p.m. (consider both John 19:30 and
Mark 15:37–39).

Third, simultaneous with Jesus's death, three awesome phenomena followed
(Luke 23:45b–46).

Fourth, other events—like Jesus's burial—were completed over the next three
hours (3:00 p.m.–6:00 p.m.), events that fulfilled the words of Zechariah
3:9d: "I will remove the sin of that land in *one* day" (John 19:31–42).

Fact: It takes much Scriptural investigation to see how all the *time elements* on
Good Friday perfectly fit together to fulfill all the prophecies of the
Old Testament. Only a careful deciphering of those clues can solve
New Testament mysteries.

Both Matthew 27:46 and Mark 15:34 pinpoint 3:00 p.m. as important. By adding the word
"about" to his statement ("*About* three o'clock"), Matthew indicates that Jesus still had time
to speak four times—and still to be ready to die at 3:00 p.m. This was crucial for his Jewish
audience to know. In fulfillment of prophecy, it was so important that Christ die at the exact
time predicted by God in the Old Testament. Why? Because two things happened on a regular
basis at 3:00 p.m., one of them daily, one yearly, but on this day, there would be two final things,
two once-in-the-history-of-the-world *things*!

Every day, seven days a week, around 3:00 p.m., a lamb was sacrificed, called the "evening
sacrifice." For centuries, this ceremony pointed forward to the death of Jesus, the Lamb of God.
At 3:00 p.m. on that first Good Friday, Jesus became the world's final "evening Sacrifice."

Also, once a year at Passover, Passover lambs were slaughtered at 3:00 p.m.

But it would be on this day, on this first Good Friday, at 3:00 p.m., that the real and final
Passover Lamb—JESUS—would die.

(That the Gospel of Mark lumped several sayings and events all together at 3:00 p.m. does
not contradict Matthew; it gave initial, primary, and sufficient information to Mark's Gentile
audience, an audience that was not acquainted with Old Testament prophecies. Those readers
were able to decipher and catch up later as their faith and knowledge grew.)

The Savior's Fourth Statement from the Cross

There was *dead silence* for three straight afternoon hours until Jesus quoted the first verse of
Psalm 22. Matthew notes it as a prophecy being fulfilled right as Jesus screamed out: *"Eli, Eli,
lama sabachthani?"* (Hebrew meaning, "My God, My God, why did You forsake Me?")

This fourth statement from the Savior's lips is the most vital and *theologically* packed of

Christ's seven sayings. Since page after page could be written to explain the statement, it seems wise just to list my teaching notes to effectively give a synopsis of the fuller meaning.

ELI, ELI, LAMA SABACHTHANI

1. Jesus quoted these words from Psalm 22:1.
2. These words represent the *high point* of Jesus's suffering!
3. God now abandoned God to save us! Christian hymn: "deepest stroke . . . was the stroke that *Justice* gave."
4. At this moment on the cross, Christ was experiencing "hell" for all.
5. Isaiah 53:4: "stricken, smitten, and afflicted *of God*"!
6. 2 Corinthians 5:21: "He who knew no sin was made sin for us" (cp. 1 Peter 2:22).
7. Hebrews 9:22: ". . . if no blood is poured out, no sins are forgiven."
8. 1 Peter 1:18-19: ". . . not by a payment of silver and gold . . ., but by the precious blood of Christ, ..."
9. Jesus's fourth statement is *beyond human comprehension* (Colossians 2:2–3).
10. Only Jesus, the GOD-MAN, could defeat the devil (analyze 1 John 3:8b).

Yes, Christ's *fourth* saying indicated the "high point" of His suffering. At that very moment, God the Father totally abandoned God the Son and made His "Beloved" (cp. Matthew 3:17; 17:5) endure the punishments of "hell" for all human beings of all times. How much the Father loved every human, giving up His Son for them; how much the Son loved every human to enter hell in their place! And as to "hell," it spells total *separation* from the physical and spiritual blessings of God. Now no believer in Jesus need go there (Galatians 3:13–14).

This fourth statement from the cross was rapidly followed by Christ's last three sayings.

The Savior's Fifth Statement from the Cross

Jesus spoke again: "I thirst."

If asked to vote, it's probably safe to say, most would vote this statement the *least* significant of the seven sayings spoken by Christ from the cross. Do not underestimate it.

Jesus had now endured the "cup" of suffering (cp. Matthew 26:39). Only one thing remained unfulfilled before He could die, the need to say, "I thirst." It was the fifth time Jesus spoke from His cross. This statement fulfilled *two* prophecies: one a direct prediction, the other an acted-out picture of the future, greater One who eventually came. In fulfillment, a drink was given to Christ at the end of His biggest battle. He was given "sour wine," as reported in Matthew, Mark, and John.

Psalm 69:21 came to fulfillment: "And they put gall in My food and for My thirst give Me vinegar to drink." Combining gall and vinegar and putting it into wine would certainly make "sour" wine. Jesus's mouth was dry from His six hours on the cross, not having had anything to drink. Like our modern drinks that place lemon juice into water, so Jesus received liquid that quenched His thirst.

Most have connected the "I thirst" saying of Jesus with its Psalm 69:21 prediction. But what about its "Samson" connection? Not so much.

Judges 15:18 portrays the mighty Samson dying of "thirst" after just winning a decisive victory over his persistent enemy, the Philistines. A few hours before, he had willingly permitted *Judean* Jews to "tie him with two new ropes" and hand him over to his *Gentile* Philistine captors (Judges 15:9–13). In direct parallel, Jesus willingly permitted Himself to be arrested and "bound" in Gethsemane and, a few hours later, to be handed over by *Judean* ruling Jews to the *Gentile* governor, Pontius Pilate (John 18:12, 28–29). Amazing parallel. (Review this parallel again.)

But there is another equally parallel connector.

When the tied-up Samson entered the Philistine camp, Judges 15:14b–19b reports:

> But the Spirit of the LORD came over him [Samson], and the ropes on his arms became like flax burnt in the fire: his ropes melted off his hands.
>
> Finding a donkey's fresh jawbone, he reached for it, grabbed it, and with it struck down 1,000 men. Then Samson said:
>
> > "With a donkey's jawbone, I piled them in heaps;
> > with a donkey's jawbone, I killed a thousand men."
>
> When he finished saying this, he threw the jawbone away. And so that place was called the Hill of the Jawbone.
>
> Then he was very *thirsty*, and he called to the LORD and said, "You have given this great victory to your servant, but now I am dying of *thirst* and will fall into the hands of the uncircumcised."
>
> So God split open the hollow place that is at Lehi ["the Valley of the Jawbone"], and water gushed out. He drank it; his spirit was refreshed; . . . .

Like Samson after his greatest battle, Jesus was also *thirsty* after His greatest battle at Calvary; and parallel to Samson, God provided a drink for His Son. (We will visit Samson again when considering the seventh saying of Jesus on the cross.)

It is of great importance that investigative clue-seekers watch for *seemingly* contradictory evidence at Calvary and seek out whether the facts are indeed contradictory or not; if not, do they hold a hidden *purpose*? We remember the

> In THE AD 1600s, Johann Gerhard also observed the same Samson and Jesus "I thirst" connective (cited in B, *ROTNC*, Part II, 44–45).

example of the "scarlet" and "purple" robe situation, and on that occasion we detected a *purpose* for that particular *seeming* contradiction.

As we now analyze Matthew 27:48 and Mark 15:36, we note another *seeming* contradiction.

> Of interest is the fact that hyssop stems only grow about three feet long; their flimsy tops needed to be cut down to support a sponge. What does this indicate? The feet of Jesus were, most likely, only a mere two feet off the ground. All Jesus's enemies were "up close and personal." This pictures His agony as even more intense.

These two Gospel writers say a wine-soaked sponge was lifted to the lips of Jesus on a "reed"-stick, while John 19:29 identifies the stick as a "hyssop stem." Can the two different terms be reconciled?

It was Passover and hyssop would readily be available to remind Jews that their ancestors had painted blood on the doorframes of their Egyptian residences—with hyssop—so God would *not* strike their firstborns with death but would "pass over" them, sparing the lives of His people. John's Gospel made sure its readers picked up the *hyssop* connective motif.

It seems Matthew and Mark wanted to place a different emphasis; they desired to jolt their readers' minds to think: "Moses and Egypt!" Do you remember that Moses, as a baby, had been placed among "reeds" in the Nile River so he would be saved (Exodus 2:3)? When rescued, Moses grew up to lead His people out of Egyptian bondage. Now Jesus, the new and "better" Moses, is associated with a "reed" at Calvary, seemingly to remind readers that He also leads the people of His new Kingdom [His tribe or His Church] out of the bondage of sin into the freedom of forgiveness.

John, writing some forty years after Matthew and Mark, may have realized that Christians had forgotten to connect the "Passover hyssop" to the "reed" instrument that held the wine-soaked sponge. That sponge would have been "red" from wine when put to Jesus's lips. Such imagery of a reed stick with *red* on top should have reminded Jews and Christians alike of those "hyssop" paint brushes, the ones that had spread red blood on the doorposts and upper frames of Israelite homes in Egypt. John made sure it would. He indicated what kind of "reed" served Jesus a drink at Calvary, a hyssop-like reed stick.

A Side Issue Concerning the Good Friday "Hyssop"

A difficult matter for evaluation: Just maybe, Jesus's cross was T shaped, as shown in the *Ben-Hur* movie. Not the usual kinds that are displayed in Christian churches: those crucifixes or crosses that have a crossbar intersecting the upright beam *(crux immissa)*. At Calvary, Jesus's body certainly was in both a perpendicular and horizontal configuration. As His body was hanging on the cross, it became the *new doorpost* and *lintel*, and the blood running through His body became paint to cover the doorposts and lintels of the hearts of all people. In truth, Christ became the "Hyssop-Man." Only on the hearts of believers, however, can His blood prove *effective*, since only believers can personally experience and benefit from God "passing over" their sins.

One thing that is surely not conjectural, however: a *hyssop* stick with red on top would scream, "Passover." And the final Passover Lamb was shedding His blood, like the first Passover lambs in Egypt had shed their blood which, in turn, was then used to paint Israelite doorframes.

But something was so different this time. God would *not* "pass over" Jesus; He would strike down His "Firstborn" in death for all the peoples of the world.

Having now internalized all that data, does that fifth statement still sound so insignificant, detectives? No, it contains valuable evidence that determines whether Jesus of Nazareth was really the messianic Passover Lamb of God, or not!

The Savior's Sixth Statement from the Cross

If Christ's fourth statement was the most important *doctrinally*, then His sixth statement preserved in John 19:30a is the most *comforting* in the ears of Christians and needs to become so in the ears of everyone in the world.

For over 4,000 years, those who awaited the coming One had yearned to hear the words, "It is finished" [Greek: *tetelestai*]. This sixth utterance of the Savior still echoes over the centuries as the most precious sound sin-ridden people can ever hear; it sounds the message of total *forgiveness*. The devil is defeated; Jesus wins; we win. The battle is won; Christ has completed His work perfectly. He can now be declared the perfect Lamb of God who has "taken away the sin of the world" (cp. John 1:29).

Oh, to be sure, that "dying" part was still left and several *postmortem* events to be fulfilled, but the "washing"-away-of-sin part was done—and for all time (Hebrews 7:26–28). Jesus now surpassed all the high priests of old; on the cross He had become both the final "High Priest" and sacrifice at one and the same time (Hebrews 9:11a, 26b, 28). And now He could "sit down" (Hebrews 8:1)—a thing no other high priest had ever been able to do in the earthly Tabernacle or Temple. Why? There had never been any "chairs" in those structures. But forty days after His resurrection, the victorious Messiah would ascend into heaven and *sit down* at the right of God the Father. It would then be "Alleluia" time forever (Revelation 19:6–8; cp. Psalm 110:1).

Truly, "It is finished!" Therefore, God does not need our human good works to do more *finishing*. He did the whole job on Good Friday just fine—without our help.

Note: Just as God "finished" His work of Creation on the *sixth* day in Genesis 2:1, a Friday, Jesus now "finished" His work on Good Friday, the *sixth* day of the week. More than a "coincidence"!

The Savior's Seventh Statement from the Cross

Luke writes, "And Jesus cried out with a loud voice, 'Father, into your hands I entrust My spirit'" (Luke 23:46).

Later in Acts 7:59–60, the first martyr of the post-resurrection era, Stephen, would cry out these same words to Jesus—and *couple* them with Jesus's first words from the cross—as he died. We detectives also need to put Jesus's *first* and *seventh* statements from the cross together, noting that *both* sayings began with the word "Father."

As you have sensed, Jesus always had something special "up His sleeve" when He said or did anything. What did He have going on as He checked out of life for three days? He was completing the *first* purpose for His coming into this world; namely, He was keeping the Ten Commandments for all humans who had been so superb at breaking them (cp. 1 John 3:4). How did He do that?

Appendix 5 *(Christianity's Heart and Core)* lists the "five reasons" that God the Father sent His Son to earth.

Do you recall Jesus's summary of the Law in Matthew 22:37–39? He said, "'Love the Lord your God with all your heart, with all your soul, and with all your mind.' This is the greatest and most important commandment. The next is like it: 'Love your neighbor as yourself.'" The Bible calls those summary commandments the two "Tables" or "Tablets" of the Law.

With Jesus's *first* statement on the cross, He was keeping the Second Table of the Law. He was loving His "neighbor," as demanded by His heavenly Father. With His *seventh* saying,

Jesus was loving His "God," thus keeping the First Table of the Law. In total, He kept the Ten Commandments perfectly *in humankind's place* on the cross. Done!

As to the *double* use of "Father," what about that? It was like a set of *bookends*, better yet, like a *ribbon* around a gift. There it was: the gift of forgiveness that – through faith provided by the Holy Spirit – could be picked up and opened to receive its contents *personally*. It's a gift people should not leave unopened. They should not ignore it, or try to win heaven on their own goodness (cp. Isaiah 64:6; Romans 3:9–18). Why waste time doing what no one, except Jesus, could do? Would you waste time rewashing dishes that are already *perfectly* clean? Christ has already washed us clean; we cannot get any cleaner by trying to add to His "finished" works. Our attempted efforts are desired by the Savior (Ephesians 2:10), but they merit us nothing; our "works" are merely our way of saying "thank you" to Him who first gave the gift. As Scripture says, "We love because He *first* loved us" (1 John 4:19).

Once more, we have found out that there is always much more investigative work to be done in God's "66" police precincts of the Bible. It is not like TV where your favorite series eventually comes to an end, to your chagrin. But the excitement of the Bible goes on endlessly.

Did you notice that Jesus entrusted His "spirit" into His Father's hands? Jesus trusted in the true heavenly Father and therefore committed Himself to His Father in death, as He had in life. "He bowed His head" and "died" (John 19:30b; Mark 15:37).

See Appendix 14, the section on "Threesomeness," to learn more about the term *spirit*.

Notice that the Father must have returned to Calvary after He had left ["had forsaken"] Jesus. How could Jesus give Himself over to the Father if the Father would still have been absent? Rather, the Father had returned; He was most "pleased" with His Son's sacrifice (cp. Matthew 3:17; 17:5).

Also note this fact about Jesus's death: He Himself makes the decision as to *when* He is to die. As He predicted in John 10:17–18:

> The Father loves Me because I give up My life in order to take it back
> again. No one takes it from Me. No, of My own free will I am giving it up. I
> have the authority to give it up, and I have the authority to take it back again.

Yes, Jesus had the "authority" to choose His time of death; He also had the "authority" to choose the time of His Easter resurrection, as we will see further down the line. And He used that *authority*.

More Good Friday Samson and Jesus Connections

Two other Good Friday observations should tantalize our attention. They both involve Samson. Why not? As Samson was unbelievably strong and had torn down the gates of the city of Gaza when the Spirit invaded his *physical* body, so Jesus proved His superior *spiritual* strength when He brought down Satan and the "gates of hell" (cp. Judges 16:3 with Matthew 16:18).

Observe another connection between the strong Samson and the mightier Jesus. Judges 16:30c relates the *results* of the dying Samson as he destroyed the temple of Dagan, which was full of more than a thousand people. It says, ". . . those he killed when he died were more than those he killed during his life." We know that total must have been over a thousand, because he killed that many alone in a former Philistine encounter (Judges 15:16).

And then there is Jesus, the parallel Conqueror of Calvary. But He does it "better." First, He killed thousands upon thousands from the cross. Who? Satan and all his thousands of evil angels, those who were now as good as dead, destined to be sealed for eternal doom and death in the "bottomless pit" of hell (Jude 6; Revelation 20:3a, 10)!

Second, a *reverse* parallel: Jesus made millions more *alive* in His death than He made alive with the resurrections He performed during His lifetime. Millions upon millions would come *alive* by faith in days to come (John 5:25; cp. Romans 1:17). In contrast, the Samson narrative features killing, whereas, the account of Jesus's Easter resurrection emphasizes "life" over "death." Jesus taught, "Because I live, you also will live" (John 14:19, a good program to buy into).

And now the "Grand Finale" of Jesus's moment of death. Samson the Old Testament connector and Jesus the Finalizer again take the "limelight"! Two more parallels: the first a very direct analogy; the second an advance by Jesus.

Judges 13:5b predicted that Samson's ministry would *"start* to free Israel from the Philistines," and Samson did make one great "start"! Samuel—prophet, priest, and last "judge" of Israel—followed with a significant defeat over a later Philistine army at Ebenezer (1 Samuel 7:10–13), while King David pretty much *finished off* the Philistines as a *major* threat, though their continued presence proved a mere nuisance for many years after (cp. 2 Chronicles 28:16–19).

But the world needed someone stronger than Samson. It needed a *Finisher* [Jesus], not just a *starter* [Samson].

And so Jesus did come and did gain a *final* victory that *finished off* all His enemies—sin, death, and the power of the devil. Yet, because God wishes to test Christians to strengthen them, He still permits Satan to hang around to tempt us all. Just as He permitted the Philistines and other evil influences to hang around to tempt and test His people in Old Testament days, so He still permits the same today (James 1:12–15; 1 Peter 5:8).

Or put it this way (on the level of our "old self," our sinful side): Temptations still have power today, but in relation to our "new self," Satan's nuisance temptations need only have a "paper tiger" effect (Romans 7:18–20; 8:31–39; Ephesians 4:20–24; *cp. Romans 16:20*). Why? Because our new nature cannot sin, even though our old nature can. No wonder Paul wrote this in Romans 7:24–25:

> What a miserable person I am! Who will rescue me from this body which brings death? Thanks be to God—He does it through our Lord Jesus Christ! So on the one hand, I serve the Law of God with my mind, but on the other ⌐I serve⌐ the law of sin with my flesh.

To the reader of Scripture, a new mystery seems to have begun. In seeming contradiction, the Bible both teaches that Christ's battle *finalized* the whole problem of sin and also that sin *still continues* to be a real enemy. In theological terms, this present problem becomes understandable when one recognizes the tension between Scripture's "now" and Scripture's "not yet" (cp. Romans 16:20a).

Closing Down

We bring Calvary's 12 noon to 3:00 p.m. time slot to a wingding of a close as we think about the *posture position* of both Samson and Jesus at the times of their deaths. The connection has been distorted for many people by Bible story pictures showing Samson "pulling" the pillars of Dagan's temple down as he died. Judges 16:29 says he "pushed" them down. That word sets up a picture-perfect setting. Samson died with his arms outstretched horizontally, the same horizontal way the arms of Jesus were outstretched when He died nailed to the cross.

Oh, just a coincidence; just ignore it! Or is it *"Evidence Just Too Coincidental to Be Accidental!!!"*? You judge.

By the way, as you have noticed, several parallels have been made between Samson and Jesus. For decades, it has been my privilege to lecture on Samson, giving presentations that have cited some fifteen identical and contrasting parallels to Christ.

A final comment is also needed concerning "The 'Good Friday' Psalm": Psalm 22. Repeatedly, its verses were fulfilled as Jesus hanged nailed to

Augustine and other churchmen throughout post-NT times also noted some of these parallels between Samson and Jesus (B, *ROTNC*, Part II, 29, 36–37, 44–45, 51–52, 56–57).

His cross. All was so dismal at Calvary on that first Good Friday; likewise, all the words of

Psalm 22 seem so dismal when first read. But do not be fooled. Just as the Passion story will end with *hope* on Easter morning at the empty tomb, so the predictive Psalm 22 also *ends* on a high note of *hope*.

The New "Friday" Man

Did Jesus need to die on a Friday? Could a Monday or Wednesday or some other day have done the job? No, it had to be a Friday. Why? Think! On what day were human beings created? That's right. Adam and Eve were created on a Friday; that "finished" God's work (Genesis 2:1), and then God "rested" on the "seventh day," a Saturday (Genesis 2:2).

Now Jesus comes on a Friday to redeem people whose first ancestors were originally created on a Friday (Genesis 1:26–31). But all humans had turned the Creation topsy-turvy through sin. A new "Friday" Man would have to appear and undo the mess—and, we repeat, just as His heavenly Father had "finished" His creative work on a "Friday" (Genesis 2:1), so the new "Friday" Man straightens out the whole iniquity mess on a "Friday," and exclaims, "It is 'finished'" (John 19:30)!

What a climactic connective!

And then, as if that is not divine enough, Jesus is buried on that same day, and readers then find Him in His grave until Sunday, which means (Are you ready, detectives?) that Jesus, as at Creation, also "rested" an entire Saturday (cp. Genesis 2:2–3), only this "rest" was in a grave awaiting a new creation day that was about to begin on a Sunday—that day of the week when Christ rose from the dead.

Yes, go ahead and say it in advance of the details that will unfold in the remaining parts of this book!

Yes, say it,

The Savior of the world not only had to die on a "Friday"; He also needed to rise on a "Sunday" to start a new world Creation. Just as the first Creation had started on a Sunday, the "first day of the week," so Jesus would start His *new creation* "on the first day of the week" (Mark 16:2; Galatians 6:15: ". . . what matters is being a new creation"; 2 Corinthians 5:17: "So if anyone is in Christ, he is a new creation").

Several of the Old Testament connective-clues for all the above can be cited at Genesis 1:5 ("one day" or Day 1; Creation started on a Sunday); 1:26–31 ("humankind" was created on a Friday); 2:1–2 ("finished" used twice; Creation was completed on a Friday); 2:3 ("seventh day"; God the Creator "rested" on a Saturday). (Note the concurrence of Irenaeus on some of the above, as quoted in B, *ROTNC*, Part II, 47.)

When the promised Messiah died, the world did not stop; rather, "just then"—all around—several strange things happened (Matthew 27:51–52). What were those things? Inspect them in the next chapter!

> **Evidence room conclusion:** If the walls of the evidence room were not covered to capacity before this point in our investigation, well, the posting of the data collected on the afternoon of Good Friday between 12 noon and 3:00 p.m. demands a whole separate room capable of holding all the Golgotha or Calvary information gathered by Bible observers.

CHAPTER 20

GOOD FRIDAY: 3:00 P.M.–6:00 P.M.

Examining Clues in the Evidence Room
When connected to Old Testament history,
how do Christ's post-death events
provide answers for New Testament detectives?

Calvary's Post-Death Happenings

If things had been relatively motionless for most of the three hours from noon to three o'clock on that first Good Friday, they certainly were not motionless during the next three hours. *Bang, bang, bang!* Events now took place one right after another.

Event One: The Temple Curtain Is Separated

The curtain in the Temple "was torn in two *from top to bottom*" (Matthew 27:51a). This large Temple curtain had separated the Holy Place from the Most Holy Place; it was composed of "72 squares" (being some two inches thick) and was 60 feet long by 30 feet wide (E, *LTJM*, II, 611). In addition, this curtain was dyed violet, purple, and scarlet—the colors of sin (cp. Exodus 24:1; Isaiah 1:18), with warrior angels [cherubim] embroidered on it.

Old Testament high priests, every one of them through the centuries, were only permitted to enter through this inner curtain once a year, and that was on the Day of Atonement, called *Yom Kippur* in the Hebrew language.

> *Yom Kippur* was also the "day" (once a year) when the *scapegoat* carried Israel's sin "outside the camp," symbolically removing blame from the people (Leviticus 16, esp. vv. 22, 29–31, 34a).

Able Bible analyzers need to recall that this curtain's presence—also *symbolically*—forbade *day-by-day* entry until the ultimate High Priest [Christ] would come. At that time, He, and He only, would make it possible by His atoning death to have this curtain barrier removed, ripped down, in order to show that human transgressions that had separated humans from their God were now totally forgiven, not for just a year but rather for all time (Hebrews 9:12, 28a; 10:14).

Christ, the ultimate High Priest, finally came on that first Good Friday, and He completed His work of redemption. But what about that foreboding Temple curtain that still symbolically separated people from God? Iniquity had now been removed, and God the Father recognized this. Looking down from His throne in heaven, He tore the curtain from "top to bottom," indicating He was now satisfied that the full price for sin had been paid.

The Father's action of tearing the veil into "two" parts showed that He was now inviting all to enter (Hebrews 9:12; Ephesians 1:7). That action also encourages Christians today to invite all types of people in the whole world to enter into fellowship with the true God and to be united, one to another. Reject no one created by God; all are invited to come inside the Christian faith. Ephesians 2:11–14 says:

> Remember, then, that once you were outwardly Gentiles, called "the uncircumcised" by those who call themselves "the circumcised" (whose circumcision is ˎonlyˏ an outward one done by human hands).
>
> ˎRememberˏ that at that time you were without Christ, excluded from citizenship in Israel and strangers to the covenants of the promise. You had no hope and were without God in the world.
>
> But now in Christ Jesus you who once were far away have been brought near through the blood of Christ. For He is our Peace: In His flesh, He has made both ˎJew and Gentileˏ one by breaking down the wall of hostility that kept them apart.

At first glance, Matthew 27:51 and Luke 23:45–46 seem to be contradictory in terms of chronological happening. The solution is to be found in realizing that right at the same time as Jesus died, the Temple curtain tore. These two events happened simultaneously.

Event Two: A Whole Lot of Shakin' Goin' On

The mighty Maker of the whole universe had just died; "the Prince" and "Author of Life" had been killed" (Acts 3:15). The Creation reacted violently! Throughout history, after sin entered Eden, all Creation had been waiting to be delivered from results caused by human rebellions against God's ways (Romans 8:19–22). The "earth quaked"; "rocks split apart" (Matthew 27:51b)! It was chaos!

> Edersheim, a superb Bible commentator who was converted from Judaism, notes that this captain would have been over twelve guards at the cross, four guards for each of the three crucified victims (E, *LTJM*, II, 582–583).

The captain [centurion] who was standing guard at Christ's cross seems to have caught the meaning of it all. As he gazed at the dead Jesus, he saw beyond death to Calvary's real meaning. He "praised God," confessing, "Certainly this Man was righteous" (Luke 23:47); then as he understood it even more, he added, "Certainly this Man was the Son of God" (Mark 15:39).

Some others standing there may have come to the same conclusion, as they shook in their sandals and were "terrified" (Matthew 27:54), but as usual, others probably went home as clueless as ever (Luke 23:48).

Event Three: Wait; It's Too Early!

Tombs opening on Good Friday? What, bodily resurrections? That should *not* have happened. No one should be rising until Easter! Scripture had predicted, "He [the Messiah] will come to Zion as a Redeemer" (Isaiah

> In the overall Scriptural picture of Jerusalem, its status as the capital of the Holy Land was meant to be an *earthly* representation of the *heavenly* Jerusalem to come down from above and be the throne area of the "KING of Kings" after the world comes to an end (Revelation 19:11–16; 21:9–11, 22).

59:20). Jesus should rise *first*; then others. Matthew must be wrong (27:52). It can't be!

But it was.

Matthew testifies to the facts:

> The tombs were opened, and the bodies of many believers [saints or ones made "holy" by the forgiving blood of Jesus] who had been sleeping were

brought back to life. They came out of the tombs *after* He had risen and went into the Holy City where they appeared to many people (27:52–53).

There it was: the passage that really befuddled me in my seminary days. Not only was the idea of Good Friday resurrections puzzling; the idea that these *live* people stayed in their tombs till Easter Sunday was even crazier. Where did Matthew come up with this cockamamie story?

But maybe Matthew was right; maybe he met a few of those resurrected people after Easter and talked with them *personally* before he wrote his book. In any event, this account remained a big mystery until I happened upon 2 Kings 13:20–21. Then all kinds of lights began to flash. The key had been found. It was another *New Testament mystery* that could be solved with an *Old Testament clue*.

> Elisha died and was buried. And Moabite bands used to invade the country at the beginning of the year. Men who were going to bury a man saw such a band, and so they hurriedly put the man into Elisha's tomb. But touching Elisha's body, he became alive and stood up on his feet.

Strange occurrence. The prophet Elisha raised a dead man *after* he himself was dead? Then the "better" light went on. If Jesus had been the One He claimed to be, then He would also have to outdo the "hotshot" prophet Elisha. He would have to raise someone from the dead *while He Himself was dead*. And it would be way too late to do it on Easter *after* He was back alive. So – while *dead* – Jesus did it on Good Friday. And this time, He really did "better" Elisha. Not one but "many" persons were resurrected by the dead Jesus—and *without touching* them.

But why did they have to stay in their tombs until Sunday? Because the resurrected Christ had to be the *first* into Jerusalem, which by this time in history was also called Zion (see R. K. Harrison, *CBD*, "Zion," pp. 654–655). (Remember, Zion had always been called "The City of David.") Repeating Isaiah 59:20, "He [the Messiah] will come to Zion as a Redeemer."

Since Zion had come to be a comprehensive term, also encompassing all the territory that surrounded Jerusalem, that would mean Jesus was the *first* back from the grave to place His living feet onto its soil. The new Shepherd King David, Christ Himself, would appear in Zion to claim His throne on Easter, as Ezekiel 34:23a had predicted: "I will raise up one Shepherd over them, My Servant David, who will feed them."

A lot to digest all at once. And Jesus is not yet back alive in our story, so we must hurry back to the cross and leave those live people in their tombs for three days until we report the resurrection of Jesus. At that time, we will journey with those resurrected people "into the Holy City where they appeared to many people."

But for the moment, the miracle of the *dead* Elisha performing a resurrection miracle is the clue to solving the Good Friday mystery of tombs opening and dead bodies resurrecting via the power of the *dead* Jesus. That God of ours is so amazing—and unpredictable!

Back to the Cross

The body of Jesus continued to hang on the cross for over an hour after He died, but the two malefactors crucified with Him remained alive. Both situations created a problem. The Jews in Jerusalem were ready to begin a new day, "an important Sabbath" (John 19:31). It would be *unholy* to leave bodies hanging on crosses on a Sabbath (Deuteronomy 21:22–23). Therefore, the Jewish leaders asked Pilate to have all three bodies taken down from the crosses and buried (John 19:31). He agreed.

The two thieves had to be put to death before their bodies could be removed from their crosses and before their burials. That meant breaking their legs. (See accompanying box for details.)

It was not unusual for those hanging on crosses to stay alive for even three days (E, *LTJ*, II, 612–613), repeatedly pumping up and down to get air to breathe. If they could *not* pump upward, they would suffocate and choke to death. So soldiers came and hastened the deaths of the two thieves on either side of Jesus by breaking their legs (John 19:32). They soon choked to death.

With Jesus, it was different; He was already dead. There was no need to break His legs. Since He was the Passover Lamb and no bones of Passover lambs were to be "broken" (Exodus 12:46; cp. Psalm 34:20), the soldiers by God's design would not break the legs of Jesus. Scripture fulfilled (John 19:33)! Instead, to make sure He was dead, a soldier "pierced" His side with a spear (John 19:34), thus unknowingly fulfilling another prophecy, Zechariah 12:10b: "They will look upon Me [Jesus] whom they have pierced." God was still running the show!

About the piercing: John twice testifies that he saw "blood and water" come out of the dead body of Jesus (John 19:34b–35; 1 John 5:6–8). Only John records this phenomenon, the separation of "blood" from "water." Many see the 1 John text giving reference to what is called "the three means of grace," namely, the word, baptism, and the Lord's Supper. They say the words in that *1 John* text, "the Spirit, the water, and the blood," support this claim. Edersheim agrees (E, *LTJM*, II, 615). I concur but see an *initial* and *primary* meaning flowing from the John 19 report *before* one should apply correct symbolism to the 1 John testimony.

There was a strange medical situation, it would seem, going on at the cross. The spear does not enter Jesus's body for a good sixty to ninety minutes after Jesus is dead. From what I have learned, bodily fluids begin to mix *immediately* after death. Blood and water mingle together. The fact that "blood" and "water" separately flow out of Jesus long after death certainly indicates one thing: the body of Jesus had *not* started to decay.

Verification of *non-decay* is emphatically stated in Acts 2:31 and 13:35! Besides, Jesus would need His body in good shape when rising on Easter Sunday. In Psalm 16:8–11, the pre-incarnate Jesus had declared that His dead body would not "experience decay"! It was so clear. Within the dead body of Jesus, blood was still blood and water was still water. And that *non-decaying* process would go right on until Jesus rose on Easter morning. As Psalm 16 also says, the body of Jesus would "rest securely" in the grave.

Of particular added interest is Brant Pitre's take on the whole "blood and water" incident at Calvary. He notes that John is reminding his readers of a particular phenomenon well-known in the days of the Lord Jesus. Pitre summarizes the Jewish Mishnah Middoth 3:2 with these words:

> According to ancient Jewish tradition, before the Temple was destroyed in AD 70, the blood of the sacrifices used to be poured into a drain that flowed down from the altar of sacrifice to merge with a spring of water that flowed out the side of the mountain on which the Temple was built: . . . (P, *CJ*, p. 170; see pp. 171–172 also).

When alert Bible detectives put the facts of John's "blood and water" report all together, it presents a most fascinating picture that proves Jesus to be the true Lamb of God who has fulfilled certain Old Testament predictions that foretold the fact that His blood-death would forgive our sins (Isaiah 53:5–7)—and did!

"File closed" on this segment of data; evidence noted. God had put His Son's body *on hold* for resurrection.

The Burial

After Governor Pilate was assured Jesus was dead, he permitted a high-ranking member of the Jewish Sanhedrin, Joseph, a rich man from the city of Arimathea, to have the body for burial (John 19:38b). This Joseph fulfilled Isaiah 53:9 which had predicted that a "rich man" would be connected with Jesus's burial.

Also, Joseph's friend Nicodemus, a secret disciple of Jesus, showed up to help (reference John 3:1–2 for background). He brought "a mixture of myrrh and aloes, about 72 pounds" for embalming (John 19:38–39). Question: How would Jesus rise with that much weight holding

Him down? (Said with tongue in cheek!) Edersheim notes that the text does *not* say all seventy-two pounds was used (E, *LTJM*, II, 618, n. 1).

Near the place of crucifixion, there was a "garden" (Hello, detectives!) and in that garden Joseph owned a "new" tomb. No one had ever been buried there (John 19:41; Matthew 27:59–60).

> Put the "garden" information in the back of your minds until Easter morning!

Investigation time: Why was it important that the burial of the Savior be in a tomb where "no one had yet been laid"? Do you remember that any Jew who touched a "dead body" would be "unclean" for *seven* days (Numbers 19:11)? To lay Jesus where a dead body had already lain would have made Jesus unclean for seven days, and He would have been unfit to function in society in three days—on Easter Sunday.

Boy, that God of the Bible is always a step or two ahead of any situation. Must frustrate the "hell" *into* of the devil who deserves it.

Three Women behind the Scenes

Jesus would never want us to forget all the valuable women who were behind His ministry. Mark 15:40 acknowledges their value, mentioning three of them by name. Verse 42 adds, "While He [Jesus] was in Galilee, they [Mary from Magdala, Mary the mother of James the Younger and of Joseph, and Salome] had followed Him and supported Him. There were also many other women who had come up to Jerusalem with Him" (Mark 15:41b).

> This financial support from females for Jesus's ministry had most likely supplied food and clothes for Jesus and His disciples as they traveled and studied together. A personal interjection: The Lord Jesus has, in turn, sent many sacrificial ladies into my life to supply support for my various ministries—married gals, widows, and those who have never married. How would God's Church effectively carry on Her work without the caring of such women? Jesus must have been so comforted seeing His support group of females at the foot of His cross.

Some of those women later trailed Joseph and Nicodemus to the grave, "following close behind" (Luke 23:55). However, we assume they were not *so* close as to see *every* detail (M, *WMS*, p. 66; E, *LTJM*, II, 618). Since they later went home and "prepared spices," they must have thought Joseph and Nicodemus had not had enough time to embalm Jesus's body, since the Sabbath was near (Luke 23:54). After a large stone was rolled across the tomb's opening, they left the grave site

(Matthew 27:60b–61; Mark 15:46–47), hurried home, and prepared spices for later embalming, but stopped per custom when the Sabbath began (Luke 23:56).

"Three"—and Counting: The Burial Period of Jesus

Jesus was now laid to rest for the remainder of Friday, all day Saturday, and part of Sunday—three days as the Jews counted time. Parts of days counted as whole days. Thus, Jonah being in the belly of the great fish "three days and three nights" could mean two *part* days and one *full* day. Faithful detectives must be careful not to misinterpret ancient meanings (treat Matthew 12:40 in this light).

Note that Jesus was at total rest *all day* Saturday. How profound! He is keeping the Sabbath commandment perfectly, even keeping the Law while dead. Go figure.

What's the Hurry?

Because of its utmost importance, no one dare miss the fact that the race was on to get Jesus's body buried before the new day started around 6:00 p.m. It's a Passover connection, easy to be overlooked by Bible investigators. Read God's "Passover" instruction at Exodus 12:11: "Eat it [the Passover Lamb] *in a hurry*." Therefore, "with haste" or "in a hurry" the body of Jesus was taken down from the cross and carried to the tomb to be buried. Hardly an "accidental coincidence" when noting that Jesus the Passover Lamb was buried "in a hurry" on Passover Day.

Done in "24"

Zechariah must have turned over in his grave with joy when the clock ticked 6:00 p.m. and a new day started—with the stone having already been rolled over the entrance of Jesus's tomb. God's prediction on the pages of his book (3:9d) had been fulfilled to absolute perfection. It now echoes through the centuries, "I will remove the sin of that land in *one* day." Mission impossible for man, accomplished in *one* twenty-four-hour period by the God-Man.

To the Triune God be the glory!

But the "Paid in Full" receipt had not yet been signed by God's resurrection pen.

Unbelief Seldom Gives Up

Those religious opponents of Jesus never gave up. Even after He was dead, they were still on His case. The post-events at Calvary had not fazed their unbelief or their hypocrisy, even one little bit. There they were at Pilate's door again – on a Sabbath Saturday when they were to be at "rest" (Matthew 27:62–64). Just like people of today: Make up your own rules as you go along!

What did they want now? Guards placed at Jesus's tomb! Suddenly, their memories were alert as to what Jesus had really said—He would rise on the third day (Matthew 27:63). So contradictory! At His trial, they had twisted that prediction around to accuse the Lord of sacrilege, accusing Jesus of promising He would destroy the physical Jerusalem Temple and then restore it in three days after demolishing it (Matthew 26:61; analyze Matthew 12:5-6 also). What a group of hypocrites and frauds!

Pilate must have cringed when he saw them coming. He would have been better off to have released Jesus, resigned, and retired to some Roman villa.

To get rid of those religious pests fast, Pilate quickly told them to choose guards and make the tomb as secure as possible; they did so (Matthew 27:65–66).

Interestingly, the Jews had a theory: Jesus's disciples were possibly going to try to steal His body and then say He had risen—and they stuck to that story for years thereafter (Matthew 27:64; 28:12–15). And the beat still goes on!

Really? That group of ragtag disciples had never come up with anything so ingenious before. Why now? It's was a better bet they would go back to fishing, not start scheming.

An Interjection before Moving Forward

Having now analyzed many of the events of Good Friday, is it not amazing that so few people, even most Christian people, know so little about "the greatest part of the greatest story ever told"? Christ is pleased you readers are getting "up to speed" on the many details of the precious Savior's ordeals.

Let's now continue to focus and find out what really happened on the "third" day.

> The "greatest story" is the story of Jesus; the "greatest part" of that story is the account of His suffering, death, resurrection, and ascension.

> **Evidence room conclusion:** The post-death scenarios recorded in the four gospels are loaded with "connectives" between OT clues and NT mysteries, all relating to Jesus and proving Him to be the Messiah. Thus, the concept of *connecting* the OT with the NT becomes paramount for any valid interpretation of the life and ministry of the Savior, to say nothing about all the other surrounding data from Genesis to Revelation.

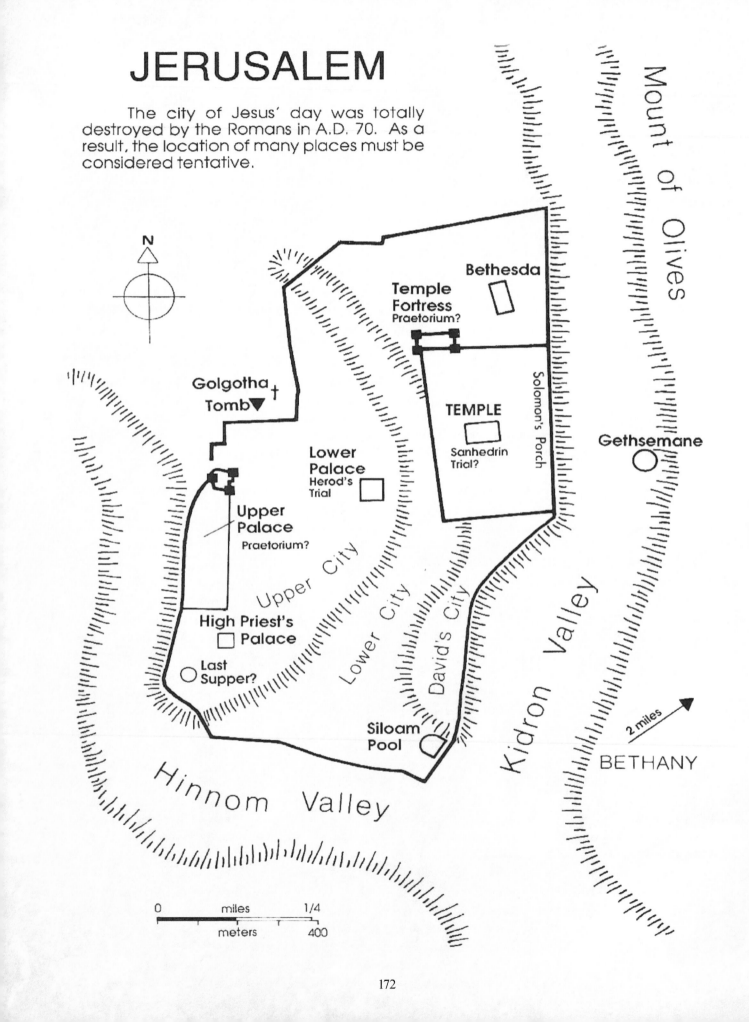

JERUSALEM

The city of Jesus' day was totally destroyed by the Romans in A.D. 70. As a result, the location of many places must be considered tentative.

N

Mount of Olives

Bethesda

Temple Fortress
Praetorium?

Golgotha
Tomb ▼ †

Solomon's Porch

TEMPLE

Sanhedrin Trial?

Gethsemane

Lower Palace
Herod's Trial

Upper Palace
Praetorium?

Upper City

Lower City

David's City

Kidron Valley

High Priest's Palace

Last Supper?

Siloam Pool

2 miles

BETHANY

Hinnom Valley

0   miles   1/4

meters   400

CHAPTER 21

VICTORY VERIFIED

Examining Clues in the Evidence Room
How do New Testament writers connect
Easter "shockers" with predictive clues?

Doom and Gloom Ended

Having now completed our investigation of most every nook and cranny of the suffering, death, and burial of Messiah Jesus, we move beyond those emotional "downers" of Good Friday to the "uppers" of Easter morning.

"Resurrection time" arrived, another supernatural phenomenon of the Bible that is totally *unreasonable* to ordinary human minds. And yet, like other *unbelievable* teachings of Scripture, it stands before us for consideration (cp. 2 Corinthians 5:7).

Considering the Unbelievable

As will be repeated below, Easter can be called the *paid-in-full* day. Jesus's physical resurrection serves as humankind's *receipt* that His death totally accomplished the heavenly Father's goal: complete forgiveness for the wrongdoings of every human being. Easter is the absolute proof that the words of Jesus—"It is finished"—were, in fact, true and effective.

That *physical resurrection* of the God-Man Jesus is affirmed over and over on the pages of the New Testament. At least seventy-eight times, words like "alive, raise, raised, resurrection, rise, risen, rose" assure readers that Jesus did come alive from the dead. (There are also many other citations where the idea of Jesus's resurrection is *implied*.)

In addition, Jesus taught that "all" people will be resurrected on the Last Day (John 5:28–29), believers and unbelievers. As to those who believe in Him during their lifetimes, Christ promised: "Because I live, you will live also" (John 14:19).

Astounding! The *resurrection* of Jesus Christ is a resounding teaching from Matthew through Revelation. It's a central doctrine of Scripture, predicted in the Old Testament (cp. Job 19:25) and verified in the New!

A New Day Dawns for Humanity

In the "Great Resurrection Chapter" of the Bible, the Apostle Paul brilliantly moves his readers from Good Friday to Easter morning with these words in 1 Corinthians 15:3–4:

> *For I brought you what I received—something very important—that Christ died for our sins as the Scriptures said He would, that He was buried, and that He was raised on the third day as the Scriptures said He would.*

To briefly repeat from our former chapter and to fast-forward to the events of Easter morning, we return to the succinct words of the Apostles' Creed concerning the Lord Jesus Christ: "suffered under Pontius Pilate, was crucified, died, and was buried; He descended into hell; the third day He rose again from the dead; . . . ."

Many Christians do not use or endorse the Three Ecumenical Creeds: the Apostles', the Nicene, and the Athanasian. Why? Because their words are not found *verbatim* in the inspired Scriptures. This is true, in part; they are not, yet, every one of their teachings is present in the Bible. For this reason, these creeds can serve as valuable tools.

Think of Late Night TV interviews that involve *religious* data. The lack of biblical knowledge concerning the most basic parts of Christianity is appalling! If these interviewees just knew the "bare-bones basics" that the three creeds condense so well, there would be hope for better Bible knowledge (cp. Hosea 4:6). In other words, the creeds are a great *teaching tool*. Maybe best to use them to summarize Christianity, imparting facts for making effective Christian witnesses!

Moving On

Having stated the above, we continue by considering the Easter or "resurrection" conclusions of the Apostle Paul in 1 Corinthians 15:12–22. He writes:

> If we preach that Christ was raised from the dead, how can some of you say, "There is no resurrection of the dead"? If there is no resurrection of the dead, Christ was not raised. And if Christ was not raised, our preaching means nothing and your faith means nothing. Also, we stand there as men who lied about God because we have sworn by God that He raised Christ, whom He did not raise if it is true that the dead are not raised. To be sure, if the dead are not raised, Christ has not been raised; and if Christ has not been raised, your faith cannot help you; you are still in your sins. Then also those who have fallen asleep in Christ have perished. If Christ is our hope in this life only, we are to be pitied more than all other people.
>
> But now Christ was raised from the dead, the first in the harvest of those who have fallen asleep. For since a man [Adam] brought death, a Man [Christ Jesus] also brought the resurrection of the dead. For as in Adam all die, so in Christ all will be made alive.

Let's place Paul's conclusions into today's lingo: It's the "same old, same old" if Christ had not physically risen from the dead!

If Jesus did not come alive *physically*, this Second Adam is no better than the First Adam—both Adams are still dead and defeated, and Satan is the victor. On the other hand, if Christ lives, then He truly is the victorious Lord and Savior. Of Satan, we can then chant, "Lo-o-o-ser!"

Present investigative question: Who truly was the loser and who the winner? To repeat so no Bible detective misses it: A new and glorious day only dawned for humanity if the Second Adam came alive *physically* on that first Easter morn. Parallel this absolute with the First Adam who at the beginning of Creation had been made alive *physically* in the first Garden of Eden! However, later that first Adam died *physically* (Genesis 5:5), and he would never come alive again—*physically*—if his better counterpart, the Second Adam, did not conquer *death* by regaining life—*physically*.

> The *physical* aspect of Christ's resurrection and its necessity will be further investigated in-depth in Appendix 10, the section entitled: "1 Peter 3:18–19 Explained."

Difficult Wording

When considering Easter morning, two initial events demand investigative research on the basis of some really *difficult* biblical data. In summary of those two events, the Apostles' Creed simply states, "He [Jesus] descended into hell; the third day He rose again from the dead."

The first Christ action, His "descent into hell," is based on 1 Peter 3:18–19:

> He was put to death in flesh but made alive *in spirit* or *by the Spirit, in which* or *by which* He also went and preached to the *spirits kept in prison.*

These two verses may arguably be the most difficult words to interpret in *all* the New Testament. If not, then certainly they are the verses with the most *varying* interpretations, views going in many directions regarding several internal aspects, so that absolute exegetical consensus will never be reached on this side of eternity (see A, *1PH*, p. 240, plus n. 10).

> Because of the complexity of the overall matter, and because most of the 1 Peter 3:18–19 discussion reaches beyond the scope of this present book, the more in-depth portions of our presentation have been relegated to Appendix 10. Those with deeper theological interest will be highly benefitted, especially if they dig into the accompanying sources that will there be noted.

For our present purposes, however, a number of items can and must be dealt with upfront:

1. Jesus did *not* enter the realm of hell *after His death* on Good Friday to suffer some more. His "It is finished" marked the end of all of His suffering. "Finished" means "finished"!

2. Jesus said He would pass into "Paradise" on Good Friday *after His death* (Luke 23:43). "Paradise" does not sound like a place where "spirits" would be described as being "in prison" (analyze 1 Peter 3:19 again). Besides, on Good Friday Jesus entrusted His "spirit" into the hands of His heavenly Father; His body becoming separated from His "spirit" and "soul." Consider Cremer, who is quoted in V, *EDNTW*, "Soul," p. 55: "*Sōma,* body, and *pneuma,* spirit, may be separated, *pneuma* and *psuchē,* soul, can only be distinguished" (cp. Hebrews 4:12). On that basis Jesus could *not* appear to the "spirits in prison" until He was *physically* resurrected (with

a body) on Easter (study Luke 16:25–26). However, when Jesus's "spirit" and "soul" reentered His dead body, His body became a "glorified" body (Philippians 3:20–21), which now had substance *and a mouth* by which He could preach to the "spirits kept in prison."

3. If Jesus had gone to the "spirits kept in prison" *without* a resurrected body, then His body would still have been in "death's" grip, and, in reality, death would *not* have been "swallowed up in victory" (see 1 Corinthians 15:51–57).

4. Jesus's redemptive act was for humankind alone, not for fallen angels (cp. James 2:19). Thus, when He visited those "spirits kept in prison," a reference to fallen angels (or as some conclude: to fallen angels *and* also to those humans already dead and condemned to hell by unbelief), He could *not* have been preaching "salvation" to them, or, for that matter, to anyone else, since no one gets a "second chance" *after death* (Hebrews 9:27; see L, *IPJJ*, p. 167); they generally get thousands of *second chances* here on earth.

    Question: Did Jesus "preach" to those spirits *verbally*? Certainly! The Greek word for *preached* teaches this. Jesus now had a glorified body equipped with a mouth. How do we know? Later that Resurrection Day He ate fish with that same mouth (Luke 24:43).

    An additional thought: Before Jesus even vocally preached one word in hell's prison, His very appearance would have sent a most effective *non-verbal* message to those spirits. His live, *bodily* presence would have been sermon enough to declare their doom (cp. K, *SCD*, p. 152). Jesus was back from the dead—and this meant total *defeat* for those evil spirits.

    The ramifications of Paul's words, quoted several paragraphs above, are so compelling and informative. Let's repeat them in part: "For since a man [the First Adam] brought death, a Man [the Second Adam] also brought the resurrection of the dead. For as in Adam all die, so in Christ all will be made alive."

    At this point, thorough Bible analyzers must recall our whole discussion of the First and Second Adams in Chapter 9 and Appendix 6. As recently stated above, and now reiterated because of its importance: If Jesus was to "better" the First Adam, then He, as the Second Adam, needed to rise *with a living body* to undo the *dead body* of the First Adam.

> Question: Would Jesus have appeared as having won the battle over "death" if His body had remained dead in the grave? Hello, is anybody at home with the theological implications of this whole vital argumentation? As A. Andrew Das so ably asserts, "Whenever the New Testament speaks of Christ being 'made alive,' it is referring to his *bodily [my emphasis]* resurrection (e.g., Romans 4:17; 8:11 and 1 Corinthians 15:22)" (D, "BNT," p. 3). Thank you, Dr. Das.

Complex Wording

The first two Easter events seem *out of order* when the Apostles' Creed says, "He descended into hell; on the third day He rose again from the dead." Those words sound like Jesus was not yet alive, that is, until *after* He came back from hell's prison. Not the intent, however! He was alive in His resurrected physical body when first going to the "spirits kept in prison." Why then does the creed make it sound like He did not resurrect until *after* His visit to those "spirits"?

Here's the intended meaning of the words "on the third day He rose again from the dead": After Jesus's initial visit to the "prison," He then rose in the sense that He now, for the *first* time, showed Himself visibly *to people on earth.* His rising on the third day is emphasized to let Christians confess that He appeared victoriously on Easter morning in visible, physical form, as He had said He would (Mark 9:31)—on "the third day" *back on earth* to His followers.

In connection with this crucial data, remember Jesus's prediction and its implications in Matthew 12:40: "As Jonah was in the belly of the huge fish three days and three nights, so the Son of Man will be in the heart of the earth three days and three nights." The point being that Jesus' *body* would not be in the grave longer than three days; it would be up and about as was Jonah once the large fish vomited him up onto the shore (Jonah 2:10).

And now an additional zinger!

Do you remember how Jesus had to *first* confront the devil in the wilderness after His baptism, that is, because Satan had *first* started the whole mess in Eden? Well, now Christ had to go *first* to the forces of hell to announce His victory. Since those evil forces had caused the initial problem of sin, it was only fitting that they be the *first* to hear of their defeat and of the accomplished victory of Jesus—and also hear that Satan's victims back on earth could now have life everlasting through faith (Romans 1:17).

So, after that "prison" visit, it was time for Jesus to appear to the *earthly* inheritors of His finished work. Thus, He, the resurrected One, now showed Himself to His followers on earth. Wow, that God of the Bible really had things all worked out—and *chronologically* too!

Easter Morning Happenings

As we move on to investigate Jesus's specific Easter appearances to individuals on earth, there is one misnomer that must be set straight. Nowhere does one read in Scripture, or in any post–New Testament first-century AD document, that Jesus came *out* the door of tomb on Easter Sunday morn (cp. M, *WMS*, p. 189). When the angel rolled the stone back, the tomb was empty; Jesus had already vacated it, without making an exit through its entrance (cp. Matthew 28:2–6). Which, in turn, leads us to many questions that God the Holy Spirit did not choose to answer, questions like, "At what time did Jesus rise from the dead?" and "Where did He get the clothes He was wearing when He made His first Easter appearances?"

What is certain, however, is that the resurrected Jesus, having passed beyond His "state of humiliation" into His "state of exaltation" (Philippians 2:5–11), now had a new "glorified body" that could do things ordinary earthly bodies could not do (cp. Philippians 3:20–21). Several examples can be cited: When so desired, the resurrected Jesus could now make His body *not* take up space; He also was able to pass through otherworld "dimensions" (1 Peter 3:19), as well as pass through the "solids" of our four-dimensional world on Easter morning and evening (John 20:3–9, 19). On several other occasions, Jesus also disguised Himself at will (John 20:14; Luke 24:16). Note the ramifications of Colossians 2:9 to these phenomena: "In Him [Christ], that is, in His body, lives all the fullness of the Deity." After His resurrection the God-Man Jesus could now do anything He pleased, at any time He pleased—"no holds barred" ("wrestling" terminology).

When Did Jesus Rise?

Jesus predicted He would rise on the "third day" (Matthew 16:21). When did that day begin? Around 6:00 p.m., the hour when Jewish days began. (Today we would call that hour "Saturday," but for Jews it began the day of "Sunday," the first day of the week.)

What does this mean?

It means that Jesus could have risen from the dead as early as, let's say, 6:01 p.m. since it was already Sunday, the "third day." A surprise? Yes, if Bible students have never thought about it! Well then, at what time did Jesus rise from the dead? Scripture does not say. But we do know it had to be some time *before* He made His visit to "the spirits kept in prison" and also *before* His first earthly appearances to various women on Easter morning (cp. quote from Johann Quenstedt in P, *CD*, II, 314).

Getting Our Attention

There He did it again, that God of the Bible! Just when you think you have Him figured out, He goes in a different direction. That is how it was on Easter morning. When back on earth from "Paradise" and from the above-mentioned "prison," Jesus made His very first appearances to *women* (Matthew 28:5–10; John 20:8–18).

Prior to Jesus's saying, "Good morning," to those first females (Matthew 28:9), "a young man," "an angel," "two men" had spoken to these ladies at the tomb.

When viewing the four gospels as a whole, it would seem that Mary from Magdala, who had come to the tomb on

> Note the three resurrection accounts concerning Jesus: "He has risen" (Mark 16:6); "He has risen as He said" (Matthew 28:5–6); "He has risen" (Luke 24:6).

Easter morning, along with *several* other women (Luke 24:10), did not initially enter the opened grave with those other ladies, and thus she did *not* hear the message of the angel(s). Rather, she just assumed the grave was empty and ran to tell the disciples the news before she knew all the details. Note that she did *not* tell the disciples that Jesus had "risen," only that someone had moved His body, indicating that she had not heard the "He has risen" message (John 20:1–2). (This is a crucial piece of evidence; see M, *WMS*, p. 179.) Later Mary returned to the grave alone, and only then did she see two angels inside the tomb. She conversed with them, and then after that, she saw the resurrected Jesus and spoke with Him in the Easter garden (John 20:11–13).

Caution, detectives: It takes great patience and careful biblical analyzation to put all the Easter facts into *chronological* order. The seeming "divergent" accounts of the four gospels is *proof positive* that the facts are not contrived by deceitful followers of Jesus (consider M, *WMS*, p. 183). *Had they been polemic falsehoods, the writers would have put them into a more plausible sync to fool their readers.* To understand this point more fully, view four confusing and varying references at Matthew 28:1–10; Mark 16:1–8; Luke 24:1–11; John 20:1–2. They will help you better understand our vital Easter conclusions.

Repetition, "the Mother of All Learning"

At this juncture, the angel's "He is risen" report makes it most appropriate to reiterate the importance of the resurrection of Jesus. If He had remained dead, this would have spelled total victory for Satan, and the faith of Christians would be empty and useless (1 Corinthians 15:13–14). Good Friday was most important because the plague of sin came to a screeching halt

(John 19:30a), but it was the Easter resurrection that gave Christ's victory validation. It was the heavenly Father's visual declaration that the debt of iniquity had been *paid in full*. Seeing Jesus alive in the flesh also ended Satan's hopes and showed God to be the Victor. PTL!!!

Women Witnesses?

Now back to the appearance of Jesus to the women, following the angel's "He has risen" announcement.

Something most strange! *Women* became the first witnesses to testify they had seen Jesus alive. Who would believe them? The disciples didn't! Yes, it was so odd that God would choose women as the *first* "witnesses" to the resurrection of His Son. Why? Women were *not* permitted to witness in Jewish courtrooms. Their words did not hold any weight. (A cultural thing of that day and age.)

God was right in line with His usual disconnect. When the Magi looked for the baby King in the Jerusalem palace, they ended up finding Him "in a house" in the lowly city of Bethlehem (cp. Micah 5:2).

And in the case of Easter, God still did it His way, not "the Sinatra way" (idiom for our older readers). Jesus's appearance *first* to women, as the "first witnesses" to see Him, demands special attention by careful Bible inspectors. No Jew like Matthew or John would have thought up that approach on their own. It reveals that God was controlling the facts by inspiration. Reminder: The Bible, first and foremost, is "His Story," not man's story. As it is quipped: Live with it!

But there is more. Even though these females were vital witnesses *within* the *Christian* community, when testimony was later given to the unbelieving Jewish communities of Jerusalem or to Gentile areas of culture, well, then the female testimony was not directly noted since, as already stated, female testimony held no weight in public. This is shown by Paul's male inclusions but obvious silences concerning women in 1 Corinthians 15:5–8 (see M, *WMS*, p. 185). It was a cultural thing that made it initially wise *not* to mention "women witnesses" upfront. Remember how the disciples themselves "pooh-poohed" the first testimonies of the women (Matthew 24:11)!

Yet, be assured that when Paul testifies that "500" persons saw Jesus "at one time," there were certainly women among them—and even before that, it would seem. When? On that first Easter evening when Jesus made a startling appearance—and even more appearances beyond that time (cp. Luke 24:33; Acts 1:13–14). To be sure, those female testimonies (that of Mary from Magdala and the other gals) became very valuable as the days of the New Testament wore on, as is shown in the writings of the four gospels, which came into existence from the AD '50s to the '90s.

Four Proofs Jesus Rose

Each year, close to Christmas and Easter stories appear that try to debunk the virgin birth or resurrection of Christ. This is to be expected from the "world of unbelief." Satan is a busy little guy. In spite of these voices of unbelief, there are masterful things to consider when probing biblical data.

Let's deal with the initial, rapid spread of the Easter story. Within "40" days after Jesus's resurrection, that is, before His ascension into heaven, Jesus appeared to some "500" persons (possibly up in Galilee, a territory less hostile to the Savior). That situation was played upon some decades later when Paul challenged his Corinthian readers to hunt up some of the majority of these witnesses who were still alive (1 Corinthians 15:6). But more astounding is the fact that within fifty days of Jesus's resurrection, some "3,000" people—on the basis of believing that the crucified One was now resurrected—were converted to this truth and were baptized on that first post-Easter Pentecost day (Acts 2:41). What, as many as "3,000" people were fooled and became susceptible to a *false* message of "resurrection"? Re-e-e-e-ally?

Now to be sure, Christians "walk by faith, not by sight" (2 Corinthians 5:7). Today's believers have not seen the living Christ in person, nor can they at this time. They just believe He is alive because the Bible says so. At the same time, Scripture says these Christians are "always to be ready to answer anyone who asks them to explain the hope," the faith, they have (1 Peter 3:15). For example, believers are to answer those who have trouble with the concept of the physical resurrection of Jesus. How? Here are *four* great arguments they can use in favor of His resurrection.

1. **Peter, John, and the "burial clothes"**

    When Mary from Magdala informed the disciples that Christ's tomb was open, Peter and John raced there. What John saw inside convinced him to "believe" (John 20:8). What did He see? "He saw Christ's linen body wrappings lying there, also the cloth that had been on His head. The latter was not lying with the linen ˌbodyˌ wrappings but was rolled up neatly in a place by itself" (John 20:6b–7). What was significant about that?

    The word *rolled up* in Greek signifies that the cloths were wrapped in a circular pattern, like whoever had been inside them just *passed through* them, without unwrapping them first. And then they had collapsed together, just a little air separating the bottom from the top. Besides, the head piece was lying separate, also still all rolled up.

If someone had stolen the body, they would *not* have been meticulous enough to fold everything up again into its original form. They would have been in a hurry to get away with the body. Or, they would have taken the body as it was, fully wrapped, and have run for their lives.

When looking and considering, John "believed" something very strange had happened that Easter morning. As implied above, Jesus must have passed right through those burial wrappings when He rose from the dead, just as He later that evening passed right through a solidly closed door into the place where the disciples were hiding (John 20:19).

2. Mary from Magdala and the "Witnesses" in the Garden Easter Morning

One of the most impressive books ever written about the resurrection of Jesus is entitled, *Who Moved the Stone?* It contains many valuable clues as to why one should be compelled to believe Jesus did rise from the dead, as Scripture claims. Its author, Frank Morison, started out to *disprove* the truth of the resurrection; the Holy Spirit stopped him in his tracks and turned him around. Morison ended up defending the biblical resurrection accounts (cite J. N. D. Anderson, quoted in M, *EDV*, pp. 183–184).

Morison's presentation really got me thinking. His most compelling arguments revolve around the "*stone*" and the "*witness*" that were *in the garden that Easter morning*. Note: a "rolled-away stone" and a "young man" (Mark 16:5), the latter, of course, who proved to be an angel from heaven (Matthew 28:5). Morison's view has its own separate validity. He is correct in saying that the enemies of Christianity would certainly have "produced" this male witness and used him against Christian claims (M, *WMS*, pp. 102, 174, 176), that is, if they could have found him. But for obvious reasons, they never did find that angel.

Morison is very convincing in saying that the opposing Jewish authorities would have been most interested in answering the mystery of the "rolled away" tomb stone. He deals with all the possibilities of persons and events that could or could not or that would or would not have accounted for the strange garden phenomena on the Sunday after Jesus's death (cp. Matthew 27:60b; Mark 16:4).

To cut to the chase, let it be said that Morison concludes that the only viable answer lies in the fact that the "young man" (an "angel" in *Matthew*) was the only reliable witness concerning the moved stone. All the Jewish officials would have needed to do is locate this young man, have him testify that he had moved the stone, and the Christian testimony could have been discredited.

To repeat: That "young man" was never found. Matthew tells you why. He was an angel from heaven—and later on Easter morning, He would have returned to heaven, never able to be located.

(For those who have trouble with the Bible's Easter resurrection report, I highly recommend they purchase Morison's *Who Moved the Stone?* It can be ordered at Amazon. Well worth the money; tons of info.)

The Jews continually said the disciples had come and stolen Jesus's body (see Matthew 28:12-15). (Alert investigators need to ask: "How could that be with guards on duty?")

But there is solid *contrary* evidence. Mary from Magdala, as the Gospel of John reports, claimed she spoke with *three* other witnesses in the garden that Easter morning—two angel witnesses, plus a Gardener-Witness, who proved to be Jesus Himself (20:11–18).

Now it could be said that the Jewish authorities never heard the testimony of Mary from Magdala and therefore would not have gone in search of the "gardener." If they had, he should not have been hard to turn up, that is, if he had just been the human gardener who tended to the garden during morning hours. But that "Gardener" was never found. Christians know why.

On the basis of the fact that the news of Lazarus's resurrection from the dead in John 11 had immediately spread like wild fire (vv. 45–47) and that other resurrections were also witnessed on that first Easter morning (Matthew 27:52–53), it is hard to believe that Mary's claim did not reach the ears of the Jewish authorities very soon after Easter.

Again: Very, very easy to undo the Christian tale of Jesus's resurrection if the witnessing Mary and the other women had been mistaken or deceitful, but they were not. In the case of the encounter of Mary from Magdala with Jesus, as to the person she mistook for a regular gardener, you know the Bible's

Remember, for Jews, Sunday was the first workday of the week. It would seem normal for a gardener to have been on duty. But why was he never produced as a counter witness?

answer. That supposed Gardener was Christ—and she recognized Him as the risen One. Again, if Caiaphas or other Jewish opponents had produced an ordinary "gardener," the "resurrection claim" of the Christians would have been over (cp. M, *WMS*, p. 102). But they never found any of the *three* garden witnesses, especially Mary's "Gardener." He had risen and ascended to heaven (Acts 1:9).

Interjection concerning another Easter concern: The little phrase "Do not touch Me" (KJV) at John 20:17, a command given by the risen Jesus to Mary from Magdala, has confused people. It should, because Jesus permitted other women to touch Him (Matthew 28:9), as well as Thomas the disciple, who was commanded to touch the remaining scars on Jesus's hands and pierced side (John 20:27). Then why not Mary from Magdala also?

The verb tense at John 20:17 must be translated, "Stop holding on to Me." This was the conclusion of Dr. Robert Hoerber, a Greek specialist and one of the revising translators of the NET New Testament (see NET, p. 527), as well as an expert consultant for the NKJV.

Mary had been hugging Jesus out of excitement at seeing Him alive. In modern language, Jesus would have been saying, "Mary, that's enough, you have checked Me out; do not continue to hug Me."

But what about the reason Jesus gave for discontinuing to "hold on"? Jesus said to Mary, "I have not yet ascended to the Father."

Does this mean Jesus, after talking to Mary, immediately ascended to heaven, and then came back to appear to His other followers and let them touch Him? Hardly! Rather, readers must realize that Jesus was *not* allowed to ascend until forty days later. Why? "Hold your horses," as is said. That discussion comes in Chapter 22.

The whole appearing of Jesus to Mary from Magdala is filled with mystery. This time, there is an "Eve" connection, more than an "Adam" connection.

In the same way, as God in former times appeared to Eve and Adam in the "Garden" of Eden, talking and walking

> Readers can again view Appendix 6 to see a listing of all the parallels between the First and Second Adams.

with them (Genesis 3:8), Jesus now appears to Mary, the *new* Eve, walking with and talking to her at the "garden" tomb. (Do you remember being told that the tomb of Joseph of Arimathea was in a "garden" that was near the place where Jesus had been crucified?)

This is the third time a *garden* is mentioned in the Passion and resurrection narratives—and this *garden* repetition is *"Evidence Just Too Coincidental to Be Accidental!!!"* Would you not agree?

3. **The big change in the disciples of Jesus**

One surprising thing should get the attention of all readers of Acts 2. What is it? With the coming of Pentecost, just *fifty* days after Jesus's Passover death, something had radically changed the original disciples of Christ. They became willing to do anything for the truths Jesus had taught them: go to any length for Him, that is, be beaten, go to prison, even die for Him; travel anywhere to spread His message, and most astoundingly, they became instant experts, so to speak, in understanding His teachings and in communicating those teachings to others; they could now evaluate things extraordinarily well, things they had fumbled around saying and doing during Jesus's earthly ministry.

What changed them? For example, how did fishermen like Peter and John suddenly develop the abilities to preach publicly and to pen profound New Testament books?

As said, the disciples must have seen or experienced something that drastically *transformed* them. That something must have been their contact with Christ, the resurrected One who was really, really *physically* alive again (place John 16:12 into the mix too). This "resurrection experience" *began* the transformation that turned those disciples into effective Gospel messengers. Then, on the first Pentecost, the Holy Spirit *forever* changed these "nobodies" into "somebodies" (cp. Acts 2:31, 32).

4. **The thousands who, just as a matter of fact, accepted the reality of Jesus's resurrection**

If Jesus did not really rise from the dead, how does one explain the fact that three thousand persons became gullible enough to fall for the Christian myth of His resurrection and thus committed themselves to baptism on that first Christian Pentecost day (Acts 2:41)?

Besides, how could the Apostle Paul have encouraged first-century AD "seekers" to investigate his claim that some five hundred persons had visually seen the *physically* risen Jesus Christ (1 Corinthians 15:6)? He stuck his neck out by challenging his readers to find these observers, testifying that the majority of them were still alive. If true, it would not have been very hard to locate a few and interrogate them. After all, many Jews from all over Palestine had been scattered because of the events of Acts 7; they could now be found all over the Roman Empire. Hmm?

In addition, how does one explain the reality of so many brilliant figures of history throughout the centuries having endorsed Jesus as the physically resurrected Savior; that is, if the whole resurrection-of-Jesus thing is a hoax? Were all these persons duped?

Of course, there have also been and continue to be hundreds of persons whom the world considered and still considers brilliant who denied or presently deny Jesus's *physical* resurrection. Guess the ball is now in your court. The Holy Spirit will guide you. How? On

> You may highly benefit by reading Appendix 10, the section entitled: "Empty 'Resurrection' Faith."

the basis of Scriptural evidence that clearly testifies that Jesus physically rose on the third day! I believe it; what about you?

Four False Theories

The following are four false theories (minus other minor ones) that have been put forth throughout New Testament times to debunk the doctrine of the resurrection of Jesus. These denials need to be confronted with a direct frontal attack. As Jesus instructed His followers, "Be shrewd as snakes and innocent as doves" (Matthew 10:16), meaning take the attack to the critics; do not stand idly by and say nothing. Most Christians have the "dove" part down "to an art form," but as to the "snake" part, not so much. (The Christian discipline known as "apologetics" takes it right to Christian opponents with dovelike love, but also with the venom of snakes, standing up for those truths that the risen Christ desires His followers to teach.)

1. **The "fraud theory"**
   It claims the disciples just lied. They knew Jesus had not risen, but they were too embarrassed to admit they had been conned by their Teacher, so they covered their tracks.

How ingenious would that have been? And are we then to believe that they continued that lie for years to come by going around the world preaching that same lie and laying their lives on the line day after day?

That takes more faith to believe than believing Jesus rose! As previously stated, it's easier to think those disciples would have gone back to fishing, tax collecting, or something else.

Anyone believing this theory would have to say that Peter was the best salesman *ever* to talk three thousand people into getting baptized on that first Pentecost, convincing people to believe in a "resurrection" that never happened. Really?

2. The "theft theory"

This conclusion appealed to the Jews, as formerly stated.

When confronting those who still endorse this theory, use this argumentation. Just ask them which disciple would have been brave enough to try to sneak by the guards, roll back the stone without making noise, steal the body, and make a clean escape? None of the remaining eleven disciples, to be sure. Besides, the idea of guards being asleep is unthinkable, especially that *all* of them would have been asleep.

The Bible deals with this nonsense by reporting that the Jewish leaders bribed the soldiers to lie and say they were asleep, and if they got in trouble for sleeping on the job, the religious leaders would get them "off the hook" (Matthew 28:12–14). The "hour of darkness" was still ruling the hearts of unbelievers (cp. Luke 22:53b). See M, *WMS*, pp. 88-89, 151 for undeniable argumentation against the "theft theory."

3. The "swoon theory"

This is a beauty! It contends Jesus fainted on the cross, was mistaken for dead, was buried, and then revived (in the "coolness" of the tomb), came out of His grave, appeared to His followers, and was assumed to have risen from the dead.

Sleuths, this one does not take much effort to dismiss. It is very hard to remain "dovelike" on this one, and not just laugh in the face of such a claim.

Even if Jesus just "swooned" on the cross and then came back to consciousness in the coolness of the grave, how vibrant do you think He would have appeared when waltzing around on Easter Day after all the torturing

He had endured, plus the fact that His side had been run through with a spear?

Need more be said to cancel any serious consideration of this false claim?

4. **The "hallucination theory"**

To some, this claim really sounds viable. It contends that many thought they had seen the risen Jesus, but, being under great emotional stress, they only *imagined* they had seen Him. This theory would be akin to the proposed "vision hypothesis" (also countered in E, *LTJM*, II, 626–628).

It is said the followers of Jesus were stressed out over the disappointment that Jesus ended up dead. Hopes had been dashed when the supposed Savior did not prove to be the Messiah people had hoped He would be. These despondent persons could not handle the disappointment. During their time of emotional turmoil, imaginations ran wild as they hoped against hope that He was alive. Did He not say He would "rise on the third day"? This continuing hope led persons to *hallucinate* and come to believe they had really seen the risen Christ (or that they had had a "vision" of Him).

This may seem legit in the case of a few overly emotional believers. But there is a big problem. First Corinthians 15:6 says "more than 500 believers at one time" saw Him. That "at one time" puts a different twist on things. It confirms that Jesus was truly resurrected. Why?

Any reputable psychiatrist or psychologist will tell *fact sifters* that there is no such thing as "mass hallucination." It just does not take place. A person or two may hallucinate over an event or over some other thing, but "500" imagining the same thing "at one time," "at the same time," well, it just does not happen!

Before moving on, it would be wise to alert all Bible sleuths to read Hank Hanegraaff's *Resurrection* (H, *R*—258 pages). (Among Hank's much documentation, there is a most significant quote from Dr. Norman Geisler on pages 106–107.) A very convincing argumentation concerning Christ's resurrection can also be found in Hanegraaff's CRI's "Equip" newsletter (H, "*E*")! In this day and age, Bible believers cannot afford to let the naysayers go unchallenged to the detriment of human souls (1 Peter 3:15b).

Of counter importance is the best seller of 1965/1966/1967 by Dr. Hugh J. Schonfield, entitled *The Passover Plot* (S, *PP*—269 pages). Fortified by Schonfield's legion upon legion of Bible references, Jesus is presented as a con artist who plotted His whole arrest, crucifixion, and reappearance. For what reason? To convince the Jews that He was the long-expected Messiah.

Schonfield concludes that the plot was spoiled by a soldier who was not in on the scheme. His spear spoiled the plan; however, the disciple conspirators who were in on the plot continued the hoax and spread the legend that Jesus had truly risen from the dead and had subsequently ascended to heaven.

To be sure, thousands fell for Schonfield's satanic-induced research and its conclusions. He successfully conned them, as well as himself, as he created a literary plot of his own, spinning a most dubious and ingenious scenario against the four gospels and their presentation of the passion of Jesus. The biblically *uninformed* were sadly duped by this book's misinformation.

Bias and unkind? Well, let's put it this way: Every human of all ages will be able to check it out firsthand when the resurrected One appears on the Last Day—and be assured, He will be very, very much alive (Romans 10:11).

Jerusalem in a Tizzy—Busy and Dizzy!

Most modern readers of the Easter account are under the impression that Easter morning was a rather quiet time. Quite the opposite. Oh, it may have been silent when those several women started out for Jesus's grave "while it was still dark" (John 20:1; Luke 24:1; Mark 16:1; Matthew 28:1).

Possibly unbeknown to many asleep in Jerusalem, it may have been quiet, even while "a great earthquake" was taking place and an angel sent by God came and rolled the grave stone back, unblocking the tomb's entrance. The guards viewed it all in terror (Matthew 28:2–4). (Note how the earthquake on Easter morning represents the whole creation's acknowledgement that its Creator was once again alive.)

By the time the ladies reached Jesus's grave, the sun had come up (Mark 16:2). Why is that fact so important? One must read between the lines.

Bible readers of today should realize that Saturday to Jews was like our Sundays years ago—relatively quiet. But Sundays in that day were like our Mondays; it was "business as usual"; Sunday was the *first* day of the week. Shops opened and coins were clinking. Plus, Jerusalem was buzzing with many "Passover" visitors who had not yet returned home to distant places; many were again trading and buying; also, the regular Jerusalem residents were now busy purchasing for their household needs. It was a busy and noisy time—nothing like Bible readers usually picture that first Easter Sunday.

There is a hint of that activity in Mark 16:8; it says a group of women "hurried away from the tomb." As they traveled to tell the disciples that a young man had talked to them and told them Jesus had risen, the text adds, "they said nothing to *anyone*." There were lots of "anyones" on the paths as they traveled toward Jesus's hidden disciples (see v. 7 also). (Mary from Magdala had previously raced from the tomb also to inform the disciples of the strangeness of the rolled-back stone.)

There was something else happening simultaneously.

Dead people who had risen on the previous Good Friday now came out of their tombs and started appearing in Jerusalem (Matthew 27:53). Soon Jerusalem would be in a tizzy. The air would be abuzz with the news of *multiple* resurrections.

Let's remember that from the cross, the *dead* Christ had raised "believers," most likely, people who were from that generation, persons who would be instantly recognizable. Imagine "Joe the Jew" returning to the shop he previously owned, and seeing the sign over the door *already* changed, exclaiming to the embarrassment of his former business partners, "*Oy vey! Vot haf you dun—and so suunto?*"

Also, Benjamin the Hebrew appears at the door of his former home and is greeted by his little boy, yelling "Abba, Abba!" Then that son runs to Mom, screaming, "Abba's at the door." His mother responds, "Come here, you need 'grief counseling.'" But with persistent tugging at her robe, she finally goes to the door, sees her dead husband alive, and faints on the spot.

Yes, it was chaos on that Sunday in Jerusalem with "many" resurrected people vacating their graves and returning to the streets of Jerusalem and cities nearby.

Oh, to have been there!

It was anything but quiet that first Easter morning. The truth of this fact is verified later Easter afternoon when Jesus—hiding His identity—joined two of His disciples heading westward to the city of Emmaus. When He struck up a conversation with them, acting intentionally ignorant as to the events of the day, the response was: "Are you the only stranger living in Jerusalem who does not know what things happened there these days?" Jesus, still playing dumb, asked, "What sort of things?" They answered (Luke 24:19b–27),

> The things about Jesus from Nazareth, who was a Prophet, mighty in what He *did* and *said* before God and all the people, and how our ruling priests and officials handed Him over to be condemned to death and crucified Him. But we were hoping He would be the One who was going to free Israel. What is more, this is now the third day since these things happened. But then some of our women startled us. They went to the tomb early this morning and did not find His body. They came and told us that they had even seen a vision of angels who said He is alive! Some of our men went to the tomb and found it as the women had said, but they did not see Him.

⌊Jesus replied⌋, "How unthinking you are, and how slow you are in your heart to believe everything the prophets said! Did not the Christ [Messiah] have to suffer these things and enter into His glory?" Then starting with Moses and all the prophets, He explained to them what was said about Him in all the Scriptures.

What event in the Bible would you select if you could go back in a "time machine" and watch events unfold? Would you choose to watch God create the world, see inside Noah's ark while it floated during the flood, view the Red Sea parting and the Egyptians drowning, eye David killing Goliath, observe Jesus being born in Bethlehem, witness Christ suffering on the cross, or gaze at the risen One appearing to Mary on Easter morning? I know what I would want to see and hear—the Emmaus event!

It was the greatest Bible teaching ever held on planet earth. The risen Christ dissected the Old Testament and gave interpretations from possibly every one of its books. We know it was impressive, because *after* Jesus revealed Himself and made a quick exit [a miraculous disappearance], the two disciples said to each other, "Did our hearts not burn within us as He was talking to us on the way and explaining the Scriptures to us" (Luke 24:32)?

The two disciples were quite impressed; they rapidly ran to tell Jesus's other disciples the whole series of events (vv. 33–35).

Those two "clueless" disciples were given all types of clues to solve the mysteries they could not formerly figure out, that is, until Jesus built a word bridge to carry them from the Old Testament into the era of fulfillment, called the New Testament. Now those two disciples were personally equipped to become teaching detectives who could show others how to investigate the Scriptures.

The Holy Spirit can help each of us become the same kind of evidence finders.

True Christian Faith in the Resurrected One

Alert investigators will note that Scripture firmly roots its evidence in *history*, in historical facts. Faithful detectives cannot separate faith from *historic* events (cp. H, *COT*, I, 14). True Christian faith does not permit one to rip Scriptural moorings out of history—and still retain credibility. It does not permit persons to deny teachings rooted in history, saying they did not happen, and then in the

Remember, for Jews, Sunday was the first workday of the week. It would seem normal for a gardener to have been on duty. But why was he never produced as a counter witness?

same breath say they still personally *believe* in Christ, a Messiah to whom Scripture gives a different testimony. What kind of police work would that be to have one set of proofs and then convict a person with contradictory evidence?

Let's get real. We live in the actual history of this world. To repudiate Christ's resurrection and say He was not raised with a physical body—with a "glorified" physical body that His disciples touched—is to undermine God's whole historic Creation and biblical accounts. It also does away with God's promise to transform our resurrected bodies to a most perfect physical state (1 Corinthians 15:20–23, 35–54). Or, as Job 19:25–27 says, our resurrected bodies will have "eyes" and "fleshly skin"

> See Appendix 10, the section entitled: "Empty 'Resurrection' Faith."

and will "see" the living "Redeemer" standing on the solid ground of His restored planet in our same universe (cp. 1 Thessalonians 4:16; 2 Peter 3:13; Hebrews 12:26b–29).

To repeat: Jesus was born, died, and rose in our history, so will we also rise historically!

Momentary Reminder to Keep Our Investigation on Target

The previous conclusions of this present book are built on certain presuppositions that govern the investigation of biblical data. There is no such thing as *absolute* human impartiality. In the case of a faithful biblical and theological starting point, it all boils down to one's view of Scripture. Does the investigator totally trust Scripture's testimony or not? For your present author, it's the whole Bible—or else, throw the *whole* thing out.

That's the approach I take with the four gospels.

Some prefer to play Matthew, Mark, Luke, and John against each other, at least in the belief that those writers either contradict one another or that they have unsolvable "divergences." Not my conclusion.

I believe Scripture, as a whole, is from God (2 Peter 1:21) and was given by inspiration (2 Timothy 3:16). It came from my God "who cannot lie" (Titus 2:1). Thus, the Bible is not "fake news" and cannot contradict itself (John 10:35). At times, it appears to have contradictions, but they are only *seeming* contradictions, until able Bible sleuths do research and offer possible solutions.

Such is the case with the so-called "divergent" facts concerning the events of Easter. With certainty, I believe the accounts of the four canonical Gospels can be reconciled, fact-wise and chronologically. The four writers are *not* at odds with one another, even

> For your aid, cite Appendix 10, the section entitled: "Easter Events in Chronological Order—and Beyond."

though they do wish to emphasize certain points that one of the other writers do not treat or to which they add additional data that initially appears contradictory. Most anyone can pick up these separate points of interest when reading the four Easter accounts. Don't get discouraged; put on your thinking caps, detectives, and dig in.

My belief that the so-called "divergent" aspects of the four gospels can be put into *chronological* order, and that the mystery of their puzzling data can be solved through diligent study, stems from my love for what is called the "harmonization" of the gospels. Be sure to see Appendix 11, entitled "Harmonizing the Four Gospels"!

Evidence room conclusion: The unbelievable surprises of Scripture just go on—page after page, event after event. Can they ever get better than those of Easter Sunday? Yes, they can and will for people who endorse the resurrected One. Apply an *extended* meaning of 1 Corinthians 2:9: "No eye has seen, no ear has heard, no mind has comprehended, what God has prepared for those who love Him." An unbelievable future awaits those who endorse the *resurrected* Savior (Romans 10:9).

CHAPTER 22

"UP, UP, AND AWAY"

Examining Clues in the Evidence Room
Can any Old Testament clues be found concerning Christ's ascension?

Introducing the "40" Phenomenon

As we wind down our whole investigative task, a few vibrant and clue-filled narratives still beckon our attention. Lean back, enjoy, and observe!

The initial narrative concerns the *ascension* account of Jesus's journey back to heaven forty days after Easter. In Acts 1:3, Dr. Luke reports,

> After His suffering Jesus also showed the apostles through many convincing proofs that He was alive; He was seen by them for 40 days and spoke with them about the Kingdom of God.

What a learning experience for Jesus's disciples! Present-day disciples are also in for such an experience as they investigate why Jesus had to hang around for "40" days after His resurrection. Yes, He had to stay on earth for another forty days after Easter before He was permitted to return to His throne in heaven.

Some scholars, for example, the credible F. F. Bruce and Peter Toon, disagree with me on this point. Contrary to my comments in Chapter 21, these exegetes feel Jesus ascended back to heaven already on Easter Sunday—and then made subsequent journeys back and forth to earth over the next forty days, appearing to His followers here and there from time to time (B, *CBA*, p. 40; T, *AOL*, pp. 11, 125).

Toon feels that Jesus Christ's new state of "exaltation" demanded His *immediate* Easter session to the right hand of God. In my opinion, he seems overly concerned with the question of the "whereabouts" of Jesus if He would have remained on earth for forty consecutive days (see T, *AOL*, pp. 10–12).

That seems to be God's business, not ours.

As our newly exalted High Priest (Hebrew 7:25), maybe Christ was praying in private places here on earth during His post-Easter absences (cp. Mark 1:35), or maybe He was visiting followers in scattered places where He had previously preached. Such persons would surely have heard of His death. Following that sad and confusing reality, a personal, visible resurrection appearance by the risen One would certainly have encouraged and cemented their faith for salvation.

In my view, this last possibility would make great sense in terms of future evangelism in the days after Jesus's ascension.

Dr. William F. Arndt says Scripture records "at least ten" post-resurrection appearances by Christ. He continues, "There may have been many more; not anywhere do we find a statement declaring that the holy writers have recorded all the occasions where Jesus after His resurrection permitted His disciples to see Him alive" (A, *GL*, p. 498; cp. John 21:25).

In any event, I challenge any conclusion that views Jesus returning to heaven earlier than forty days after His resurrection. The next section will prove my contention—all totally based on Old Testament evidential clues.

Why "40"?

To begin our "clue" search, we recall that Jesus had to fulfill the Scriptures by doing things "better" than God's previous prophets. In the case of Jesus's ascension into heaven, He had to do things *better* than Moses and Elijah, those two prophets who had appeared with Him on the Mount of Transfiguration before His death (Matthew 17:1–2).

We start with Moses, who climbed Mount Horeb, a mountain in the Sinai mountain range, seven different times. On two of those occasions, he stayed on that mountain for forty days. Prior to the last of those two forty-day stints, while still *off* the

> The Bible is filled with all kinds of 40s! Take a Bible concordance and look them up; you will be surprised. Two of those events, both comprised of the words "40 days," are parallel to Christ's *ascension* account.

mountain, Moses asked to see God's "glory" (Exodus 33:18). Later, back up the mountain, Moses was given a small glimpse of God's glory; God also spoke His glorious Name over Moses (Exodus 33:21–23; 34:5). That "glory" appearance—at the end of the forty-day period—was so consuming that Moses's face shined ever so brightly, and it continued to glow for days to come when back *off* the mountain; eventually, it faded away (34:4–6, 28–35; cp. 2 Corinthians 3:7).

For those interested in viewing additional "ascension" data, Appendix 13 will be of interest. It compares the ascensions of Enoch, Elijah, and Jesus, in terms of *numeric* separations. Exciting stuff.

Moses's experience was the Old Testament's most major *eye* or *seeing* revelation (Exodus 33:19–23, especially the last verse), maybe the best *hearing* miracle too (Exodus 34:5).

According to 1 Kings 19, Elijah also had a "glory" moment. After a forty-day journey to the same mountain and arriving at "*the* cave" where Moses had seen the LORD around 600 years before (vv. 8–9), Elijah also received a marvelous revelation from God. After God sent "a mighty wind, an earthquake, and also fire" (all three proving *empty* of God's presence; see vv. 11–12b), the LORD personally came to Elijah in the whisper of a "gentle Voice" (v. 12c).

Elijah's experience seems to have been the Old Testament's most major *hearing* revelation, possibly even greater than when God "pronounced the Name 'the LORD'" before Moses (Exodus 34:5). You will have to decide.

My cautious but inclined interpretation: Moses had the greatest "seeing" revelation from God in the Old Testament and Elijah had the greatest "hearing" revelation.

Could Jesus "top" the experiences of these two leading Old Testament prophets?

Yes! He ascended *bodily* to heaven forty days *after* Easter, as we will see in our upcoming review of Daniel 7. As He appeared before His welcoming Father, the "Ancient of Days" (cp. S, D, p. 351), He bodily encountered both the greatest *seeing* and *hearing* revelations—ever! And remember, Christ's *seeing* and *hearing* realities still endure to all eternity, never to "fade" away (Hebrews 13:8). Careful Bible observers will recall that Jesus viewed His

Vital: Other more technical matters concerning the ascension of Christ are dealt with in Appendix 12.

heavenly Father in *all* the fullness of His Father's "glory" (examine Colossians 2:9; Hebrews 1:3a)—a phenomenon not permitted Moses and Elijah during their earthly ministries.

Christ's *God-revelation* was so very much "better." He became the "greater" than Moses and Elijah—*combined*. And it all had to happen at the end of a forty-day period, the same amount of days after which Moses and Elijah had their supernatural encounters with the LORD. *"Evidence Just Too Coincidental to Be Accidental!!!"*

As If Gravity Ceased

The day came for Jesus to leave earth. He took His disciples out to the Mount of Olives, the mountain that housed the city of Bethany and the Garden of Gethsemane. This mountain had been predicted to be the place from which Jesus would ascend. In Zechariah 14:4a, in a figurative way, the "splitting" of the Mount of Olives from "the middle" on toward the "east" and "west" proved to be a prophecy about the "Gospel" being carried east and west by the disciples *after* Jesus's ascension into heaven. Difficult prophecy (cp. v. 4b).

What we do know is that Jesus stood with His feet on that mountain, gave His parting instructions to His disciples, and, as if gravity had ceased, He gradually floated into the sky and was soon out of the sight of those same disciples, a cloud covering Him from view (Acts 1:9–12).

We know from this former Scripture what happened on this side of the cloud. Would you like to know what happened on the other side? Daniel 7:13–14 reveals hidden clues to enlighten us who are still on the *earthly* side:

> In the visions during the night, I [Daniel] saw one [One] coming with the clouds of the heavens like a son of man [like a Son of Man], and He came to Ancient of Days and was presented before Him.

See S, *D*, p. 337 where Dr. Steinmann sets this passage into superior poetic form.

> And He was given glory, power to rule, and a Kingdom, so that all peoples, nations, and those of every language should serve Him. His authority is everlasting and will not pass away, and His Kingdom one that will not be destroyed.

My usual capitalization of the title "Son of Man" in Daniel 7:13–14 is based on the interpretation of numerous New Testament passages that Jesus applies to Himself (e.g., Matthew 9:6; Mark 14:62; Luke 17:30; John 3:14; also see Revelation 1:13–18 where Jesus appears as "one like a son of man"). See an expanded list of the New Testament "Son of Man" usages in P, *CD*, II, 71.

When reading Daniel 7:13–14, sharp Sherlock-types immediately spot this "son of man" designation. Dr. Edward J. Young strongly concludes that Daniel's Aramaic phrase, "like a son of man," is "messianic"; he also notes that it was the earliest interpretation among ancient church fathers (Y, *PD*, pp. 163–165). For them, it referred to MESSIAH Jesus.

The word *like* is also significant. Steinmann alertly observes that its inclusion in the phrase "*like* a son of man" shows that this heaven-arriving personage "possesses a true human nature and human appearance. At the same time, . . ., 'like,' implies that he is far greater than an ordinary man" (S, *D*, p. 339). Superb detective work!

Bible critics go to great lengths to empty the phrase "like a son of man" of any *messianic* implications within the Daniel 7 context (e.g., H, *TDOT*: "*ben 'ādhām*," III, 159–165). For me, this reveals anti-biblical bias at its extreme, even in light of the fact that "Perhaps no phrase in Daniel has elicited more comment by scholars . . ." (S, *D*, p. 355).

Interpreting Daniel 7:13–14

The Bible's Daniel 7 passage tells how "one like a son of man" enters heaven and is presented to the "Ancient of Days," God the Father Himself. It's a *coronation* [*enthronement*] scene (having been predicted in Psalms 2; 89; and 110); Jesus is crowned "*KING of Kings and LORD of Lords*" (cp. Revelation 19:16). His earthly victory over Satan has won Him "glory, power to rule, and a Kingdom."

Look at those very last words above—*in reverse*. Are you clue-spotting scrutineers awake? Those words should be ever so familiar, now constituting the last words of the Lord's Prayer, namely, "For Thine is the *Kingdom* and the *power* and the *glory* forever and ever. Amen."

Jesus had *not* added this ending to His teaching of the Lord's Prayer in Matthew 6 and Luke 11. However, many Christian congregations use these words to give honor to Jesus, as well as to His Father.

It would not have been appropriate for Christ to have added those words *until* His work of salvation was completed. But now on Ascension Day, He stood victorious before His most "pleased" Father in heaven. According to Daniel 7:13, this One "like a son of man" was present in terms of His *human nature*. In that human state, He was given His "Kingdom, power, and glory." True, according to His *divine nature*, Christ had always possessed the "Kingdom, power, and glory," but now, in terms of His glorified, resurrected human body, He received those three entities for a job perfectly done. Thus, He now reigns *bodily* to watch over all His followers— believers in heaven and also those still on earth.

Having briefly and more clearly tracked the "glory" of Jesus to the other side of the cloud, you are now ready for a closing passage in honor of you, the reader, from 2 Corinthians 3:17–18. It ties in with Christ's ascension and the Holy Spirit's presence in the present Church on earth—and also, let's not forget to couple this with the Old Testament revelation to Moses.

> This Lord is the Spirit, and where the Spirit of the Lord is, there is freedom. And all of us, as we reflect the Lord's glory in our unveiled faces, are being changed by that glory into the same likeness, namely, to the very same glory which comes from the Lord, who is the Spirit.

Evidence room conclusion: The clues from Daniel 7, along with those from the accounts of Moses and Elijah, help Bible detectives know how to interpret Jesus's ascension reality.

Clues Applied; Mysteries Solved

Confidently, faithful Bible detectives can now say that the evidence is in. Jesus accomplished everything perfectly, and He now reigns to the glory of the whole Trinity. Yet, we investigators, trapped in our four-dimensional world of height, width, depth, and time can only present the facts of Scripture to the minds of the masses within our own time frame. On the Last Day, together with all believers, we will greet our "Lord in the air," in eternity; then we will all be in total harmony as to the interpretation of the totality of biblical evidence (1 Thessalonians 4:17; 1 Corinthians 13:12). In the meantime, we "walk by faith, and not by sight" into the arms of Him who showed Himself to be the authentic One, the only true Savior of this world (2 Corinthians 5:7).

Wait a minute! I also need to note something of great significance. They named Him "Jesus" at a directive from heaven. By analogy, at the beginning of our book, we compared Him to Dr. Seuss's Horton. How apropos! The primary meaning of the name Jesus is "Helper." Its secondary meaning is "Savior." Horton helped save the *Whos* of *Whoville*. Jesus is the Helper "*Who*" wants to spiritually "help" ["save"] all us "Whos" in our earthly "Whoville," the place He created and has now redeemed.

Welcome to His new earthly and heavenly Whoville.

Before Locking Down the Evidence Room

Appendix 15 is presented to let Bible bloodhounds sniff out an additional Old Testament clue from a spellbinding narrative found in the New Testament book of Acts.

With Appreciation

Good to have had *you* along to read *Solving New Testament Mysteries with Old Testament Clues: Evidence Just Too Coincidental to Be Accidental!!!* My honor to have talked with *you* about GOD things. Thanks!

Keep private-eyeing the Scriptures (John 8:31–32); God is continuously *texting, trending,* and *tweeting* you on its pages (Romans 15:4). Happy continued investigating!

In Revelation 2:10 Jesus says, "Continue to be faithful until death, and I will give you the crown of life."

As a reader analyzes the whole of *Solving New Testament Mysteries with Old Testament Clues*, two realities should become apparent. Chapters 1–22 present two theological types of presentation simultaneously; one easier to comprehend, while the other is much deeper in content. In parallel, but also in contrast, Appendices 1–15 present an even lighter side as well as a deeper side pertaining to valuable Scriptural truth.

Thus the importance of this connective box between the chapters and appendices of this book.

Point of contact: My literary argumentation has shown why Jesus *said what He said* and *did what He did.* As such, the whole essence from cover to cover has verified the claim of the Lord Jesus that He was *who* He said He was; namely, the God-Man, the Son of God, sent to earth by His heavenly Father to be the Redeemer of the world to save humankind from sin.

With that basis of understanding, I feel honored to introduce you the reader (if you are not already aware) to Ravi Zacharias and his book, *Jesus and Other Gods.* (In addition to Ravi, several other leading apologists [defenders of the faith] of our day and age come to mind: Norman Geisler, Ken Ham, Josh McDowell, Albert Mohler, and Lee Strobel. There are several more.)

Ravi, born in India, is an expert on Hinduism, Buddhism, and Islam. His 195-page writing is must reading. Z, *JOG*, p. ix says it all, "This book is a defense of the uniqueness of the Christian message" (also view p. 5).

My present book is a more *overall* presentation of the Savior's claims, whereas Ravi's writing is much more pinpointed and challenging to the serious intellectual and ordinary non-Christian who is not afraid to consider new and uncomfortable data or truth (Z, *JOG*, p. x). In particular, Ravi confronts those who need to evaluate Hinduism, Buddhism, and Islam in the light of Christian claims.

Sidebar: Before departing from my praise for the Zacharias book, I desire to demonstrate Ravi's prowess for the defense of sane thinking. In one of his live presentations, a young student stood and told Ravi and his audience that there is no such thing as "absolute truth." This contradicted Jesus who claimed He was "the Truth" (John 14:4). In a calm manner, Ravi asked the student, "Where did you come up with that 'absolute truth'?" (It takes a second for that to sink in.) The student had just destroyed his own argumentation. It was vintage Ravi at work for his Savior!

APPENDIX 1

THE "WHO" REFERENCES PERTINENT TO THE IDENTIFICATION OF JESUS, PLUS OTHER EXTENDED DATA ON NEW TESTAMENT GROUPINGS

For the best of detectives, here is a list of the "who" and "whom" passages that seek to identify *Jesus* as the "expected" One *Who* fulfilled pertinent predictions from the OT, including those already treated. Duplicate texts are coupled in parentheses when they appear in the first three "Synoptic" ("seeing-from-the-same-point-of-view") Gospels. Thus, the *"who"* references: Matthew 21:10; **Mark 1:24** (Luke 4:34); 2:7 (Luke 5:21 – twice); **Luke 7:49**; **9:9**; 10:22; **John 1:19**, 27, **30**, 33; 4:10; 5:13, 15; 8:25; 9:21, 36-37; 12:34; **21:12**. The *"whom"* passages: **Matthew 3:17** and 17:5 (Mark 1:11); 11:27; **16:13**, 15 (Mark 8:27, 29; Luke 9:18, 20); Mark 14:71; Luke 9:9; **John** 1:15, 26, 45; 3:26, 34; 5:38; 6:29 [v. 68]; 7:25; 8:53; 17:3; **18:4**, 7; 19:37; 20:15. (References in **bold** indicate the *nine* selections used in Chapter 3 as prime proofs that Jesus was the *"who"* and *"whom"* sent from heaven by the Father.)

Basic reasoning: Why would anyone ever want to follow the "Jesus" of the NT unless He really was *Who* He said He was—"Someone" way beyond *special*?

Flavius Josephus (c. AD 35–100), the famous Jewish and non-Christian historian, records what seems to be the only ". . . extrabiblical evidence in the first century AD for Jesus's existence" (J, *WJ*, *Antiq.* 20.9.1), so concludes the scholar John P. Meier (M, *MJ*, p. 68). Meier's research extensively covers some forty-eight [48] pages (56–104) to reach this conclusion—and this is all based on two passages from Josephus. He adds the possibility that the *Annals* of the Roman, non-Christian historian Tacitus (c. AD 56-c. AD 118) may also give witness in the second century AD to Jesus being a historical figure, but Meier remarks that Tacitus "adds nothing really new" (M, *MJ*, p. 92).

Dr. Andrew Das—with reference to John P. Meier's analysis of the authenticity of the preservation and meaning of the Josephus text noted above—conveys the following in his classroom teaching notes: "This account of James (and Jesus) from Josephus is therefore original and not the result of an early Christian insertion" (D, *JOG*).

Another more well-known quote from Josephus can be found at J, *WJ*, *Antiq.* 18.3.3., but its more descriptive content seems to have been enhanced *after* the time of Josephus, surely by someone with Christian leanings (M, *MJ*, pp. 61–62).

When all the smoke is cleared, it needs to be stated that by the time Josephus wrote (post-AD 70), Jesus was already a famous *Who's Who* in the eyes of the Roman world, as the NT had already verified (Acts 17:5–7). Today there are very, very few persons in the world who doubt the *historicity* of Jesus from Nazareth. His virgin birth, resurrection, and ascension may be questioned by the *unbelieving* world, but that same world does not generally question His human birth, crucifixion, and death.

Where are your inclinations as you continue to consider this book's investigation and presentation of "*Evidence Just Too Coincidental to Be Accidental!!!*"? Maybe too early to say!

APPENDIX 2

VERIFICATION OF THE HEBREW USAGE OF *'ETH* AS AN APPOSITIONAL

The Genesis 4:1 translation, viewing *'eth* as an indicator of *prepositional* usage ("from" or "by" or "of" or "with the help of," as in "I have gotten a man 'from' or 'by' or 'of' or 'with the help of' the LORD") or as an *appositional* indicator ("I have gotten a man, the LORD") has been undergoing exegetical investigation in biblical commentaries for centuries. In recent times, the late William F. Beck, a most able Hebrew scholar, endorsed this *appositional* usage in his 1976 *An American Translation* (AAT). Thus, the adoption in this present book.

The fear of those avoiding *'eth* as an apposition centers around assigning Eve too much understanding of God's future plans; that is, before NT times. As already stated, we will discuss the whole phenomenon of "progressive revelation" in Chapter 5 when we deal with an Abraham experience in Genesis 22, as interpreted in part by Hebrews 11:19. In advance, however, let it be said that the words of Eve do not necessarily mean she understood the *full* import of what she said; God could have put the words in her mouth with the idea that He would reveal their fuller meaning to later generations (cp. 1 Peter 1:10–12).

But for the moment, one needs to view the parallel *'eth* in the next verse of the Eve saga, namely, Genesis 4:2. It uses *'eth* twice, like an appositional in a *direct object* position, just as the AAT has translated verse 1.

When Eve had a second son, he was named "Abel." It would follow that *'eth* in two consecutive verses would call for an identical usage: "Then she [Eve] gave birth to his [Cain's] brother, Abel."

So, let's try the *prepositional* way in contrast: "Then she [Eve] gave birth to his [Cain's] brother *with the help of* Abel." Total nonsense! What? Abel helped Eve have Abel? Did his kicking in the womb aid Eve in giving birth?

Additional *prepositional* translations also do not fly: "Then she [Eve] gave birth to his [Cain's] brother '*from*' or '*by*' or '*of*' Abel."

The only rendering of Genesis 4:2 that makes sense is, "Then she [Eve] gave birth to his [Cain's] brother, Abel." This translation, parallel as it should be to verse 1, sees "Abel" as an *appositive* or particle in a *direct object* setting. Why not 4:1 also? "I have gotten a man, the LORD."

It seems the import of 4:1 demands we regard Eve's statement as an indicator of *trust*. The following references show a fuller gamut of views for readers to investigate: J, *G*, pp. 58–59; H, *GWG*, pp. 233–239, K, *G*, p. 74; L, *EG*, I, 189–190; L, *LW*, I, 241–242.

In conclusion, I refer readers to Dr. Jonathan Sarfati's undisputable argumentation in favor of the translation, "I have gotten a man: the Lord") (S, *RC*, pp. 216–217).

A Valuable Observation

With the whole naming of Eve's second son comes something of great theological interest. Eve must have learned fast that Cain, her first son, was a sinner, a real piece of work, who could not save anyone, including himself.

How does one know? Well, Adam and Eve named their next son Abel. Do you know what that name means? It comes from the Hebrew verb *hbl*, translated "vanity" or "empty" in the biblical book of *Ecclesiastes* (1:2). In other words, Eve's second son was named "Good-for-Nothing." Bummer, but reality!

Contrary to Genesis 1:26 where we learn that Adam and Eve were originally created *holy* in the "image of God," Genesis 5:3 teaches that *after* the Fall into sin people could only produce children in their "own sinful image." Since Adam and Eve had no children *before* they were expelled from their initial home, the Garden of Eden, they therefore could only bear children who subsequently picked up their sinful natures. In theological terms, their offspring *inherited* sinful natures, not "holy images" (cp. Psalm 51:5; Jeremiah 13:23; Ephesians 2:1). A *future* coming One, as Eve learned more fully as Cain grew, would need to come and serve as the sinless Savior (cp. Genesis 4:25).

A LISTING OF THE MOST RECOGNIZED MESSIANIC PROPHECIES

Many of the most interesting parts of Holy Writ relate to *predictive* prophecy, especially those passages foretelling the coming of Messiah Jesus—His character and work. This present book touches upon several of those passages, finding mystery-solving clues.

> For readers interested in a fuller layout of messianic prophecies, two listings are presented below. The first indicates the most known texts, those universally accepted in staunch Bible-believing circles. A second list provides additional references for those with even more inquisitive minds.
>
> David Limbaugh's more recent book, *The Emmaus Code* (L, *EC*—404 pages), is a must-read, a gem in the field of presenting and dealing with many, many messianic prophecies.

Ranking the Top Twelve Messianic Prophecies

Messianic prophecies are an organizing principle for Christ-centered "Biblical Theology." See P, *EBP*, p. 681: Over one-fourth of the Bible constitutes prophetic material (8,352 verses of 31,124 verses); of these, 445 biblical prophecies of the 787 were fulfilled *before* Christ's First Coming (p. 680).

Fourteen key messianic prophecies of the OT:

Genesis 3:15:	The *foundation* of all messianic prophecy ("The *proto-evangel*")
Genesis 12:1–3:	The *key* to all messianic prophecy, the basis of the "new covenant" (see Jeremiah 31:31–34)
Genesis 49:8–12:	The "*fountainhead*" of all messianic prophecy (E. W. Hengstenberg)
Deuteronomy 18:15–18:	The coming *"Prophet"* who is to fulfill all messianic prophecy
2 Samuel 7:11c–16:	The *heart* of all messianic prophecy
Psalm 2:1–12:	The "You are My ['begotten'] *Son*" messianic prophecy: "Anointed" or "Messiah" (v. 2). The term "Messiah" ["Anointed One"] is only used of Jesus *four* times in the OT (Psalm 2:2; 45:7— verb form; Daniel 9:25–26; some say the Daniel reference represents the only pure usage of the term "Messiah.")
Psalm 22:1–31:	The *Good Friday* Psalm
Psalm 110:1–7:	The *most quoted* messianic prophecy in the NT ("fourteen times"; see L, *EC*, p. 257)
Isaiah 7:14:	The prophecy of Jesus's *virgin birth*
Isaiah 9:6–7:	The *names* of Christ and character of His coming *rule*
Isaiah 52:13–53:12:	The *clearest or most revealing* of all messianic prophecy
Jeremiah 23:5–6:	The messianic prophecy that best proclaims the *essence* of Christianity ("the substitutionary atonement of Christ")
Daniel 7:13, 14	Heaven's side of the Acts 1:9 ascension cloud
Daniel 9:24–27:	The best prophecy predicting the *time* of Jesus's ministry and death
Micah 5:2	The prediction concerning Christ's "Bethlehem" birthplace
Zechariah 3:9d:	The coming One who rids the world of sin in *one* ["24-hour"] *day*

A Listing of Some "Messianic Prophecies"

(The more recognized predictions are in **bold** typeface!)

Genesis 3:15	Proverbs 8:22–31	Jeremiah 32:6–12
Genesis 9:25-27	Isaiah 2:2–4; 4:2–6	Ezekiel 34:11–16, 23–24
Genesis 12:1–3 (15:18)	**Isaiah 7:14** (10–16)	Ezekiel 47:1–12
Genesis 49:10 (8–12)	**Isaiah 9:6–7** (1–7)	Daniel 2
Numbers 24:17	**Isaiah 11:1–10**	**Daniel 7:13–14**
Deuteronomy 18:15–18	Isaiah 25:6–9; 26:1, 19	Daniel 9:24–27
2 Samuel 7:11c–16	Isaiah 28:5	Hosea 1:10–2:1
2 Samuel 23:1–7	Isaiah 28:16	Hosea 2:14–23
1 Chronicles 5:1–2	Isaiah 30:20	**Hosea 11:1***
Job 19:23–27	**Isaiah 35:5–6**	Joel 2:28–32
Psalm 2	Isaiah 35:8–10	Amos 9:11–12
Psalm 8	**Isaiah 40:1–11**	**Micah 5:2** (1–3)
Psalm 16	**Isaiah 42:1–11**	Haggai 2:6–9
Psalm 22	**Isaiah 49:1–6**	Zechariah 2:10–11
Psalm 34	**Isaiah 50:4–9**	Zechariah 3:1–10
Psalm 40	**Isaiah 52:13–53:12**	Zechariah 6:12–13
Psalm 41	Isaiah 55:1–5	**Zechariah 9:9–10**
Psalm 45	Isaiah 59:16–21	Zechariah 11:12–13
Psalm 68	**Isaiah 60:1–6**	**Zechariah 12:10** (9–14)
Psalm 69	Isaiah **61:1–3**	Zechariah 13:7–9
Psalm 72	Isaiah 62:2; 65:15	Zechariah 14:3-5
Psalm 78	**Isaiah 63:1–14**	**Malachi 3:1–3**
Psalm 89	Jeremiah 8:22	**Malachi 4:2**
Psalm 109	**Jeremiah 23:5–6**	
Psalm 110	Jeremiah 31:15	
Psalm 118	**Jeremiah 31:31–34**	*Cp. Numbers 24:8–9

APPENDIX 4

ALL THOSE WEIRD NAMES

Both Matthew 1:1–17 and Luke 3:23b–38 give genealogies of Jesus's family line, but they seem so different from one another. It is beyond the scope of this appendix to list all the differences; two will suffice.

Luke's genealogy is longer; it traces names *backward* all the way from Jesus to Adam, even to God Himself. Why? Because Luke's purpose is wider than Matthew's. He desires to present Jesus as Savior of *all* people, not just Jews (cp. 1 Corinthians 5:15, written by Paul the apostle with whom Luke traveled).

Matthew's listing moves *forward* as he starts with Abraham and moves toward Jesus.

Most of the names in the two lists differ when viewing those descendants who lived between the time of David and Jesus. Reason: Matthew traces King David's messianic relatives forward from his son King Solomon down through Joseph, the carpenter, Jesus's earthly, *legal* father, and then he takes it one step further on down to "JESUS" Himself.

On the other hand, Luke trails Jesus's ancestors up from Jesus *through Nathan*, another son of King David, to David himself. (This Nathan is not to be confused with Nathan the prophet of the same era.) In so doing, Luke's line *implies* "Mary" the virgin, Joseph her husband, and Jesus her Son all descended from the line of David, Judah, and Abraham. Luke even traces the line of Jesus all the way back to Adam and God Himself. This assured readers that "Jesus" was of the right stock to be Messiah and Savior.

Oh, by the way, there is another clever clue for observant sleuths. Spot it at Luke 3:23b: "Jesus was ˌtheˌ son (*so it was thought*) of Joseph, ..." Have you caught it? The "so it was thought" interjection! The *human* Jesus was only from the Holy Spirit and the virgin Mary, not in any way from Joseph, biologically speaking. Matthew 1:16 also teaches that Joseph was not the biological father of Jesus.

The Family Line of Jesus Christ

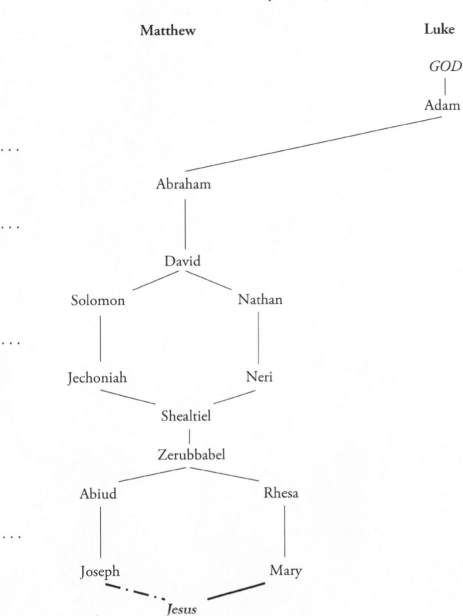

Matthew   Luke

GOD
|
Adam

...   Abraham
|
...   David
Solomon   Nathan
| |
... | |
Jechoniah   Neri
Shealtiel
|
Zerubbabel
Abiud   Rhesa
| |
... | |
Joseph   Mary
Jesus

Joseph was not the *real* father of Jesus. Rather, Jesus was the earthly Son of His mother Mary, through the "virgin" process executed by God the Holy Spirit. Biologically speaking, Joseph had nothing to do with the human conception of Jesus. Instead, Joseph should be called the *legal*, not the *real* father of Jesus.

Do you now see why Scripture must be read and analyzed very carefully?

In light of Jonathan Sarfati's research, Bible scholars will want to investigate the so-viewed "Cainan problem" of Genesis 11 and of Luke's 3:36–37 genealogy in S, *RC*, pp. 295–297. Not such a difficult mystery after all.

Recording Matthew's Genealogy for Counting Purposes
Matthew 1:1–17 (NET, 1990)

A record of the family history [family line or genealogy] [Greek: *geneseōs*] of Jesus Christ, a descendant of David ‚and‚ a descendant of Abraham:

> **Abraham** was the father of Isaac,
> **Isaac** was the father of Jacob,
> **Jacob** was the father of Judah and his brothers.
> **Judah** was the father of Perez and Zerah
> > by Tamar, ‚who was their mother‚.
>
> **Perez** was the father of Hezron,
> **Hezron** was the father of Ram,
> **Ram** was the father of Amminadab,
> **Amminadab** was the father of Nahshon,
> **Nahshon** was the father of Salmon,
> **Salmon** was the father of Boaz
> > by Rahab, ‚who was his mother‚.
>
> **Boaz** was the father of Obed
> > by Ruth, ‚who was his mother‚.
>
> **Obed** was the father of Jesse,
> **Jesse** was the father of King **David**.

> David was the father of Solomon by her,
> > ‚who had been the wife‚ of Uriah.
>
> **Solomon** was the father of Rehoboam,
> **Rehoboam** was the father of Abijah,
> **Abijah** was the father of Asa,
> **Asa** was the father of Jehoshaphat,
> **Jehoshaphat** was the father of Joram,
> **Joram** was the father of Uzziah,
> **Uzziah** was the father of Jotham,
> **Jotham** was the father of Ahaz,
> **Ahaz** was the father of Hezekiah,
> **Hezekiah** was the father of Manasseh,
> **Manasseh** was the father of Amon,
> **Amon** was the father of Josiah,
> **Josiah** was the father of **Jechoniah** and his brothers
> > when the people were taken away to Babylon.

After they had been taken away to Babylon,
Jechoniah was the father of Shealtiel.

Shealtiel was the father of Zerubbabel,

Zerubbabel was the father of Abiud,

Abiud was the father of Eliakim,

Eliakim was the father of Azor,

Azor was the father of Zadok,

Zadok was the father of Achim,

Achim was the father of Eliud,

Eliud was the father of Eleazar,

Eleazar was the father of Matthan,

Matthan was the father of **Jacob**,

Jacob was the father of **Joseph**, the husband of Mary;
she was the mother of **JESUS** who is called CHRIST.

So there are in all

14 generations from Abraham to David,

14 generations from David to the Babylonian Captivity,

14 generations from the Babylonian Captivity to Christ.

Background for Solving the "42" Indicator

Problem! Matthew claims *three* groupings of fourteen names each, for a total of forty-two names. Yet, there are only forty-one names, only thirteen in the final group. Mystery or error? Did a name drop out because of a copyist error? Unlikely, since scribes were so careful; this type of number error would have been picked up immediately—and corrected in following manuscripts.

Let's consider a miscount by Matthew. What, Matthew, whose former occupation was that of a tax collector, could not count to *fourteen* three times without making a mistake? Come on; someone must come up with a better solution than that!

Alert detectives should realize that a mystery is here present to be solved. Clues are needed. Two can be picked up from both the OT and NT. They include numeric components: "7" and "6"! (Note that three 14s [42] equal 7 x 6. Easy to miss!)

To begin, "7" is the Bible numeral for "perfection," the most used Scriptural number with

> "Seven Eyes" and "Seven Spirits" are code names for the Holy Spirit.

symbolic meaning. Example: The Spirit of God is defined both as the "*Seven* Eyes . . . on one stone" ["cornerstone"] (Zechariah 3:9b) and the "*Seven* Spirits who are before His [God's] throne" (Revelation 1:4–5), since the numeral "7" stands for holy perfection, as in the *Holy* Spirit.

The numeral "6" stands for "created" things, as in, God created all things in *six* days (Genesis 1:31, Exodus 20:11).

Now 7 x 6 = 42. Of what should that remind you when dealing with the NT book of Revelation? There the Apostle John equates 1,260 days (11:3) with forty-two (42) months (11:2) and then again with "time, times, and a half-time," meaning, year, years, half-year. The terms *times* and *years,* both in the *plural*, indicate "two years" (12:14). (In the Jewish culture of Bible times, a year consisted of 360 days; thus, 1,260 days or 42 months was equal to 3 and ½ years.)

Important: All *three* arrangements indicate the entire *length* of the NT, a timespan during which the Church or Kingdom of heaven will be persecuted by Satan for believing and spreading the Good News of Jesus's saving work (apply Revelation 12:6; 13:1–8, especially v. 5; and 11:3). Stay alert, detectives: Remember that Matthew's Gospel is all about the "Kingdom of heaven," God's people, the Church (e.g., 13:1–53—The "Seven *Kingdom* Parables").

The book of Daniel (12:7) initiates this symbolic number trail for God's usage in Revelation when he speaks of the "shattering" time of NT persecution. There Daniel speaks of "three-and-a-half seasons," once again equivalent to "time, times, and a half-time"! To summarize: Matthew and Daniel have four different ways of saying the same thing.

> For those interested in understanding the whole story of Revelation and Daniel, in the context of the above numbers, see Brighton's work which provides brilliant and fascinating insight (B, *R*, pp. 287–291, plus pp. 299–300). Also note Becker's *Revelation* to understand the "42" usage by John the apostle (B, *RDTS*, pp. 165–166). This Becker commentary, in my opinion, is absolutely the best explanation—ever—of the book of Revelation for faithfulness of interpretation and ease of understandability for the minds of religious leaders and laypersons alike. Brighton's work is magnificent for religious scholars who want to examine every nook and cranny of Revelation.

Solving Matthew's Genealogical Mystery

In line with my inquisitive nature, the initial "42" *clue* was kick-started in the classroom of Dr. "Red Fred" Danker of Bauer, Arndt, Gingrich, Danker lexicon fame. The class was discussing the various interpretations of the "14-14-14" in Matthew 1:17. Danker suggested the possibility of the *missing* fourteenth (14th) name in the third subset to indicate "the Church," the people of God who make up Christ's Kingdom both in heaven and on earth. Sounded fascinating. Years later, a reading of Isaiah solidified its truth for me.

Some 700 years before Christ's coming, it was foretold that Jesus would have "children." In Isaiah 53, the clearest chapter in all the OT concerning Jesus's suffering, death, and resurrection, verse 10 predicted that the coming One would die, yet later "see those born to Him" since He would "enjoy a long life."

> Of course, Jewish tradition takes the whole of the Isaiah 53 context as foretelling its nation's plight of suffering and its destiny to be the Jewish *saviors* of the world. Their rejection of Jesus of Nazareth as the true Messiah obviously is *not* the endorsed belief of the Christian Church nor is it the true interpretation of Isaiah 53. See Acts 8:31–35.

But how do the two seemingly contradictory items mesh? Scripture indicates Jesus never married; yet, one reads, "He will see His children"? (No, no, He did not have kids out of wedlock! That would make Him a fornicator and then *not* a candidate to be the Savior from sin when He Himself had become a sinner!) 1 Peter 2:22 declares: "He never sinned . . . ." Nor did Jesus marry Mary from Magdala, have children with her, and move to London, England! Only religious dreamers come up with such unsubstantiated conclusions.

Rather, the clue and answer lie in an OT custom termed "levirate marriage" (cp. Deuteronomy 25:5–10). This strange tradition ordered a man's brother to marry and produce a baby with the widow of his brother who had died *childless* (cp. Genesis 38). The first son born after that union would then be regarded as the heir of the dead husband; in this way, the dead man's genealogy and name would be carried on. Compare Matthew 22:24.

Who was bound by this law? Later history seems to indicate a more inclusive relationship than that of "brother" only, as is shown in Ruth 3:12 ("nearest relative"). In Ruth's case, a *reverse* levirate comes into play. The widow Ruth becomes the levirate agent whom Boaz, Jesus's distant ancestor-to-be, marries. These newlyweds produce Obed, who has Jesse, who has David, who later becomes King David. Thus, the family line of Jesus continues via the levirate arrangement. That God of the Bible does have strange ways to accomplish salvation for sinners. His twists and turns demand that Bible detectives stay on their toes!

There it is, an OT *clue* that leads to solving the 14-14-14 NT mystery! Have you caught it? Jesus died, rose, ascended back to heaven, and left no children behind. But He had a "nearest Relative," the Holy Spirit, the heavenly *Levirate* agent, the Third Person of the Trinity. The

Holy Spirit steps in to raise up *spiritual* children for Jesus (Romans 8:15–17 and 1 Corinthians 12:3). Thus, believers become Christ's *children* by faith in Him, as worked out by the Holy Spirit, Christ's Levirate agent. These children of the Lord Jesus, through conversion by the Holy Spirit, are made "born-again" Christian members of the Messiah's Kingdom (cp. John 3:3).

All *Christians* make up the missing *fourteenth* generation, the last listed in that third subset of Matthew 1. There in that very first chapter of the NT you can find God's "love letter" to you and me, the children of Jesus. Complex love (cp. Isaiah 9:6: Jesus is called "everlasting Father"). Amazing! ("Everlasting Father" means that Jesus has the qualities of a father, not that He is God the Father. He is God the Son who also possesses "fatherly" qualities.)

APPENDIX 5

CHRISTIANITY'S HEART AND CORE

The "five" reasons God's Son came to planet Earth:

- To "fulfill" the OT prophecies relating to Him (cp. Matthew 1:22);

- To give "glory" to His heavenly Father through *what He said* and *what He did* (John 4:34; 5:19, 24; 12:49–50);

- To come "under law" and keep it in the place of all people who could not keep it (Galatians 4:4);

- To "redeem" all peoples through His sacrificial, substitutionary death (Galatians 4:5);

- To "undo the works of the devil" (1 John 3:8).

APPENDIX 6

JESUS, THE RECAPITULATOR [REPEATER]

How was the *First Adam* a "type" [prefigurement] and "picture parallel" to Jesus, the *Second Adam*?

A. "Splitting the Adams" as to *type* and *Antitype* [Adam and Jesus] in Romans 5:12–19 (quote marks indicate words from this NT text):

   1. Adam's "sin" brought "death" into the world; Jesus took the sting of "death" out by bringing back "life" through His "righteousness"!

   2. Adam's "*disobedience*" brought "condemnation"; the "*obedience*" of Jesus brought "justification"!

   3. Adam's "sin" fell on "multitudes"; Jesus's "overflowing grace" fell on "multitudes."

   4. Adam's "failure condemned all people" to die; Jesus's "free gift of righteousness which brings life" enables all believers to "live and rule" by "grace."

B. "Splitting the Adams" as *parallel pictures* (extended applications) in Romans 5:12–19:

   1. God's direct creative actions caused both Adam and Jesus to become human beings.

   2. Both Adams came into the world without sin; initially, they both possessed the sinless "image of God." After sin, Adam lost his "moral" image, but through *continuous* holiness, Jesus retained His original and sinless human "image of God."

   3. Adam and Jesus had special relationships with their heavenly Father; both were humanly unique—by the *direct* hand of God; Jesus was *more* unique, being both the "eternally begotten" Son of God, as well as fully human in one Person, the God-Man (Colossians 2:9).

4. Both Adams were *initially* and *personally* tempted by Satan: the First succumbed (lost); the Second overcame (won). This is why Jesus, following His baptism, *initially* had to confront the devil in the wilderness *before* picking His disciples. These handpicked, chosen disciples later became "new Adams" and thereby representatives of the "Second Adam," as well as forerunners of all NT believers, each new believer, in turn, becoming by faith a "new Adam" themselves (Colossians 3:10). Whew!

5. Adam ate from a *tree*; Jesus died on a *tree*.

6. Adam was *naked* when he sinned; Jesus was *naked* when he died for sin.

7. Adam brought sin into the world in "one day"; Jesus took it out in "one day" (cp. Zechariah 3:9d).

8. Both Adams came under the "curse" of sin; God's Law convicted both (cp. Galatians 4:4–5).

9. Adam passed *blame* to others; Jesus took the *blame* for others.

10. Adam and Jesus both *carried* sin, but differently!

11. Both Adam and Jesus were the *greatest* of sufferers (cp. Jesus with Adam and Eve and also with Job?). You have to think this one through—carefully. Hint: Adam had 930 years of life on earth to think about the consequences of his sin, the death after death of his multiple descendants. Much grief!

12. Both Adams had a *curse* of "thorns" put on them; Adam's *thorns* created hard work; Jesus's *thorns* brought discomfort to Him but "comfort" to us (cp. Genesis 5:28–29 with John 14:16).

13. Both Adams had existences where "gardens" played a significant role in the drama of sin.

14. Adam was put out of the Garden of Eden; Christ was permitted back into the "new" garden ["Paradise"] (Luke 23:43).

15. Adam spoke to a *woman* [Eve] in the Garden of Eden; Jesus spoke to a *woman* [Mary from Magdala] on Easter morning in the resurrection garden.

16. Adam had children *after* he was defeated by sin; Jesus had children *after* He defeated sin (cp. Genesis 5:3–5 with Isaiah 53:10–12, esp. v. 11c–d).

(See L, *EC*, p. 27 for further "recapitulation" examples from the Old Testament.)

APPENDIX 7

JUDAH OR JESUS?

Interpreters seem evenly divided over this question: Do the *six* usages of the masculine "He" or "he" in Genesis 49:11–12 refer to SHILOH or Judah? Exegetes almost always opt for an "either/or" solution in difficult situations. This seems to safeguard the hermeneutical principle that limits a text to having "one sense" of meaning—and only *one* sense. A vital principle! For example, it keeps one from *allegorizing* Bible texts, one method by which many massacre the intended textual meanings of God. In all ages, fanciful handlers of Scripture have been tempted to interject all kinds of notions not truly present in biblical passages. The "one sense" principle guards against "adding" to Scriptural meaning.

At the same time, the "either/or" approach can limit or "subtract from" the fuller or fullest meaning of a text. Why can a passage not contain a "both/and" conclusion? It would seem to me that a text can have two *levels* of meaning, while still maintaining a single, overall sense. What does that mean? Genesis 49:11 and 12 serve as a good illustration, but careful vigilance must dominate all interpretation of the text.

Back to the question, "Do these verses refer to Jesus or Judah? Why not *both* on two different levels? The "donkey" and "donkey's colt" surely remind us of the fact that Jesus rode into Jerusalem on Palm Sunday. But what about the tying of these two animals to a "vine" and a "choice vine," to the best part of a grape arbor? Did Jesus do that after His ride? It would seem something additional is meant.

Or what about *the washing of "His"* and *"his" garment and clothes in red wine,* or what about a possible extended meaning as to *"His"* and *"his" white teeth and dark eyes*? Tough stuff! Already, these terms have been cited, indicating Jesus as the fulfillment of their meaning. But is there a further fulfillment, a "both/and" possibility? This would seem to be the case! Again, what does it mean?

To grasp the answer, one must recall the most *foundational* prophecy of all Scripture. It is Genesis 12:1–3, the original covenant-promise of God. There Abraham, as representative of God's holy Church or people, is given a *threefold* promise: (1) "land"; (2) "seed" (a collective: "descendants" as well as an ultimate "Descendant"); and (3) "blessings" for all believers. The latter plays into our "both/and" assertion—Jesus and the people of His saved Kingdom.

On level 1, Genesis 49:11–12 promised that SHILOH would receive "blessings" through His resurrection (cp. Acts 3:13a). On level 2, Judah, who represents believers of all ages, seems to be the recipient of Christ's distributed spiritual and physical "blessings," this being inferred by an extended meaning demanded by the text (e.g., "vine" and "choice vine").

Those who only see Judah as the subject of verses 11 and 12 point this out. Judah receives "blessings." As far as these interpreters go, they are correct. But Acts 3:25 includes Jesus in the whole mix. By quoting Genesis 12, this Acts passage says that all who endorse the promise given Abraham are *blessed* heirs of Abraham through the redemptive work of the coming Descendant Jesus (also see Galatians 3:15–18). This arrived One now shares all His blessings with His people [Judah]. 1 Corinthians 3:22–23 agrees, " . . . everything is yours . . . you belong to Christ . . .," meaning Christ shares all His "blessings" with His people who, based on Genesis 49, are "the new Judah."

Thus, in Genesis 49:11–12, each "He" refers to SHILOH and each "he" refers to Judah, God's people. Thus, the masculine pronouns—at one and the same time—do double duty, a "both/and" situation. For example, not only SHILOH but also SHILOH's people receive the abundance of the twofold health (v. 12), as they eat the spiritual and physical "blessings" of Jesus's saving actions—by faith.

APPENDIX 8

THE GREATEST:
MOSES OR JOHN THE BAPTIZER OR YOU?

There is no doubt about it. John 1:17 chooses Moses as the greatest OT prophet: "For the Law was given through Moses, but grace and truth came through Jesus Christ." Moses, the greatest of OT times; Jesus, the greatest of the NT era!

But what does one do with Jesus's conclusion that John the Baptizer was the greatest (Matthew 11:11a)? It's a mystery to be solved.

Jeremiah 31:31–34 certainly sets up Moses's covenant, called the "old covenant," as an absolute contrast to the "new covenant," the latter made operational when Jesus instituted the Lord's Supper. Hear God speaking in that Jeremiah passage:

> The time will come, says the LORD, when I will make a "new covenant" with Israel and Judah. It will *not* be like the "¸old¸ covenant ¸of Moses¸" that I made with their fathers when I took them by their hand to lead them out of Egypt – My covenant that they broke although I was their master, says the LORD. But this is the "covenant" I will make with Israel after those days, says the LORD: I will put My law within them and write it on their hearts, and so, I will be their God, and they will be My people. And no more will anyone have to teach his neighbor or his brother, and say, "Know the LORD," because they will all know Me, from the least to the greatest of them, says the LORD, because I will forgive the wrong they did and not remember their sins anymore.

Almost a whole chapter is needed to explain the full history and meaning of this text. It should be ranked in the "top five" of all Bible passages. Let it suffice to make a few points.

First, the two covenants are presented as being diametrically opposed to one another.

The "old covenant"—the Law, used here in its *narrow* sense, implying the Ten Commandments of Moses, and spoken of by Paul in that same *narrow* sense in Galatians 3:17—could *not* be kept perfectly by humans, as is illustrated by Jews in OT days and by humans of all time periods. The Law always ends up being broken.

On the other hand, the "new covenant"—the "Gospel" or "Good News"—did provide that "Someone" who could and did keep God's Law *and* who at the same time did forgive all lawbreakers.

"Who" was that "Someone"? It was the Lord Jesus, He who was predictively given the name "Covenant" in the OT (Isaiah 42:6). Galatians 4:4–5 substantiates it: "But when the time finally came, God sent out His Son to be born of a woman and to be born under law, in order to pay the price to free [redeem] those under law . . . ."

Second, let's contrast Moses and Jesus by repeating John 1:17 in paraphrase: "For the 'old covenant' was given through Moses, but the 'new covenant' came through Jesus Christ." In short, Moses represented the Law, while Jesus represents the Gospel. Moses represented failure ("My covenant [covenant of Law] which they broke"); Jesus represents hope ("I will forgive the wrong they did and not remember their sins anymore").

Though it was God who gave the Old Covenant, Moses is regarded as the human who instituted it. None of God's other OT prophets started a covenant of this magnitude. Therefore, all OT prophets were "carbon copies" of Moses; they were all under that same Law, as they served as spokesmen for God.

Only Prophet Jesus was different. He instituted a "new covenant" or "last will and testament" (Matthew 26:28), a second "covenant" or "testament," parallel to that of Moses, yet very, very different. Moses and John the Baptizer are similar; Moses and Jesus not so! Remember: When Gabriel came to Mary and then later to Joseph the carpenter, he did *not* tell them to name their Son "Moses Jr." That would have meant Jesus was to bring Commandments 11 to 20, and no one could keep Commandments 1 to 10. The world did *not* need another "law giver"; it needed a "law keeper" and deliverer! That is one of the reasons Jesus was named after Joshua, Moses's successor, whose name meant "helper" or "savior."

But on another level of discussion, we continue our evaluation of Moses and John the Baptizer. Moses was great, but Jesus names John the Baptizer "greater" than Moses and all the other OT prophets (Matthew 11:11a). How dare Jesus contradict me! Ha, ha! Breathe. He does not contradict; rather, He stresses an entirely different point.

It's once again time to play detective.

To start, one must realize that John the Baptizer is an *OT* prophet, even though we read about Him on the pages of the NT. You need to know John was dead by the time Jesus announced the beginning of the NT era with His "new covenant" comment at the Lord's Supper. John had already died shortly after Jesus's ministry began (cp. Mark 6:14–29). In a sense, even Jesus was an *OT* "prophet" until the time He won salvation on Calvary's cross, that is, on that same day He "took the cup" and declared He would "shed His blood for the *forgiveness* of sins" (Matthew 26:28 again).

So how could Moses and John the Baptizer both be the greatest OT prophets? In fact, should we not declare Jesus to be the greatest? If you notice, Jesus took Himself out of the running when He declared that John the Baptizer was "greater than all those born of women." Jesus was born of a woman, but His was a very different type of a woman's birth—a virgin birth. So, His birth falls into a category far different than that of Moses, Elijah, Isaiah, and even John the Baptizer.

Back to our main question, "Who was greater, Moses or John? Both! Moses was the greatest in terms of his being the OT personage who *originated* the Old Covenant. But John the Baptizer was the "greater" than Moses in that he was the *only* OT prophet who saw Jesus *in the flesh*. All other OT prophets were dead by the time Jesus was born, but not John. He was alive and kickin'! The other prophets were long gone; they had recorded the "promise" of the coming One, but only John the Baptizer saw the *partial* "fulfillment."

And now the real surprise, also from Jesus's lips: ". . . the least in the Kingdom of heaven is greater than John" (Matthew 11:11b). That's a reference to us. How can we be greater than the great Moses and John the Baptizer? Easy, we live on the other side of Calvary and the empty tomb. None of the prophets, including John the Baptizer, witnessed the death and resurrection of Christ. They were dead, but we are not. We can see the risen Christ through the eyes of faith, and that makes us "greater" than any OT prophet, so says Jesus!

Wow, these mysteries just keep on getting solved!

APPENDIX 9

WHO WERE SOME
OF THE ACCUSING AGITATORS
IN THAT GOOD FRIDAY CROWD?

Readers of Scripture may be surprised to learn that a very special group of priestly accusers may have been in the Good Friday crowd that influenced Governor Pilate's ultimate decision. These *non-Jerusalem* priests would easily have been *willing* participants to aid the ruling priests and elders of the Jerusalem Temple to call for the release of Barabbas and the crucifixion of Jesus (cp. Mark 15:11; Matthew 27:20).

Now for something that few Bible scholars have considered! I cite the work of the late chronologist Gene Faulstich. He concluded that the "Nazareth" group of priests (Happizzez, the 18th division—1 Chronicles 24:15) was getting ready to come on duty the day *after* Jesus's trial, that is, on the Saturday *after* Jesus's Good Friday death (cp. G, *ALD*, p. 9).

So in American idiom, it is asked, "What's that got to do with the price of tea in China." Well, that complex data concerning the Nazareth priests presents a significant line of reasoning that competent Scriptural detectives should want to examine.

To reach his eventual "Nazareth" conclusion, Faulstich analyzed the various divisions of OT Jewish priests. Scripture reports that over a period of around 450 years (between the days of Moses and those of King David) the volume of priests grew from 22,000 (Numbers 3:39) to unmanageable numbers. Jewish Levitical priests now over flooded the Tabernacle as they carried out their various duties, probably tripping over each other.

King David remedied the situation. He divided the priests into twenty-four orders. Each group served twice yearly at the Jerusalem Temple, as outlined in 1 Chronicles 24. These two weeks of service were *not* consecutive; they were separated six months apart. In between their two weeks of Tabernacle, and later Temple, service, the priests went back home and served the other weeks in one of the forty-eight Levitical cities (or other cities) that were scattered throughout the Holy Land (cp. Numbers 35:7; Joshua 21).

E. W. Faulstich's ultimate conclusion has to do with a particular event during Jesus's trial before Pontius Pilate. If truly applicable, it is fascinating beyond coincidence.

Faulstich observes that the Bible-labeled "Happizzez" group of priests from Jesus's hometown of Nazareth would have arrived in Jerusalem during Holy Week. Some of those priests would be good candidates to desire Jesus's crucifixion since He was hated by many in Nazareth (Luke 4:14–30). Those who were enemies of Jesus would have been *willing* participants in "stirring up" the crowd at Jesus's trial before Pilate (Mark 15:11).

These "Nazareth priests" may have been jealous of Jesus's popularity, or maybe, as former childhood playmates, they had viewed Jesus as a "goody-two-shoes" since He never sinned by participating in youthful or teenage pranks. Now, it may have been "get even" time. In any event, as Jesus said, "I tell you the truth, no prophet is accepted in his hometown" (Luke 4:24).

Now comes the zinger: If that Nazareth division of priests did *not* come "on duty" until the day *after* Jesus died, it is significant that Jesus was already "off duty" as our sacrificing Priest by that Saturday since His work was already "finished" on Friday. The sacrifices to be offered by the Nazareth priests, or whatever priests in the weeks to come, would have been null and void by then, obsolete to be sure (Hebrews 9:12). Why? Because Jesus would now be serving as the final High Priest after "the order of Melchizedek" (cp. Psalm 110:4 with Hebrews 7:17).

Stand in awe of this fact!

Additional data of interest: Above, I have mentioned the Happizzez, the 18th division of priests. Bible sleuths should also recognize the 8th division of the twenty-four groups of priests, the one called "Abijah," the order of priests that came from the city of Hebron, John the Baptizer's hometown. Recall that Zacharias, John's father, was from the "Abijah" group of priests. He was offering incense at the Jerusalem Temple when the angel Gabriel appeared to him to announce the coming birth of his son John (Luke 1:5); and as God's plans would have it, Zacharias was there at just the *right time*, since each priest was privileged to perform certain tasks only *once* in their lifetime. Interestingly, it is estimated there were 830 priests in each division (E, *LTJM*, I, 134, plus n. 1). No wonder priests only got one shot at things in their short twenty years of service (Numbers 4). (Larger divisional numbers than the 830 can be compared in J, *JW, "The Life of Flavius Josephus,"* p. 1, fn. *a*.)

APPENDIX 10

CONFLICTING MATTERS CONCERNING CHRIST'S EASTER RESURRECTION

(For seasoned Bible enthusiasts only!)

About This Appendix

This is the most *technical* appendix. It is designed to deal with many *resurrection* aspects. The first delves into the difficulties of 1 Peter 3:18–19. (Its content is quite complex and is intended to feed readers who are very acquainted with the Bible and Christianity.)

Several sections of the present appendix expand on certain Easter and resurrection topics already touched on in Chapter 21.

In addition, some new topics will be introduced for the purpose of intrigue and reader exploration.

In concert with the comments made in this book's To the Reader, this present appendix will emphasize meanings via an over-usage of various types of English format. For example, the terms "Paradise, Heaven, Hell" will generally be capitalized when in certain groupings; also, excessive *italics* and "quotation marks" will be employed for purposes of meticulous clarification. To repeat, this is done since one of this book's target audiences is made up of *second-language* persons in Africa and other foreign countries where I have taught.

In initial outline form, let's preview the major areas of this appendix:

A. Concerning 1 Peter 3:18–19 (see printed-out text below):

   1. To be contrasted: "*in the spirit*" with "*by the Spirit*"!

   2. As to the "prison" visited by the resurrected Jesus, *where* and *what* was it?

   3. Who were the "spirits" Jesus visited "in prison"?

B. Examination of Scripture's Perplexing Narrative of the Events of Easter Sunday—and beyond That Day

C. Theologically "Empty" Views Concerning the Resurrection of the Lord Jesus

D. "From Here to Eternity"

    1. Where are Paradise, Heaven, and Hell located?*

    2. Seminar notes on this topic!

*As stated again below, contrary to general principles of capitalization, this present Appendix 10 will capitalize *Paradise*, *Heaven*, and *Hell*.

1 Peter 3:18–19

The following are the two major translations of 1 Peter 3:18–19. They represent varying views that contain all the words that come into interpretive play:

> [18] "For Christ died once for our sins, the Righteous One for the unrighteous, to bring us to God. He was put to death in flesh but made alive **in spirit**, [19] in which He also went and preached to the spirits kept in prison . . . " (NET) [similarly, ESV, NASB; NIV (also see alternate reading in RSV that is referenced to 4:6: "to the spirit")].

> [18] "For Christ also suffered for sins once for all, the righteous for the unrighteous, that he might bring you to God. He was put to death in the flesh but made alive **by the Spirit**, [19] in which he also went and made proclamation to the spirits in prison . . . " (CSB) [similarly, CJB, (also see alternate reading in ESV, KJV, NASB, NIV, NKJV: "in the Spirit")].

Approaching 1 Peter 3:18–19

As stated in Chapter 21, it is beyond the scope of this book to go into every aspect of the various views expressed by theologians concerning the correct interpretation of the *whole* of 1 Peter

3:18–19, a passage traditionally used as absolute proof for "Christ's descent into hell." (For those who confess the Apostles' Creed, this doctrinal point is of vital importance.)

Page after page has been written to express the various views of this and that biblical interpreter. Present readers need to be reminded that 1 Peter 3:18–19 are the two verses with the most varying interpretations in the NT. We note the valuable assessment of Paul J. Achtemeier concerning 1 Peter 3:18–22: "There is little question that these verses constitute the most difficult passage in the entire letter"; and as to verse 19 itself, "This verse is one of the shorter, but surely the most problematic, in this letter, if not in the NT canon as a whole, and eludes any agreement on its precise meaning" (A, *IPH*, pp. 240, plus n. 10, and 252, respectively).

Since this is true, I will do my best to introduce readers to pertinent information, speak firmly where Scripture gives verifiable evidence, and painstakingly provide an abundance of references where readers can go to draw their own Scriptural conclusions. Be assured that all *essential* Easter matters in this present appendix will be defended in a most dogmatic way on the basis of solid Scriptural truth. The Bible should not be contradicted with wild theories that itch ears (2 Timothy 4:3), and, to be sure, some of the interpretations of this section of Scripture are truly "over the top." However, in regard to varying opinions that contain solutions that do *not* contradict other passages of God's Holy Word, I will choose to remain relatively neutral.

The Debate

Please do yourself a favor and reread 1 Peter 3:18 above and be very familiar with its content.

Alternative 1: Should the Greek words "*zōopoiētheis pneumati* in verse 18 be translated "made alive **in spirit**"? Do they indicate that Christ's "spirit" was now reunited with His dead body ("made alive")? Do they stand in paralleled contrast to the words "put to death **in flesh**" in the same verse?

To be considered: Recall that Jesus had "entrusted" His "spirit" to His Father" when He died at Calvary. Thus, on Easter morning His "body and spirit" (now back together) passed into a "state of exaltation." Thus, our initial translation of 1 Peter 3:18–19 possibly favors a *contrast* between "flesh" (state of humiliation) and "spirit" (state of exaltation). (Parallel support for this conclusion would rest upon Philippians 2:8–9.)

Alternative 2: Should the Greek words "*zōopoiētheis pneumati* in verse 18 be translated "made alive **by the Spirit**"? Do they indicate that the Holy Spirit raised Jesus Christ from the dead by putting His "spirit" and "body" back together?

To be considered: The translation "made alive **by the Spirit**" possibly finds support on the basis of Romans 8:11, and if a capitalized "Spirit" is meant by Peter, then the Holy Spirit raised

Christ from the dead and led Him in triumph to preach to the condemned "spirits" kept "in prison."

Inconclusive: Both translations of 1 Peter 3 seem Scripturally solid. Therefore, I doubt that Christian interpreters who favor one or the other of these differing views would be willing to bet their *eternal* salvation on either conclusion. For that reason alone, my final comments will leave this valuable discussion open, submitting it to God's wise domain and your investigative analyzation.

1 Peter 3:18 Further Examined

The words "made alive in spirit" or "made alive by the Spirit" must mean Jesus's body came alive *physically* when He resurrected. (Jesus's "spirit" never died, only His "body.") In both body and spirit, Christ then visited the "prison" of "spirits" who were condemned to all eternity. To expand the explanation, His "spirit" and "soul"—both of which had gone to "Paradise" after death (cp. Hebrews 4:12)—were now reunited with His non-decayed "body" (Psalm 16:9–10); He was "bodily" alive. The resurrected God-Man had now passed from His "state of humiliation" into His "state of exaltation" (see Philippians 2:5–11). Even if the text teaches that "the Spirit" raised Jesus from the dead and led Him in victory to the "spirits in prison," it still remains true, as stated, that the Spirit would have reunited Jesus's "spirit and body," both of which would now have passed into a "state of exaltation."

In this new state of existence, Jesus "always and fully" used power sent from His "divine nature" over to His "human nature." (As such, Christ's *human nature* had nothing to share with His *divine nature*, since the divine nature lacked nothing and therefore was not in need of anything that could be supplied by His *human nature*.)

In His new "state," Jesus now *regularly* did what He pleased. He no longer needed to *humiliate* Himself to accomplish redemption. That process was "finished." Now He could disguise Himself when desired; walk through solids when advantageous; do whatever to prove He was alive *bodily*, as, for example, when He ate "fish"—and the watching disciples could *not* see the fish go down His throat, since He was then again "flesh and blood," not just a "ghost." A doctor, like Luke, would be impressed with that—and was (24:36–43).

And if you think that is "deep," that's the easy stuff. 1 Corinthians 15:35–55 (especially v. 49) compares Jesus's resurrected body to the body all Christians will receive in heaven, a "spiritual body" (v. 44). Cannot wait to see how God pulls that one off!

The simplest it can be put on this side of eternity is to say that the risen Jesus also passed from the tomb into the "prison" of the condemned "spirits" with a "glorified" body, a body compared to our future, eternal bodies (cp. Philippians 3:21: ⸢The Lord Jesus Christ⸣ ". . . will change our humble bodies and make them like His *glorified* body . . .").

A Solid Dilemma

As your present Scriptural lead investigator, I most always have a definite opinion grounded on biblical data. However, in the case of "made alive **in spirit**" or "made alive **by the Spirit**," I cannot make up my mind; both views seem solid, and personally, I wish I could choose them both because they each have their strong points.

Alternative 1 again: I appreciate the translation "made alive *in spirit*." It makes a beautiful parallel with "put to death in flesh." If correct, it magnificently parallels Jesus's "states of humiliation and exaltation." This would be a perfect fit and parallel to Philippians 2:5–11. As such, Peter would be teaching that Christ died in His "state of humiliation" ("in flesh") but rose in His "state of exaltation" ("in spirit"). Support in favor of this **Alternative 1** can be viewed in K, *SCD*, pp. 151–152.; L, *IPJJ*, pp. 152–160; S, *FESP*, pp. 196–197; Dr. Martin Scharlemann's agreement is noted in A, *1PH*, p. 250, n. 130.)

Alternative 2 again: I equally relish this view. Jesus being raised by the Holy Spirit would be *another* great passage proving that all three Persons of the Trinity raised Jesus from the dead (see 1 Corinthians 15:15; John 10:18; Romans 8:11). Besides, if Peter's text teaches that the Holy Spirit led Jesus to the "prison of spirits," it parallels the Spirit *first* leading Jesus into the wilderness after His baptism to confront the devil, since the devil had been the *first* to bring evil into the world. Considering the implications of John 1:33, it would be most fitting that the Spirit should *first* lead the risen, victorious Christ into hell's domain to confront the evil spirits who had started the whole mess of human sin. Thus, I also like "Spirit" being capitalized. Support in favor of this **Alternative 2** can be examined in A, *1PH*, pp. 239, 250 and D, "BNT," section "II. Verse 18."

On the overall matter concerning "spirit" or "Spirit", also compare P, *R*, pp. 126–128. Tough, yet intriguing, stuff!

"He *Preached* to the Spirits Kept in Prison"

This next discussion is even more multifaceted than the former. Some of its wild speculations demand dogmatic rejection, while other parts are legitimately up for grabs. In reference to the latter, I refer investigative readers to the section below that will deal with the *locations* of Paradise, Heaven, and Hell, entitled "From Here to Eternity."

Some contend that Jesus went to hell or the "prison" of the condemned on Good Friday to suffer additionally for our sins. How can that be? He claimed, "It is finished!" Why would He have to do more *finishing*? Bad robot! Bad theology!

The *fourth* Christian creed, the Apostles' Creed, confesses "He descended into hell." The first three Christian creeds *[my numeric designation]* are found in the Bible:

A. Deuteronomy 6:4: "Listen Israel, the LORD, our God, the LORD are ˛a united˛ One" [N, *JT*, p. 113] (the three "GOD" words in this passage have *Trinitarian* implications);

B. Matthew 16:16: "You are the Christ [Messiah], the Son of the living God";

C. Philippians 2:11: "Jesus Christ is Lord!"

Deuteronomy 6:4 was the Trinitarian confession of God's people in the OT.

Matthew 16:16 became the required confession for any *Jew* who wished to become part of the believing Christian community following the first Pentecost in the Christian era.

Philippians 2:11 served as a "must" public testimony for any *Gentile* or *Greek* who wished to enter the Christian community in post-Pentecost times.

Interjection: In NT, post-Pentecost days, converted Jews had to confess *publicly* that they had come to believe Jesus of Nazareth *was* the Messiah whom the Jewish nation had long expected. As for Gentiles, they had to confess *publicly* that the only "Lord" they would now worship was the Lord Jesus, no longer Roman or Greek "gods," such as, Jupiter or Zeus, or the pantheon of gods common to Gentiles.

Now back to the Apostles' Creed. Concerning Jesus, it confesses that He "suffered under Pontius Pilate, was crucified, died, and was buried; He descended into hell, and on the third day He rose again." As stated in Chapter 21, the *time* factors seem *out of order*, that is, if one correctly contends that Jesus "descended into hell" or "went and preached to the spirits kept in prison" right *after* He resurrected.

Once again, observe that the true thought of the Apostles' Creed is that Jesus did visit the spirits kept in prison *after* He came alive physically; then following that, He *later* showed Himself to be *physically* alive by appearing to persons back on earth—outside the tomb.

Both events attest to the fact that Jesus was *physically* alive, possessing a body that had "flesh and bones," and that He was not just a "spirit" or "ghost" as were the "spirits" in prison (Luke 24:38–43).

Why?

If Jesus appeared to the condemned "spirits" in prison *only* as a "spirit" (without a resurrected body), what proof of His victory would that have been to the spirits condemned in eternity's prison? The *physical* resurrection of Christ served as proof that He, the new or Second Adam, had overcome sin and death and had now opened the gates to a new paradise.

(Bible investigators need to analyze this fact most carefully. Satan and His horde certainly would have continued to claim victory if Jesus had *not* appeared before them in *live, bodily* form.)

And as to those humans back on earth who also witnessed Christ's Easter resurrection, how could they have seen or touched Christ Jesus if He was not *bodily* alive?

Therefore, the creed does make it clear that Jesus visited "hell," a place which Peter calls a "prison," *before* He showed His resurrected body outside the tomb. (This should take care of the "time" concerns, at least for many.)

> See L, *IEPJJ*, p. 163: "The Scriptures know of only one . . . 'prison,' that confines 'spirits,' namely hell, 'hades,' 'the Gehenna of the fire'" (Matt. 5:22; 18:9)." Rabbis, and others, wrote about a "prison" or "dungeon" for the lost wicked (S, *FESP*, p. 199).

In Chronological Order, Easter Events—and beyond

1. Jesus rises from the dead some time following sunset. (This would be considered Holy Saturday to moderns; however, it was already Sunday in Jesus's culture; the "third day" after His death and burial.)

2. Jesus visits "spirits kept in prison" (1 Peter 3:19; cp. Isaiah 63:1–6).

3. Numerous women start out for Jesus's grave while it is still dark (John 20:1).

4. An "angel" rolls away the stone from the grave entrance; a "mighty" earthquake occurs; the guards at the tomb are frightened and flee (Matthew 28:2–4).

5. The women arrive at Jesus's grave after sunrise and see that the grave stone has been moved away (Mark 16:2–4). (Note: These women would *not* have known guards had been placed at the grave on Saturday.)

6. Without entering the grave, Mary from Magdala, one of those women, runs to tell the news of the rolled-away stone to the disciples, not suspecting that Jesus has

resurrected. Remember, she never looks inside the tomb before running away and holding the assumption that the tomb is empty and someone has moved Jesus's body (analyze John 20:1–2 in light of Mark 16:5–6).

7. The remaining women enter the grave and see two angels, one of whom tells them Jesus is alive. They leave to tell this *resurrection* news to the disciples (Mark 16:8; Matthew 28:8).

8. Following Mary's report, Peter and John race to and arrive at Christ's grave and see the folded burial clothes; they then leave (John 20:3–10).

9. Jesus appears to the women who have recently left the grave site, minus Mary from Magdala. They become the first humans to see Him alive (Matthew 28:8–9). (The contradiction seen at Mark 16:9 ["showed Himself *first* to Mary"] provides a side reason that many textual experts conclude that Mark 16:9–20 is *not* part of the original text, based on the solid fact that "a few of the older manuscripts and early translations omit" these verses [NET, p. 105, n. 16 *b*]. View the recent movie production "Fragments of Truth" [2018] to verify this conclusion.)

If the textually contested ending of Mark 16:9-20 is authentic, then numbers 9 and 10 of this listing must be flip-flopped on the basis of verse 9 of the Mark text or at least combined as "one scene," as explained by Edersheim in his extensive analyzation (E, *LTJM*, II, 621-622, plus n. 2 and 633, n. 2). Stoeckhardt, the brilliant 19th century German exegete, stated the contrasting position followed in this chronological listing (S, *BHNT*, pp. 298-300, NO. 144.8; NO. 145.1, 4, 5).

A most complex exegetical situation! (See Appendix 11, end of p. 266.)

10. Mary returns to the garden, enters the grave, and converses with two angels, and then back outside the grave, she sees Jesus, whom she initially mistakes for a regular gardener; however, she eventually recognizes Him when He says, "Mary" (John 20:11–18).

11. Verified by Matthew 27:52–53, the "resurrected" persons of Good Friday leave their graves and start appearing in Jerusalem!

12. Jesus walks with two disciples on the "road to Emmaus," initially hides His identity, but later reveals Himself at supper (Luke 24:13–33).

13. Jesus appears to Peter (1 Corinthians 15:5).

> The rotation of #12 and #13 remains uncertain. Possibly, these two appearances by the Christ should be flip-flopped. Others would say they should be *combined*, feeling that Simon Peter was one of the two men who were on the road to Emmaus (in particular, see Luke 24:34).

14. Jesus appears to His disciples on Easter evening, doors being locked and Thomas being absent (John 20:19–24).

15. A week later, Jesus appears to the disciples a second time when Thomas is present (John 20:26–29).

16. Jesus appears to "more than 500 Christians [literally: brothers] at one time" (1 Corinthians 15:6: when and where?).

17. Jesus appears to His half-brother James (1 Corinthians 15:7a: when?)

18. Jesus appears to "*all* the apostles" (1 Corinthians 15:7b: when?)

19. Jesus has breakfast with His disciples in Galilee (153 fish; "Peter, do you love Me?") (John 21:1–14).

20. Jesus meets "the Eleven" in Galilee ("The Great Commission"—Matthew 28:19–20).

21. Jesus ascends to heaven from the Mount of Olives forty days after His resurrection (Acts 1:9).

22. Jesus—via a heavenly vision—appears to Stephen as he is stoned to death (Acts 7:55).

23. Jesus appears to Saul [Paul] on the road to Damascus (Acts 9:3–5).

24. The apostles witness to the world concerning the "resurrected" Lord Jesus (cp. Acts 2–28 and the NT epistles which provide much geographical data).

25. Christ Jesus will visibly appear again when He comes a second time [His Second Advent] on the Last Day (Revelation 1:7).

Why Christ "Visited the Spirits Kept in Prison"

We now move on to the *reason* for Jesus's "prison" visit. If it was *not* to suffer further, as concluded above, then what was its purpose? To "preach to the spirits kept in prison," *prison* being one of Scripture's definitions of *hell*.

Cult leaders most often have formed their theology around the teaching that there is *no eternal* damnation, contending that a "loving" God would never condemn anyone to an *everlasting*, non-ending punishment. They can speculate all they wish, but the truth is that God is God and He has revealed the reality of hell in Scripture, whether one believes it or not. To agree with those, like the preterist John Bray, who believe that "eternal destruction" in 2 Thessalonians 1:9 does not mean *punishment forever without end* (B, *FW*, pp. 2–3), is so unscriptural; it also creates doubts in believers' minds as to whether they will live with Jesus *forever*. How can "forever and ever" mean one thing in Revelation 20:10c and something different in 22:5d? This is wishful

> Those who deny the reality of hell stand on very thin ice since Jesus's preaching ministry taught hell's existence multiple times. For example, see Matthew 5:22 and Luke 16:23; Peter the disciple concurs in 2 Peter 2:4.

thinking that does not exist in the mind of God. The problem with four-dimensional creatures, like us, is that we cannot yet think of "time" in terms of "eternal time." Everything then will be in the "now"—no past or future—just "present" torment or happiness.

The argument that a "loving God" would never send anyone to *hell* is a cop-out. Why would God send His Son to the hideous agony of the cross if there was no "hell" to endure or escape? Sir Francis Bacon: "People prefer to believe what they prefer to be true."

When visiting the "spirits," did Jesus preach them *out* of eternal damnation? Cannot be, for Jude 6 concludes: "And there were angels who did not keep their position of authority but left their estate. He put them in *everlasting* chains and gloom to be kept for the judgment of the great Day." Jesus did not preach the "Good News" of the Gospel to the spirits in prison; it was too late for them. What Luke 16:26 confirms for lost humans also applies to all evil spirits:

> . . . there is a wide chasm fixed between us and you [between those in heaven and those in hell], so that those who might want to cross from here [from heaven] over to you cannot do it, nor do any from there [from hell] come over to us [in heaven].

The "Up" and "Down" Problem

Did Jesus "ascend" or "descend" on Easter morning when He "*went* and preached to the spirits kept in prison"? Reality: The Greek term for *went* in 1 Peter 3:19 is the same term used in Acts 1:10–11 to describe Jesus's "ascension" into heaven. This would seem to contradict the Apostles' Creed: "He *descended* into hell." Das and Achtemeier most ably provide a complete discussion of the "up" and "down" situation at D, "BNT," section "III. Verse 19" and A, *IPH*, pp. 256–258, respectively.

Maybe I underestimate the importance of the matter, but overall it seems like a "tempest in a teapot." I note that Achtemeier, who strongly favors Jesus "ascending" to the spirits in prison, not "descending," does conclude that the Greek term translated *went* "refers to a journey, no more" (A, *1PH*, p. 257).

Yet, with the above being stated, and noting that certain NT passages speak of Jesus "descending" into the netherworld (Romans 10:7; Ephesians 4:8–10; also possibly Philippians 2:10; see S, *FESP*, pp. 320-321), there can be a sound reason why Peter uses an "ascension" word (*went*), instead of an expected "descended" term at 1 Peter 3:19. With the ascension of Enoch (Genesis 5:24) on his mind—and Jesus being the "new" Enoch bringing condemnation into the gates of hell's prison—one would expect Peter to use an "ascension" term since the first Enoch *ascended* and is reported in Jude 14–15 as prophesying coming "judgment" or "doom" on the "ungodly" (strongly implied by D, "BNT," section "III. Verse 19"; compare also 1 Enoch 67:8–13).

Both Das and Achtemeier, noted three paragraphs above, take the two events of 1 Peter 3:19 and 22 (Christ's prison visit and His ascension) as "one "journey" (D, "BNT," section "III. Verse 19" and A, *IPH*, p. 258). If so, then the Apostles' Creed would be *non*-chronological, yet historically factual. It would give interesting interpretive value to Psalm 68:18:

> You [the Lord Jesus] went up on high.
> You took prisoners captive.
> You received gifts from men.
> Surely the LORD God has made the rebellious submit.

But combining the events into "one" trip seems to muddy the waters. As stated in Chapters 21 and 22, I would separate the two events of Easter and the Ascension by forty days. Based on Hebrews 9:11–12, it could be stated that Jesus already had entered heaven itself *while on the cross* to purify the "MOST HOLY PLACE" that had been contaminated by Satan and his demon followers shortly after the original Creation was completed (cp. even Job 1:6). That was not a *physical* ascension; it was a blood-cleansing action right from the cross. Subsequently, in

Chapter 21, it was concluded that Jesus could *not* have "ascended" on Easter morning (reference John 20:17) since that event had to wait for forty days to parallel the "revelation" experiences of Moses and Elijah (recall Chapter 22).

Very complex investigative analyzation, to be sure!

With all the Scriptural passages cited by Das and Achtemeier, both as to "descent" and "ascent" into the "prison" or "netherworld," (and they have done a most thorough job), one should suspect that Scripture is communicating to *finite* minds that are bound by geographical limitations, minds that generally think of heaven and hell as "up" or "down." (With that in mind, this becomes a good time to anticipate our future section entitled "From Here to Eternity"—with its discussion of eternity's "dimensions." It will aim to show how earth, Paradise, Heaven, and Hell are most likely not "up" or "down," but possibly in different realms that can be experienced only one at a time. This probing of Scripture may help investigators better comprehend a possible solution.)

Who Were the "Spirits" in Prison?

If former comments in this appendix have been complex, this new section promises to reach an apex of varying opinions. We now return to 1 Peter 3:19. Countless words have been written concerning the *identity* of the "spirits in prison." (Wild speculations run alongside other more sane Scriptural possibilities.)

On **level 1** the main debate revolves around whether Jesus only preached to *evil* angelic spirits or whether these "spirits" also included human unbelievers who were lost for eternity. Achtemeier (A, *1PH*, p. 255), Das (D, "BNT," section "III. Verse 19"), and Selwyn are convinced that the term *spirits* in the NT is limited to evil angelic beings. However, since Peter references the "ungodly people" of Noah's time in 2 Peter 2:5 (possibly also in 1 Peter 3:20), speaking of Noah as a "preacher of righteousness," there could possibly be a basis to draw a valid *parallel* between Noah's preaching and that of Jesus to those same lost people (view Selwyn thoughts at S, *FESP*, pp. 198–199). The only difference would be that Noah had previously condemned sin (preaching the need for "righteousness"), calling for repentance, and proclaiming the availability of forgiveness, whereas Jesus would only have preached His victory over sin and unbelief. Imprisonment in *hell*'s corridors had already spelled hopelessness for those there, with no further possibility that their eternal sentence would be commuted. If "spirits" is intended by Peter to include both evil angelic beings *and* human unbelievers who had now died, then Jesus's Easter preaching spelled eternal doom for both groups. So sad! May we *personally* not hear such preaching directed at us from Jesus on the Last Day.

On **level 2** the question becomes whether the "spirits" only included those evil angelic spirits who *in the days of Noah* influenced the evil that caused the worldwide flood and its judgment. This view is multileveled and includes many different interpretations of Genesis 6:1–4.

This particular discussion revolves around *who* the "sons of God," the "daughters of men," and the "*Nephilim*" of Genesis 6:2 and 4 were. I am not very sympathetic with two aspects of the many views offered. These I will discuss very dogmatically and then move on in a more neutral manner and let you the investigator research the sources cited so you can come to your own conclusions.

A. What about Evil Angels Having Sex with Human Women (Part 1)

1. After much thought, I cannot entertain even one iota of agreement with those who take "sons of God" to be evil demon spirits who took on human bodies, came into our earthly realm, and then had sexual relations with "the daughters of men," subsequently producing "*Nephilim*" ("tyrants" and/or "heroes" [AAT], "giants" [KJV, NKJV]).

   a. In light of Genesis 1:11–12, 21, 24–25; 6:20; and 7:14, "kinds" can only reproduce "after their own kind." Certainly, a demon spirit "kind" does not have the same DNA as humans and therefore could not have impregnated human females (H, "WWN," p. 56). Besides, Jesus's words in Mark 12:5 teach that holy angelic beings do not marry or have sex in their realm of being. It would also imply the same to be true of the evil angels, I would think.

   b. Added to this, evil angels are "spirits" who do *not* possess the sexual, fleshly apparatus capable of impregnating women, nor is there any indication in the Bible that they would have the miraculous ability to obtain such.

   c. But most of all, nowhere in Scripture do we observe even *one* example of evil angels being able to *incarnate* themselves, even to take on the mere appearance of a human being (cp. H, "WWN," p. 58). Only Hollywood and caricatures that picture Satan with a pitchfork present such fantasies. True, the holy angelic being Gabriel was able to take on the appearance of a "man" (Daniel 9:21), but that does not say angelic demons can do the same. To give Satan or one of his unholy minions such powers would nullify the *uniqueness* of Jesus's coming in the flesh and being "incarnated," a phenomenon that we call "the Trinity's greatest miracle" ever. Why would one diminish Jesus's incarnation by imagining that Satan or demons can mimic the same?

d. Note that Gabriel, when taking the appearance of a man, did not become a "man" in the real sense of the word. He only took on the "appearance" of a male human being. Rather, only Jesus, coming out of the "spirit" world, obtained a real human body (1 Timothy 3:16; cp. John 4:24).

e. Many say the phrase "sons of God" refers to both good and evil angels in Job 1:6 and 2:1. Such argumentation is on shaky ground. In both cases, "sons of God" are mentioned apart from "Satan" and his presence before Almighty God. Note Job 38:7, where it is most clear that the created angels (when all were still holy), were called "the sons of God." It would seem strange to continue to refer to *fallen* angels as "sons of God." Others will disagree.

f. But more important is the absolute fact that *believing* humans are also called "sons of the Most High," "sons of Israel," "sons of the living God," and "sons of God" in several places in both the OT and the NT (see H, "WWN," pp. 56–57).

If the "sons of God" in Genesis 6:2 are the now-imprisoned angels, the most they could have done in Noah's day is have influenced humans to sin sexually by *spiritually* moving them to disobey God's Law, which is written in human hearts (Romans 2:14–15). This would seem to be the case as it is yet today. Evil angels tempt humans to commit fornication and adultery. They also tempt humans to become "yoked together with unbelievers" in marriage (2 Corinthians 6:14). Thus, very often, believers are pulled down by unbelieving partners to give up their saving faith (cp. 1 Corinthians

10:12). This seems to have been the situation in Genesis 6, believers intermarried with unbelievers and their children became unbelievers too.

2. More needs to be said.

    a. The basic argument concerning evil angels having sexual intercourse with human women is taken from a writing called *1 Enoch* (15:2–5), coming from somewhere during the last two centuries BC. (The patriarch Enoch was from the seventh generation after Adam and was taken to heaven alive according to Genesis 5:24.) Even though 1 Enoch never reached Scriptural or even apocryphal status in the Christian Church, many bow down at its altar and overly endorse its pontifications, in part, because 1 Enoch 1:9 is quoted in the NT at Jude 14–15. At best, 1 Enoch is listed among the books labeled Pseudepigrapha ("false writings"). Only the Ethiopic Church regards 1 Enoch as canonical (B, *BP*, pp. 171, 215). (See S, *IIP*, pp. 142–144 for a summary of 1 Enoch.)

    b. Concerning the belief that Genesis 6 teaches that evil angels had sex with human females is debunked by Selwyn when he concludes: "The idea that human sin derived from this miscegenation was a product of much later Jewish thought . . ." (S, *FESP*, p. 201). By the way, contrary to "clear Jewish tradition," any teaching that evil angels were—via their generating progeny with "daughters of men"—the cause of Noah's flood is untenable (note A, *1PH*, p. 256; see 1 Enoch 10:10; 15:3; 2 Enoch 18:2–5). Genesis 6:5–7 teaches that the cause of the flood was evil humankind, not evil angels (see S, *FESP*, p. 201). However, Achtemeier (A, *1PH*, p. 261) seems correct in observing that 1 Peter 3:20a "reflects" the 1 Enoch "tradition" as involving evil angels in the flood scenario. Yet, that does *not* say Peter is teaching that these angels *directly* produced children by having sexual intercourse with human women. As stated above, these angels were only the "spiritual" cause, not a direct sexual cause, of the flood.

B. What about 1 Enoch?

1. That several intertestamental writings and their traditions were known to first-century AD Jews is a well-acknowledged fact among modern-day Bible scholars. The bone of contention concerns the usage of these writings by NT authors. Or, to probe by way of a question: Was the NT dependent on books like 1 Enoch, or were books like 1 Enoch expansions of OT truths, enhanced by personal theology developed beyond any guidance from the Holy Spirit? Of course, the latter would be diametrically opposed to the limits set down by 2 Timothy 3:16: "All Scripture is inspired by God"; 2 Peter 1:21: ". . . no prophecy was ever spoken because a man decided to prophesy but men said what God gave them to say as they were directed by the Holy Spirit."

2. Google "Books of Enoch-Encyclopedia of the Bible-Bible Gateway"; it records:

Parallels with 1 Enoch from practically every section of the NT can be cited, though it is probably going too far to say that every NT writer must have been familiar with the book. Perhaps the most familiar reference to 1 Enoch in the NT is the famous passage in Jude 14–15. In addition to this apparent literary dependence, however, many of the concepts familiar to us from the NT appeared either first or most prominently in 1 Enoch. Thus, for example, the spiritual nature of the messianic reign. Thus also the titles used to refer to the Messiah, such as "Christ" or "The Anointed One," "The Righteous One," "The Elect One," and "The Son of Man." The NT concepts of *sh*ᵉ*ōl*, resurrection, and demonology also bear striking similarities to those of 1 Enoch.

3. To conclude with the above quote that "many of the concepts familiar to us from the NT appeared either *first or most prominently [my* *emphasis]* in 1 Enoch" is highly questionable—at least in terms of the conjecture "*first.*" These "concepts" were already contained in the canonical books of the OT. If we had space in this appendix, references to Christ's coming "messianic reign," plus titles, such as "Christ" ["Messiah", "The Anointed One"], "The Righteous One," "The Elect One," and "The Son of Man" would be shown, in detail, *not* to be *firsts.* The writers of 1 Enoch—and there were multiple authors—copied, as for example, from Daniel 7:13 ("Son of Man"). Of course, if one falsely dates Daniel c. 165 BC, instead of in the sixth-century BC, one can give 1 Enoch much credit.

Also note that King David did not need to wait for the authors of 1 Enoch to enlighten him as to the various flavors of the concept of *sh⁽ᵉ⁾ōl* when some 800 years before he wrote Psalm 16:10 and 86:13. Additionally, Dr. Steinmann has furnished solid biblical data pertaining to the authentic date for the penning of the book of *Daniel* (S, *D*, pp. 1–19; see also S, *AP*, pp. 171–179, 349).

4. 1 Enoch is given way too much credit for soundness of truth; rather, it should be given credit for its original embellishments! From where did information, such as that at 1 Enoch 20:1–8, originate? Scriptural investigators should stick to facts laid out in such OT books as Genesis, Isaiah, Ezekiel, Daniel, and Zechariah, books penned long before 1 Enoch danced off into never-never land with questionable data concerning, for example, *angelology.* The reality of the matter is that 1 Enoch should be compared to our present-day Top Ten best *fictional* sellers.

Also, as for recorded truth in 1 Enoch, even fictional stories incorporate occasional truths. Did the Holy Spirit pick up one of these truths and give it to Jude? Or were there wholesome traditions passed down from days before the flood that survived in oral tradition that the Holy Spirit used to inspire NT writers?

5. A reality: Just because the Holy Spirit communicated a piece of real truth to Jude from a part of 1 Enoch does not mean 1 Enoch's content, as a whole, was truthful or inspired.

C. In Conclusion Concerning the "Sons of God":

1. The only correct interpretations of Genesis 6:2 and 4, it appears to me, is to say that (a) believers ("sons of God") intermarried with unbelievers ("daughters of men"), and their children became unbelievers, the *Nephilim*. Or, (b) the chosen line of Seth (Sethites, Genesis 4:25–26) intermarried with the unbelieving line of Cain (Cainites—Genesis 4:16–22), and their children became the "wicked" ones (*Nephilim*) referred to at Genesis 6:5.

2. Most likely, *nephilim* comes from a root verb (*nāphal*), meaning "to fall." Along with Bodie Hodge (H, "WWN," p. 53), I take the term *nephilim* to mean "fallen ones," who, in turn, could have been progeny that turned out to be all types of people who "fell away" from God. Some could have been "giants" in size; others, "heroes" or "men of renown," as in "tyrants," tycoons, famous inventors (cp. Numbers 13:33; Genesis 4:19–22). But one thing characterized these *nephilim* offspring in God's eyes as He became more and more disenchanted with them (Genesis 6:5–7); it was their rebellious sin and unbelief.

Note Genesis 6:4: "In those days [Noah's day], *as well as later*, there were *Nephilim* on the earth." This would indicate that the post-flood Nimrod, the empire builder, would also fit the *"nephilim"* description, since he most likely spearheaded the Tower of Babel anti-God project (Genesis 10:8–12; 11:1–4). Did evil angels again incarnate themselves *after* the flood to impregnate more "daughters of men"? Hardly what the text intended to communicate!

3. A rapid understanding of the 1 Enoch tradition and its "likely" influence on 1 Peter 3:19 is concisely presented by Achtemeier (A, *1PH*, pp. 255–256, including notes 188–192). Also see Hodge (H, "WWN," p. 61) for an enlightening discussion of the book of Enoch as it cites Chapters 6 and 7 upon which Jewish non-biblical tradition, as well as Josephus, built their conclusions that the "sons of God" were fallen angels who came down and impregnated human women. (Your Google reading experience, as given under H, "WWN" (Hodge) in our Bibliography, will be well worth your time.)

Final Thoughts Concerning "the Spirits in Prison"

As to the "spirits" in prison, it would be hard to imagine that Satan was *not* among those confronted by Jesus on Easter morning. He started the whole sinful mess. If an interpreter only identifies the "spirits" as sexual deviants, it is inconceivable that Satan was not the instigator behind it all, and thus he would be in the same "prison" that Jesus "visited"—and so we conclude he was! Besides, if Satan was not already in the "prison of hell," how could he later be "set free" from that prison's "bottomless pit" "for a little while" [KJV: "a little season"] (Revelation 20:1–3)?

Because of the plethora of information presented in books and articles concerning 1 Peter 3:18–20, it seems wise at this point to turn things over to your investigative abilities and direct you to references that provide further data concerning the various areas of concern.

The whole article on 1 Peter 3:18–22 by Das has a wealth of contextual information that is most insightful (D, "BNT"). The in-depth commentary analysis by Achtemeier is a masterpiece of exegesis (A, *1PH*, pp. 239–274). In my humble estimation, Selwyn's comments meticulously cover all the varying opinions on 1 Peter 3:18–20 with scholarly open-mindedness (S, *FESP*, pp. 195–203). Lenski is also of value (L, *IEPJJ*, pp. 152–169).

I am going to remain somewhat neutral as to whether "spirits" refers only to evil angels or to both evil angels and lost human beings. Since the NT seems primarily to refer to evil angels as "spirits," I, along with Selwyn (S, *FEP*, p. 198), slightly favor this position—and with good reason.

To repeat: If Jesus had to confront Satan *first* after His baptism (since the devil had initiated the whole mess of sin), then why would Christ not *first* visit Satan and his imprisoned hoard on Easter morning to announce His victory? That He could have confronted lost humans at the same time would be possible, maybe probable, though *secondary* in thought. (Comments on the term *spirits* is ably presented in *AGAGNT*, p. 711.)

Thus ends our presentation of Jesus's Easter morning "visit and preaching to the spirits kept in prison," its meaning and triumphal significance.

Empty "Resurrection" Faith

Another crucial, crucial Easter factor now demands our utmost concern and treatment. Much needs to be condensed into a few pages.

We begin by remembering that right after the beginning of this world, the devil turned everything topsy-turvy as he tried to dethrone God and set himself up as #1. His total success was stalled by God's plan of redemption that was eventually carried to initial completion against Satan at Calvary. The reality of *Forgiveness* was set in stone. Yet, God's *test period* for humanity was not at an end (cp. Romans 16:20); the devil would still have "a little while" ("a little season"—KJV) to throw everything, including the spiritual kitchen sink, at the Trinity's people.

For some fifty-six centuries—until the AD 1700s when the Age of the Enlightenment set the worst forms of *humanism* into action—the world's human population was *theocentric* (God- or deity-centered), at least to the extent that each society believed in some type of higher being, whether the true One or not. Then came a big shift in the worldview of thousands in the societies of the so-called "newly enlightened." To be sure, the vast majority of humanity continued to believe in some type of god who rules over the universe as well as over the lives of individuals. Still, humanism—with its companion *macroevolution*—gained much ground. In its worst form, labeled *secular humanism*, this human philosophy moved the true God to a much lower elevation than the Bible was and is willing to go. Read "Secular Humanism" for a total scope of the subject (M/S, *HTR*, pp. 459–478).

The fangs of the "old serpent" (Revelation 12:9) began to reach even deeper into *Christian* circles. It came in the forms of *existentialism* ["whatever you believe to be true for you yourself, then that is surely true"] and *neo-orthodoxy* [the so-called *new* orthodoxy, which was anything but orthodox]. For example, neo-orthodoxy invaded European theology where theological students began to graduate with too many "Bs" in their Easter bonnets—Buber, Barth, Baillie, Brunner, Bultmann. Traditional Bible interpretations began to be ripped from their Scriptural foundations by such theologians who distorted Christian truth.

(Another "B" is dealt with below in the section entitled "The Bonhoeffer Enigma").

For those interested, it can be noted that whereas the term *existentialism* was applied to "theological" aspects, John Dewey's *pragmatism* ["whatever works for you without causing personal consternation or guilt, then do it"] became an acceptable practice in the daily lives of many. Secular school systems—secondary education through higher education—became permeated with this bogus-type of thinking which often ended up forcing its practitioners into the offices of psychiatrists and psychologists, and sometimes into the throes of suicide. In an extended form, *pragmatism* can say that theft, adultery, fornication, and lying are fine if they work for you and do not leave harmful aftereffects, but if they do, cease the practice.

Think: Politicians continually apply Dewey's pragmatism. When in farming country, they promise growers what they want to hear, while in the next breathe, they promise city dwellers the opposite. If it works, then do it; it will get you more votes.

In the same way, consider the philosophy of *existentialism*. If you believe there is a god, then there is a god, and if you do *not*, then there is no god.

Let's see how those twin philosophies work out in the real world of sane thinking. Go and stand in the middle of a road where an eighteen-wheeler is coming right at you at a high rate of speed. Then tell yourself the truck is not there because you, existentially and pragmatically, do *not* believe the truck is there. No matter what you believe, you will still be dead.

Loosely reminds me of an associated parallel in American society. It is said that "he who dies with the most toys, wins. Someone added with humor and truth: "Yet, he is still dead."

Back to Christianity's Neo-orthodox Invasion

To be sure, Satan's deceptions in neo-orthodoxy's new *humanistic* Eden proved to be clever. Neo-orthodoxy kept the old acceptable theological terms but filled them with new meanings. In addition, secular terms also came into vogue within seminaries. "Myth" became a key catchword that took on new connotations, far from its former meanings that had been associated with Greek mythology. All of a sudden, miracles like Christ's virgin birth and His resurrection became doctored-up doctrines in "sheep's clothing." Many in the church were fooled: old words became packed with new meaning for the young, while older church members heard the same terms and took them for old truths.

Let me explain.

Note two German words for *history: Historie* and *Geschichte* or *Heilsgeschichte.* The first—*Historie*—denotes everyday history, like a person going to the store to buy milk. Theologian Bultmann put Jesus's crucifixion and death into this category. However, he put Jesus's resurrection into a *supra*-historical realm, the realm of *Geschichte* or *Heilsgeschichte* ["salvation history"]. In short, the "Jesus" of regular history died and is still buried somewhere in the Holy Land; yet, the "Christ" of faith lives in the hearts of believers, even to this very day (alive only by faith, but non-resurrected physically).

In other words, the "Jesus" of *Historie*, that is, the Jesus of everyday history is *not* the same as the "Christ" of *Geschichte* or *Heilsgeschichte* salvation history. Under such circumstances, the ears of both young and old hear the term "resurrection" on Easter Sunday with contradictory meanings. When older believers hear, "*Christ* is risen," they believe their (neo-orthodox influenced) preacher is saying, "*Jesus* is risen," while the young people have been trained to make a distinction between the names "Jesus" and "Christ." These young moderns only hear that "Christ" is alive by faith, while they now believe that the "Jesus" of Good Friday is not really risen; He is still dead and decayed, lying in some grave around Jerusalem yet today.

I have another term to cover this type of false Scriptural interpretation: *Gobbledygook*, pure nonsense.

Nowhere does Scripture indicate the right to rip Christ's resurrection or His ascension narratives out of the context of ordinary history. The well-known and respected church historian Philip Schaff comments that from beginning to end the NT presents Christ's resurrection as "historical fact" (S, *HCC*, I, 172). He adds: "It is either the greatest miracle or the greatest delusion which history records" (S, *HCC*, I, 173; also consider S, *HCC*, I, section 8: "*Central Position of Christ in the History of the World*," 56–59). Edersheim comes at the whole "history" necessity from another angle: "If the story of His Birth be true, we can believe that of His Resurrection; if that of His Resurrection be true, we can believe that of His Birth" (E, *LTJM*, II, 621).

I interrupt to tell a true story, humorous if not so sad. A pastor, influenced by the false approach mentioned above, went to make a home call to one of his shut-ins. He forgot his Bible and asked to use the one belonging to this parishioner. When opening it, he was dismayed to see passages cut out and even whole pages torn out. He asked, "Why?" The response: "Pastor, every time you questioned the truth of a passage, larger text, or chapter of the Bible, I followed your teaching and cut them out of my Bible."

Why not, if she trusted her pastor? Sad reality.

Though personally not in agreement with much from the pen of the famous German theologian Wolfhart Pannenberg, one who strangely denied the doctrine of Christ's virgin birth and yet held firmly to His physical resurrection, his following statement calls open-minded thinkers to attention: "Whether the resurrection of Jesus took place or not is a *historical [my emphasis]* question, and the historical question at this point is inescapable. And so the question has to be decided on the level of historical argument" (quoted from M, *EDV*, p. 188).

(Pannenberg is known as a "critical" Bible scholar which means—via the "critical method" of modern textual consideration—he can endorse Christ's physical resurrection and yet question the validity of His virgin birth. Why? He judges the Scriptural evidence for the former *more substantial* than that of the latter. This is pure human subjectivity, and it must be viewed as flawed when one considers, as mentioned above, that it is a medical *doctor* who reports and endorses the "virgin birth" of Jesus, and that doctor is none other than Luke, a great research scholar who writes very sophisticated Greek in his books of Luke and Acts. Certainly not a quack doctor.)

And to prove that the infection of neo-orthodox and post-modern thinking still permeates today's Christianity big time, note the following nonsensical quote from John C. Holbert, April 20, 2014:

> It remains finally impossible for me to believe that a very dead Jesus somehow has burst back into the world of the living. Yes, I know that "with God all things are possible," but my scientific credulity only strains so far. I simply cannot accept that on this day *[Easter]* we are announcing and celebrating . . . that a corpse has been resuscitated—again, that the focus of our attention is on the living body of Jesus. Since I believe that all of this is a sacred narrative, a story theology, I cannot focus on Jesus; my focus must always be on God. God, it seems, on Easter Day and on every other day is finally the God of life, fully opposed to the powerful and ever-present forces of death (H, "*RN*").

I suspect your investigative skills have detected that Holbert does *not* believe that Jesus is God. That tells the whole story as to why his resurrection theology is so out of line with the testimony of Scripture (cp. John 20:28).

My personal conviction after all is said: Either a person believes the "whole" of Scripture's *historical* report or "none" of it, even if it only seems partially true or wrong at times.

Let's note the authoritative Thomas Arnold (1795–1842), who held the chair of modern history at Oxford University:

I have been used for many years to study the histories of other times, and to examine and weigh the evidence of those who have written about them, and I know of no one fact in the history of mankind which is proved by better and fuller evidence of every sort, to the understanding of a fair inquirer, than the great sign which God hath given us that Christ died and rose again from the dead (A, *"ER"*).

To be recorded is a question raised years ago by Carl F. Henry in *Christianity Today*. Without naming names, I repeated that same question to one of my famous professors from Europe: "If you would have been outside the tomb of Jesus on Easter morning when He was speaking to Mary, and you had had a camera, could you have snapped Christ's picture? The professor did not answer the question, and another professor signaled me to be quiet. The whole class got the point. A physically risen Jesus could have had His picture taken; the neo-orthodox Christ of faux faith never existed physically to be photographed.

"History can be removed from Christian theology only by the total destruction of theology itself." You can view this conclusion when you google "Karl Barth and Contemporary Theology of History." Here the prolific theologian Dr. John Warwick Montgomery deals with Barth's whole separation of *Historie* and *Geschichte* or *Heilsgeschichte* and his separation of history from theology. (The above quote can be found on page 45 of Montgomery's essay on Barth's theology.)

With all the above being said, what is your investigative verdict? Is your "resurrection" faith *full* or running on *empty*?

The Bonhoeffer Enigma

Why was Dietrich Bonhoeffer not grouped with all the "Bs" above? What justifies that? He was a most famous of student of Karl Barth. Some even claim him to be the greatest "Lutheran" scholar since Luther, and many evangelical leaders also see him as a great Christian champion. Some of his advocates are so entranced by his writings that they almost place him in heaven at the right hand of Christ. (Obviously, over exaggeration to make a point!) Mostly, Bonhoeffer is remembered as a theological figure who put his Christian convictions into action by standing up to the atrocities of Hitler and Nazism. His most famous works are *The Cost of Discipleship* and *Letters and Papers from Prison*.

On the other side of opinion come those who see Bonhoeffer as a heretic, a false teacher in sheep's clothing. They would claim that Luther would disown him (and Bultmann) in a heartbeat, both of whom they label as pseudo-Lutheran teachers. So we ask, *How do Bonhoeffer's theological views* or *writings generate such diametrically opposed evaluations?* (I will repeat this question below after giving you resources to check out varying reviews.)

You will find opposing opinions of all kinds: (1) Bonhoeffer endorsed Christ's virgin birth; no, he denied it though he claimed to believe in the "Incarnation of Christ." (Try to figure that contradiction out, if you can!) (2) He taught the physical resurrection of Jesus; no, he did not, that is, not in a consistent sense. (3) Bonhoeffer confirmed the ascension of Jesus into heaven; no, you have to know that he did not believe it in a true historical sense. (4) He was *not* a "universalist"; yes, he did think everyone makes it into heaven. Wow, what contrasts! (You will be surprised at the evidence that can be given on both sides.)

Here are some places where you can go to get a feeling of the situation. Google "Buber and Bonhoeffer on the Resurrection of Jesus" and then click on the various links, especially "Bonhoeffer Speaks Today: Following Jesus At All Costs." Also, google "Bonhoeffer" and choose the link, "Metaxas's Counterfeit Bonhoeffer," as well as google "Barth and Bonhoeffer on the Resurrection of Jesus." After this evaluation, and most importantly, Google two other designations: "The Troubling Truth about Bonhoeffer's Theology" and "Dietrich Bonhoeffer-General Teachings/Activities." At the end of the latter, Dr. G. Archer Weniger is quoted as saying, "If there is wholesome food in a garbage can, then one can find some good things in Bonhoeffer, but if it be dangerous to expect to find nourishment in a garbage can, then Bonhoeffer must be totally rejected and repudiated as blasphemy. It is worse than garbage" (*FBF Information Bulletin*, May 1977, p. 12).

Again, *How do Bonhoeffer's theological views* and *writings generate such diametrically opposed evaluations?* The answer lies in Bonhoeffer's *neo-orthodox* approach which uses theological language that is different from the everyday language of regular humans. In fact, that is why one can make Bonhoeffer's theology say just about anything after reading all his statements. So sad!

In theology, some say the *greatest* sin a teacher of God's word can make is to be *unclear*. Bonhoeffer seems to be a master of this when his various writings are compared. They certainly are *not* crystal clear and the trumpet he sounds for God does not give a certain sound to prepare Christians for battle (cp. 1 Corinthians 14:8).

His theology seems to have changed from time to time, and yet not in the overall scheme of things; he always seems to have remained a type of neo-orthodox theologian. What he believed when he died is anyone's guess, and as to entrance into heaven, well, we never know where any of our fellow humans go; only God knows that.

In my opinion, and others can rightfully claim greater expertise as to Bonhoeffer's overall theology, I suspect that Bonhoeffer was influenced in his seminary years by theologies and philosophies that continued to guide him, even after he seemed to have shaken off some of them. The sad reality is this. When one runs with the big theologians, it is hard to reject former teachers completely with the fear that you will lose your standing among your revered peers. Such was the case already in Jesus's day: "Yes, they [the Pharisees] loved to be praised by people more than by God" (John 12:43).

Much of the evaluation problem concerning Bonhoeffer is that people view him (and rightly so) as a great man of courage who gave his life for his political and moral principles, standing up to Hitler and then being martyred on the last day of World War II. This sacrifice would be, as your research will show, in line with Bonhoeffer's high regard for Christ's Sermon on the Mount.

Yet, that sermon is not the *essence* of the saving Gospel, is it? Which brings me to two significant factors in Bonhoeffer's theology. It seems to be missing—in a glaring way—reference to the importance of personal forgiveness for each person *as an individual* through the shed blood of Jesus. It seems to me Bonhoeffer prefers to see salvation as a *corporate* thing, rather than *individual*. In this connection, readers of Bonhoeffer's works will find that he has a totally different view of "church" than did the Apostle Paul and Luther; a view, it appears, somewhere between a Lutheran and a Roman Catholic position.

But most disturbing is Bonhoeffer's failure to consistently endorse Christ's *physical* resurrection. In places he confesses it, and then in other places where one would expect him to state it, he most often falls short of saying it *directly*. Bonhoeffer also seems to avoid absolute *doctrinal* conclusions. Case in point. He is accused of teaching universalism, that is, in the end "all" people will enter into God's grace and salvation, *but* he always avoids going that last step of endorsement, though readers expect it to follow as a logical conclusion to what Bonhoeffer has been saying. Readers are left hanging as they expect a foregone conclusion. Thus, a reading of Bonhoeffer usually fails to offer a final, definite foundation for *individual* certainty of salvation; only vague hopes linger.

It's easy to admire a man like Bonhoeffer who held high moral views beneficial to humankind, but political correctness is not the biblical basis for sound teaching and Christian salvation (Romans 3:28).

In so many ways, Bonhoeffer remained a student of Barth; yet in reality, some of his teachings reflect a pre-Pannenberg approach. In short, Bonhoeffer can be made to fit the views of many varying positions within Christian denominationalism. Thus, as an evaluator, I would say that what Bonhoeffer taught with the right hand, he took away with the left.

> For the benefit of the experienced theologian, I would sum things up by saying that Bonhoeffer was much better at dealing with Romans 12–15 than teaching Romans 3–8. In terms of more current events, and this may explain Bonhoeffer's present popularity, his teachings fit well with today's yearning for "social justice" and "world peace."

To end this present section, I relate a humorous yet sad incident that followed a lecture at a famous Lutheran university. A friend of mine was leaving a lecture hall and was behind two young students who were ecstatic over the lecture. This friend was lost as to what the professor had said, so he interrupted the fellow students, asking, "What did Professor X say?" The answer, "We don't know, but it was beautiful." Guess that's the arena the Bonhoeffer's of this world have left us: Questionable content with emotional beauty that promises some type of hope, maybe even some type of hope based in a "christ" of our own creativity.

(See R, *DB* for a most balanced evaluation of the *pros and cons* concerning Bonhoeffer's theology.)

Warning: Welcome to the following discussion that will look at a possible concept of "Paradise" *in contrast to* "Heaven." Remember that Jesus did say to the thief on the cross, "Today you will be with Me in Paradise" (Luke 23:43). He did *not* use the term "heaven," a term with which He was well-acquainted, as He often did speak of the "Kingdom of *heaven*."

Let me be clear up front. I will draw no dogmatic conclusion at the end of the discussion. This section is merely "exploratory"—but worthy of discussion by Scriptural inspectors since it is a category brought up on the pages of Holy Writ.

But you need to realize one thing with absolute certainty: Whether your departed loved ones who trusted in Jesus Christ for eternal salvation are in Paradise *or* the Paradise of Heaven (explained below) between death and His Last Coming, they are at perfect "rest" in the arms of the Savior, as is expressed in Daniel 12:13.

This is every believer's "comfort"—now and forever.

"From Here to Eternity"

The present subtitle—"From Here to Eternity"—is taken from a novel (1951) and also a subsequent movie of the same name (1953). It nicely fits this section which examines the "heavens" of Genesis 1:1 and discusses the possible "locations" of "Hell, Paradise, and Heaven" in light of various Scriptural references. (Contrary to common usage, we shall usually capitalize these three locations.) Let's begin with a valuable quote from Yoel Natan (N, *JTS*, p. 142):

> Both Augustine and Einstein agree that there was less than
> 'nothing' before God began to create, and Augustine, along with the
> rest of the Christian Church, would affirm that until God began

to create, there was nothing but God only, neither an empty black universe nor even what we think of as heaven.

1. Following God's creation of "time" ("In the beginning"), He created "the heavens" (Genesis 1:1; Hebrew term "heavens" is plural, contrary to the singular in the 1611 KJV translation: "heaven" (NKJV update: "heavens").

   The *first* heaven would be the sky and atmosphere around our earth; the *second* heaven the place we know as the universe's solar system, and the *third* heaven the place *possibly* created for the angels from the beginning and/or for those holy angels as well as for the souls of believers who are no longer alive on earth between their death and their resurrection on the Last Day.

   Recall that there must be at least three "heavens," since Paul was taken up into the "third" heaven (called "paradise"—2 Corinthians 12:2, 4).

   Also note that God does not need a place to dwell as He is *everywhere* at-one-and-the-same time, even being in "hell" with His angry face; He is omnipresent (Jeremiah 23:24). Yet, recall that 1 Kings 22:19 seems to talk of God's throne being in heaven.

2. Question: Could "the heavens" indicate that God also created various *layers* of space, places, or dimensions, not only space "going out" but even places encompassing other *dimensions* beyond our *four* dimensional world of height, width, depth, and time? This is a key question pertaining to our upcoming discussion.

   By employing Scripture's symbolical numbers of *communicative* significance, could we say that "the third heaven" is where holy angels reside until Judgment Day? Would this also be the same place where the souls and spirits of departed believers pass when entering eternity? If so, this "third heaven" would be labeled Paradise, the place entered by Jesus and the saved thief on Good Friday.

   This present section will suggest that this holy location is in a *dimension* other than our *four* dimensional one. For sake of investigation, let's say the "paradise" ("Paradise") of 2 Corinthians 12 could be in a seventh (7th) dimension, while "Hell" may have been created in a sixth (6th) dimension for evil angels as punishment due to their sinful rebellion before the Fall of Adam and Eve (Matthew 25:41)?

But beyond that, could the statement of God, "I am going to create *new* heavens and a *new* earth" (Isaiah 65:17; cp. 2 Peter 3:13; Revelation 21:1), indicate a twelfth (12th) dimension where believers, the Church or people of God, will later live to all eternity, a dimension into which the good angels (on the Last Day) will escort the saved beyond their present fourth- (4th-) and possibly seventh-(7th-) dimensional existences (cp. Mark 13:27)?

Maybe even a tenth (10th) dimension could exist for believers between the time of their deaths and the Last Day, if the "Paradise" Jesus mentioned on the cross is *not* the same as the present residence of the holy angels or the same as the paradise Paul visited (2 Corinthians 12)?

(Remember: The 2 Corinthians passage does not say who or what Paul saw in "the third heaven." Did he see angels or not; did he see both angels as well as believers who had been transported into that dimension from earth via death; and do angels at this time occupy one dimension and believers another dimension between death and the Last Day?)

Speculation: The holy angels who now seem to dwell in "the third heaven," an area I labeled the seventh (7th) dimension, would certainly also reside in a new twelfth (12th) dimension to all eternity—a dimension called "Heaven." This thinking is based on the idea that maybe even the holy angels of God have not yet witnessed the fullest glory of God, a thing that possibly no one gets to see until the Final Day when the gift of the ultimate *heaven* is revealed to all (cp. 1 Peter 1:12b).

Some would ask, may a Christian dare speculate and ask such questions? Luke 16 would say "yes," as long as one does not become overly dogmatic and force his thoughts on another. Luke 16:19–31 seems to encourage Christians to probe for *fuller* answers already on this side of eternity. Recall that Luke 16:26 says that there's a "great chasm" (NET, KJV: "great gulf") that exists, *a divide* that prevents humans in either Paradise, Heaven, or Hell—being in different dimensions—from crossing over to those in counter places or dimensions.

That both good and evil angels could cross over from earth to different realms in Bible times, or *vice versa*, and then back again, is taught in passages such as Job 1:6–7 (holy angels, plus Satan, meet with God in His domain); 2 Kings. 2:11 (good angels take the form of horses and a chariot coming to earth to take Elijah the prophet to "heaven"); 1 Kings

22:19–22 (a lying evil spirit attends a meeting in "heaven"). This latter passage speaks of an appearance before God's heavenly throne, one of the several places where God dwells according to His omnipresence.

For further study, view Revelation 9:1–11 (evil spirits are portrayed as figurative horses that fight against believers on earth); Luke 16:22 (good angels carry a believer to Abraham's side in eternity); Psalm 68:17–18 and Ephesians 4:7–13; Deuteronomy 33:2; Matthew 25:31; and Isaiah 66:15 ("thousands upon thousands" of good angels in the form of chariots or other images accompany God, even Christ, on very important occasions); Hebrews 1:14 (good angels cross over to help believers on earth, even aid Jesus in Mark 1:13).

It needs to be repeated that God Himself spans *all* the dimensions of *observable* and *unobservable* space; this is supported by those Bible passages that teach the *omnipresence* of God (1 Kings 8:27; Jeremiah 23:24; Ephesians 1:15–23; cp. Psalm 103:19, particularly Psalm 139:8).

Scripture teaches that certain *evil* angels can *already*—before Judgment Day— be limited in their movements (Mark 5:10) and that *all* evil demons and their leader, the devil, will eventually be restricted to *Hell's* eternal dimension. Sometimes this is only *implied* (Daniel 10:13; Revelation 12:[4], 7–8; Luke 8:30–33) and at other times it is *dogmatically taught*, as in Jude 6; Matthew 25:41; and Revelation 20:10. Also, created angels can only be in *one* place at a time since they are *not* omnipresent; yet, holy angels are always with God since He is always present in all dimensions (consider Matthew 18:10).

3. As God created "the third heaven" on Day 1 of Creation ("heavens"), could it be that He created all the angels on that day also so they could "sing" and "shout for joy" at the amazement of His every act of creation—from beginning to end (Job 38:7)?

4. A further thought concerns "black holes" in space: Could these be comparable to places where the "degrees of Hell" are dished out (Luke 12:47–48)? "Black holes" certainly parallel the words of Matthew 8:12 where Jesus speaks of *unbelievers* being thrown into "outer darkness." On this basis, one could picture unbelievers being sucked into *Hell's black hole(s) of darkness*, outer space's reality which the television production *End Day* calls "gravity gone mad." This imagery would *not* be farfetched since Jesus must also have created these *black holes of darkness* since He created all things (evaluate John 1:3 and Matthew 25:30). (I am indebted to the late Noah W. Hutchings of Southwest Radio Church Ministries ["Watchman on the Wall"] and a telephone conversation I had with him concerning his original thoughts on these "black holes" of eternity.)

5. Connected to this comparison of *Hell*'s place(s) of darkness, the concept of "time" comes into play. Again, the first of God's creations was "time" ("In the beginning"). On Judgment Day "time" will come to an end (Revelation 10:6e: "Time will be no more," including the whole context of vv. 5–7). Those in the *black hole(s) of Hell* will wait in vain for the next second to tick, hoping that God will change His mind and show them mercy, a mercy that will never come since "mercy" ends at death when one enters an *endless, timeless* future, called eternity (2 Corinthians 5:10; Hebrews 9:27).

All of the above should move one to sit back and think deeply and seriously.

6. Initial Conclusion: The term "the heavens" (*hashāmayīm*, a Hebrew plural) in Genesis 1:1 suggests way more than a casual glance would suggest. It is full of *observable* phenomena as well as *unobservable* dimensions.

7. Something else yearns for further discussion. It relates to the possible distinction between "Paradise" and a *final* "Heaven"—with two eternal dimensions involved. (As you can imagine, it demands *very* careful handling so the Christian faith of those who have lost loved ones is not disturbed.)

Question: Is there a *possible* difference between the "Paradise" which Jesus and the redeemed thief entered on Good Friday ("Today you will be with Me in Paradise.") and "Heaven" itself.

What? They could be different? Heresy, comes the cry. Maybe not! Let's discuss it.

We start back in the first paradise at Eden. Was there something even better in store for Adam and Eve had they passed God's test and had not eaten from the forbidden tree? Have you ever thought about it?

Eden was a perfect place, to be sure, but could God have had an even greater, more magnificent place in mind for that first couple in their future? With

God, nothing is impossible, so it could be that He would be able to have a more glorious place beyond that first perfect place—Eden.

Think: Adam and Eve in their perfect state had sinless human bodies, but did they have "glorified" bodies as of yet, ones like those promised in Philippians 3:20–21: "the Savior . . . will change our humble bodies and make them like His glorified body . . ."? One aspect of our "glorified bodies" is that they will no longer be able to sin. Adam and Eve certainly did *not* possess that reality. For them, as for us, that is a future phenomenon. (Certainly deep thinking, but remember Scripture says little concerning the period of time between a person's death and Judgment Day. In fact, it says little about Heaven itself. God guards it like a secret *gift* package that no human gets to view ahead of time.)

An extended truth of 1 Corinthians 2:9 would also seem to apply to Adam and Eve, even before they fell into sin: "No eye has seen, no ear has heard, and no mind has comprehended, what God has prepared for those who love Him." What do you think?

If so, maybe there was a better place beyond that first paradise of Eden. That first garden was most likely wiped out by Noah's flood. But Jesus spoke of another "Paradise" garden while on the cross. That's the one I suggested as being in the seventh (7th) or tenth (10th) dimensions. But what if there is an even better paradise, called Heaven, waiting for an ultimate revealing on the Last Day, a place that even the holy angels may not yet have seen (cp. 1 Peter 1:12)?

This may not be as farfetched as one imagines. Remember: Paul said the things he saw in the "third heaven" of "paradise" ("Paradise") were "things that no human being *can* express or is allowed to talk about" (2 Corinthians 12:2, 4). How much more true that would be if the *ultimate* heaven to be revealed on Judgment Day is even more astounding? Paul possibly hinted at this in 1 Thessalonians 4:13–18 where he comforts the faithful with the fact that no believers will get ahead of other believers when it comes to seeing the glories of the final revelation on the Last Day. This may be saying that there *is* something even better beyond the "Paradise" to which the forgiven thief went on Good Friday. I would conjecture and place that better heaven in a twelfth (12th) dimension, selected as to number on the basis of the Revelation 21:14, 21 symbolism:

"And the wall of the city had twelve foundation stones." "And the *twelve* gates were *twelve* pearls."

Does make one think and dare to wonder about the fullness of the coming glory! Hope to see you in the Heaven of heavens to check it out together.

The basic message beyond our conjecturing, however, is quite scripturally clear: Once in Heaven, forever in Heaven; once in hell, forever in Hell.

The fact of the matter is that Jesus *physically* visited the evil spirits in prison on Easter morning in His "state of exaltation," *announcing His victory* and preaching *judgment* [*condemnation*], not salvation, to those eternal prisoners (cp. Isaiah 63:1–6).

That God of the Bible, well, He truly is "Something Else"!

The humorous, yet tragic, side of the whole story pertains to the devil who had "outfoxed" himself. He had concluded that he would win the whole battle if he could move his human minions to put Jesus to death. That was his downfall. God outfoxed him. That was exactly what God the Father needed to have happen to win the victory. Have His Son put to *death*. And after that, the Father then made His Son alive again to seal the victory (Romans 10:9; 1 Corinthians 15:15).

Picture it this way! The moment Jesus died, the devil and his evil angels partied like they had never celebrated before. Victory seemed to be theirs. That party lasted a good twenty-five straight hours until the risen Christ Jesus arrived in *Hell*—unannounced and uninvited. The party came to a screeching halt when Jesus crashed that party. Now the devil knew the game was over and that he would be "in *everlasting* chains and gloom" (Jude 6; cp. James 2:19b).

By the way, Bible probers, do not forget to make the "Adam" connection to Jesus, in reverse. Just as Satan *first* contacted Adam on earth in an effort to destroy him, so the resurrected Jesus *first* contacted Satan and all his followers in "prison" to announce destruction to those enemies of His Kingdom. The new King was alive and well.

That visit into the realm of hopelessness being over, Jesus appeared back on earth to make appearances to "doubting" believers, or, in the case of His half-brother James, to persons who would turn from total unbelief to belief (1 Corinthians 15:7; cp. John 7:5).

As a possible teaching aid, I here add my *seminar* handout that covers the above in outline form.

"From Here to Eternity"

A. Where It All Started for Me—Genesis 1:1; 2 Corinthians 12:2–4

B. "I Wonder As I Wander"—Luke 16:25–26

   1. My conclusion: Luke 16:19–31 is definitely a "parable" told by Jesus.

   2. This parable stands as the last of seven parables that run from Luke 14–18. Seven of them! Too coincidental to be accidental, to be sure. Note that both accounts in Luke 16 begin with the "same words." See Lightfoot's powerful argumentation in favor of not ripping Luke 16:19–31 out of the context of its six previous parables—and then all of a sudden deciding to interpret this seventh illustration in a literal way after treating the former six in a figurative way (L, *LP*, pp. 132–138).

C. The "Dimensions" of Death and Eternity

   1. The "Up" and "Down" of it all.

      a. Ephesians 4:7–10 (NET footnote 4a–9); Philippians 2:10 (S, *FESP*, p. 321: "things under the earth")

      b. See Luke 10:18: "I watched Satan fall from heaven . . . ."

   2. Professor Martin Naumann: "dimensions of eternity"

      (A "place," not just a "condition"; cp. "new heavens; new earth"—Isaiah 65:17; Revelation 21:1.)

   3. Hell: 6th dimension

      a. One description among several: Matthew 8:12 ("outer darkness")

      b. Dr. Noah W. Hutchings: "black holes"

   4. Paradise: 7th dimension? (What if "Paradise" is less than the final "heaven"? Is it "heresy" to ask? Compare 2 Corinthians 12:2–4 with an extended meaning of 1 Corinthians 2:9.)

      a. The saved "thief" of Calvary is still in "Paradise," it would seem. Even now the saved go there, it would seem. Luke 23:43: "*paradeiso*," not "*ouranos*" ["heaven"].

      b. Little is said about the time between "death and Judgment Day":

         (1) OT dead entered into "eternity"!

         (2) Fair to suffer longer than others?

         (3) Subset: Luke 10:13–15 ("up to heaven," "down to hell").

      c. What if Adam and Eve had passed the "tree" test? Would there have been something different and better beyond?

(1) Could God have had a place *more magnificent and glorious* than the first paradise, which Genesis 2 calls the Garden of Eden? If He so willed, yes (Luke 1:37)!

(2) Was God completely revealed in all His uncovered glory in the first "garden"? Hardly! If so, Adam and Eve would have understood the fullness of "holiness" and never sinned, it would seem.

(3) What Adam and Eve also did *not* have in the first garden paradise:

(a) No end to temptation;

(b) No end to hunger and thirst (cp. Revelation 7:16);

(c) Not "confirmed in bliss"; no presence of *realized* "immortality" (cp. Matthew 18:10; 1 Corinthians 15:51–52);

(d) Did not yet "wear the likeness of Man from heaven" (?), it would seem (1 Corinthians 15:49 needs more evaluation); and

(e) Did not have "glorified" bodies (cp. Philippians 3:21), that is, bodies that had "*eternal* abilities." "Glorified" may mean our bodies in Heaven will receive various qualities like those of Jesus's glorified body (cp. John 20:19).

What does this mean? Won't we receive bodies that are *not* subject to the *natural laws* of this present world, bodies that are no longer bound by gravity, time elements, or digestive restrictions, but rather bodies that will benefit *beyond* the perfect Adam and Eve, benefit by what we might cautiously call an eternal *sacramental* eating from the new Tree of Life or "Wood of Life" in heaven? Adam and Eve did *not* have a Tree of Life that could both (1) "make them live forever" and (2) also "remove sin" at the same time, so they would not live *eternally* in their initial sin (evaluate Genesis 3:24).

The "tree" of the cross ["wood"] in Revelation 22 can do *both*; it is more powerful than that first Tree of Life in Eden (cp. Genesis 2:9 with Revelation 22:2).

(f) Did not possess the reality of "shining like the sun", having the "degrees of glory" (Matthew 13:43; Daniel 12:3).

5. **Heaven:** 12ᵗʰ dimension, *if* different than "Paradise" (consider Revelation 21:14, 21)

   a. Consider 1 Thessalonians 4:13–17.

   b. If the "new heavens and new earth" will really be *new* as of Judgment Day, are believers who have already passed from our world into eternity *presently* in that new "Heaven," or are they in "Paradise," awaiting their *final* transport to the "new" Heaven? Something to think about!

6. **Paradise and Heaven,** a powerful argument that they are the same: Consider the seeming fact that the "Paradise" entered by the repentant thief on Good Friday was free from further temptation. (Needs to be said to be fair and not dogmatic.) Besides, our loved ones could already be in the final Heaven, just not able to experience its *fullest* glory as of yet. (This point gives readers the *flipside* of the initial part of my presentation.)

7. **Paradise and Heaven:** Whether the same or differing, one thing is certain. No one at this moment according to their human nature (except Jesus Himself) has a view of the *full* glory of the Triune God. Even the holy angels seem to be waiting to see this fullest glory at the "unveiling of God's sons [believers]" (Romans 8:19; consider 1 Peter 1:10-12 in an expanded form).

D. Summary

1. The above is based on passages of Scripture that should cause serious Christians to ponder *where* their departed loved ones are already *joyfully* residing in eternity, as well as move them to think about their own eternal residence. In addition, it provides a framework to consider how all the saved will see the *ultimate* glories of Heaven at one and the same time, no one encountering the "Final Attraction" before someone else, though Moses, Elijah, Isaiah, Ezekiel, Paul, and John did get glimpses of the "Previews of Coming Attractions" in their lifetimes (cite various Bible accounts). And so, no one gets to unwrap the *final* "Heaven" gift before others. At this time, not even those in "Paradise" (or shall we say, the paradise of Heaven) are witnessing God's *full* glory before Judgment Day, seemingly not even the holy angels (see C.7. above).

   Upper, not bottom, line: Come to heaven with me and we will check it all out together.

   Fact: Not one person on earth—not the greatest theologian or pastor or layperson—will be able to say when seeing heaven on the Last Day: "It's just how I always pictured it!" All of us will be totally overawed!

2. A "comfort" repeat: Be absolutely assured that departed Christians, already in the eternity of Paradise or Heaven, are at total rest and peace, completely in the arms of Jesus, without any needs or cares or lacks of comfort (Psalm 23:6 and Hebrews 4:9–11).

E. Some Practical Questions Often Asked:

1. What age will I be in heaven? (Alternate: Will there be babies and old people in heaven?)

2. What if my spouse or children do *not* make it to heaven, will I know it? Compare Revelation 21:4.

3. Will we be able to ask God questions in heaven? Consider 1 Corinthians 13:12.

4. How will we see the Father and Holy Spirit if they do *not* have bodies? (See John 14:9.)

5. Existence between death and Judgment Day? (See Luke 16:19–31; Revelation 6:9–11.)

6. My final question? Knowing there are "degrees of punishment" in eternity (Luke 12:47–48), will there also be "degrees of glory"? Examine John 14:2–3: "rooms" (NET); "mansions" (KJV); Daniel 12:3. Will we be happy in heaven if someone else receives more recognition?

7. Your question(s)?

_____

_____

_____

_____

_____

_____

APPENDIX 11

HARMONIZING THE FOUR GOSPELS

The Legitimacy of Gospel Harmonization

Many scholars vehemently oppose the "harmonization" of the four gospels, declaring it to be in violation of the individual intents of each Gospel writer.

Yes, I agree that one must never lose sight of the main audience and particular purpose of each canonical Gospel. At the same time, what can it hurt to let readers of Scripture view the order in which the events took place in the life and ministry of Jesus? What excitement takes place in the lives of readers when they encounter the four gospels like a novel, Matthew and Mark and Luke and John synchronized together as one flowing account!

What am I talking about?

> Early in NT Times, a scholar named Tatian (c. AD 120–173) produced a *Diatessaron*, meaning "through four," that is, "A harmony of the Four Gospels written to make one continuous narrative; . . ." (L, "D," p. 298).

> Others also arranged such harmonies through the centuries. Nearer our day and age, A. T. Robertson's *A Harmony of the Gospels* was circulated by Harper & Brothers Publishers in 1922. (Robertson was a brilliant Greek scholar, quite capable of being fair to each of the texts of the writers of the four gospels and their intents.)

I became a big fan of harmonies through the work of Dr. William F. Beck. His translation was entitled *The Christ of the Gospels* (St. Louis: Concordia Publishing House, 1959). Give yourself a literary treat and obtain a copy from Amazon. You will experience the events and meaning of the life of Jesus as never before.

(All three men referred to above—Tatian, Robertson, and Beck—were excellent NT Greek scholars.)

It was the work of Beck, namely, the last portion of His harmony that moved me to take his pamphlet, "He Died and Rose FOR ME," and have my team of scholars prepare and once again publish it under the auspices of NET Publishing (Cleveland), using the title "The Greatest Part of the Greatest Story; the History of Jesus from Cross to Crown." It became the basis for being able to line up such things as the rotation of Jesus's statements from the cross, as well as the chronological order of the Easter events. (Now translated and available in Swahili also.)

A big contribution of this new edition was the inclusion of all the individual Gospel references in the columns of each page, so that readers could see where all the various parts of the narrative of Jesus's suffering, death, and resurrection could be found. In this way, the *individuality* of each of the four canonical Gospel writers was safeguarded.

Gospel harmonies, I believe, bring much clarity and interest back to texts concerning the life and ministry of our Savior, contents that most often go unappreciated.

> Try a four-gospels "harmony"; you'll enjoy. It is a literary instrument that can become a powerful way to get young people to read the Bible. I have witnessed this in Christian classrooms and homes. A really great gift for a non-Christian family too! See Bibliography reference code B, *CG*.

ADDENDUM: On page 235 at # 9., there is a discussion of whether Mark 16:9-20 is original to Mark's book. I took a neutral position, citing various opinions.

Since we have presently discussed the *harmonization* of the four canonical Gospels, it now seems appropriate to add a quote by A. Andrew Das. After he discusses the difficulty presented by Mark's ending, he concludes: "Mark 16:16 also summarizes in a nice way what can be shown about baptism *on the basis of several other passages in Scripture*" (D, *BGF*, p. 127; *my italics for emphasis*).

In other words, whether Mark 16:16 is original or not, the same baptism truth can be picked up from other portions of the New Testament. Also, some other portions of Mark's ending can be substantiated by other New Testament texts. But what about Mark 16:9, "He [Jesus] showed Himself 'first' to Mary from Magdala"? In my humble opinion, it is hard to harmonize verse 9 with John 20:2. Mary's statement in John ("we don't know where they laid Him") seems to indicate strongly that she had *not* gone into the tomb and heard the angel say, "He is risen" (Matthew 28:6).

The exhaustive research of Cascione and Lunn is very, very compelling in favor of the longer ending of Mark. Google: "New Evidence for the Long Ending of Mark – YouTube https://www.youtube.com/watch?v=HhmccXgEL-E"!

The ball is now in your court to investigate this Scriptural difficulty.

APPENDIX 12

FURTHER ANALYZATION OF CHRIST'S ASCENSION

This appendix deals with differing opinions concerning various aspects of the physical ascension of Christ. It encourages you to recall the words of Daniel 7:13 from Chapter 22: "In the visions during the night, I [Daniel] saw One coming with the clouds of the heavens like a Son of Man, and He came to Ancient of Days and was presented before Him."

The Historic Reality of Christ's Ascension

Both the OT (via prediction) and the NT (by numerous statements) verify that Christ's ascension was a *historical* event. There are way too many passages to record them all word by word in this appendix. A few will suffice. Following those selected examples, a listing of additional ones will be given by reference only.

> **Psalm 68:18a–b:** "You went up on high. You took prisoners captive." *(In Ephesians 4:8b–c, Paul identifies the human subject to be Christ by using the pronoun "He" twice.)*

> **Luke 24:50–51:** "He [Jesus] took them [His disciples] out to a place where Bethany lay ahead of them. Then He raised His hands and blessed them. While He was blessing them, He parted from them and was taken up to heaven."

> **Acts 5:30–31:** "You hanged Jesus on a cross and murdered Him. But the God of our fathers raised Him and took Him up to His right hand as Leader and Savior in order to give the people of Israel repentance and forgiveness of sins."

> **Romans 8:34:** "Who will condemn? It is Christ who died, and more than that, He rose; He is at the right hand of God, and He prays for us."

> **Hebrews 1:3b:** "After He had made a cleansing from sins, He sat down at the right hand of the Majesty in heaven."

Other references: Psalm 89:3–4, 20, 25–27, 29; Acts 7:55; Colossians 3:1; 1 Timothy 3:16; Hebrews 4:14. All three Ecumenical Creeds of the Holy Christian Church (the Apostles', the Nicene, and the Athanasian) contain the same testimony in similar words, such as "He ascended into heaven and sits at the right hand of God the Father."

"He Sat Down at the Right Hand"

Where is God's "right hand"? He does not have a right hand since He is a "spirit" (John 4:24). Therefore, the term "right hand" does not indicate a certain location. It "is a metaphor for a position of honor, bliss, authority, power, and glory" (T, *AOL*, p. 16; so also K, *SCD*, p. 156). To all eternity, Jesus now occupies this position in His state of "exaltation" according to His human nature, as the Athanasian Creed so eloquently says it: "Although He [Jesus] is God and man, He is not two but one Christ: one, however, not by the conversion of the divinity into flesh, but by the assumption of the humanity into God . . . " (LSB, p. 320).

The "Cloud" Phenomenon

I strongly contend that Daniel 7:13–14 pertains to Christ's ascension. If so, how can one reconcile Acts 1:9: "a cloud (singular) took Him away" with Daniel 7:13: "One coming with the clouds (plural) of the heavens like a son of man"? Good question.

A biblical investigator's first inclination is to take the Daniel 7:11–12 vision as *following* the Last Judgment, the latter being cited in Matthew 26:64. Or let's state it in this manner: Some would say Daniel 7:13–14 does *not* refer to Christ's ascension at all; rather, timewise, it follows a former Final Judgment event conducted in heaven, the one already completed in Daniel 7:11. If that is true, then Daniel 7:13–14 would be a reference to Jesus's coronation *at the end of time*, not an enthronement at the time of His ascension.

But good Bible detectives should realize that this does not make biblical sense. If Jesus's Last Day judgment scene pictures Him sitting at the "right hand of Power," "Power" being a reference to God the Father (CJB, CSB, ESV, NASB, similarly the NIV), then the Matthew 26:64 reference cannot *chronologically* follow the Daniel 7:11 event.

Why?

How could Christ come "to" the Ancient of Days (Daniel 7:13) in the heavens when He is already at the right side of His Father, the Ancient of Days, at the time of the earthly Judgment Day? The words of Jesus in Mark 14:62 ("And you [Caiaphas] will see the Son of Man sitting at the right hand of Power and coming with the clouds of heaven.") shows that the Father is already with Jesus when Christ returns to earth with the clouds of heaven on the Last Day. At that time the Son of Man does *not* come "to" the Father, but He is already with the Father—and that reality runs all the way from Ascension Day right on down to His Last Coming.

There seems to be another aspect also. It possibly lies in the interpretation of the terms "cloud" and "clouds."

Some like Toon (T, *AOL*, pp. 5, 117) and Bruce (B, *CBA*, p. 41) identify the ascension "cloud" in Acts 1:9 as the *Shekinah* "cloud" of the OT (Exodus 13:21; 19:9; 40:33–38), the "glory" cloud that afforded protection for the Israelites during their wilderness journey.

This interpretation appeals to me; and yet, my theological research causes me to feel uneasy about it.

Why?

Jesus truly was present in that OT *Shekinah* "cloud" (1 Corinthians 10:1–4; cp. Exodus 34:5). And remember, His presence was most significant when that "cloud" hovered above the "atonement cover" of the "Ark of the Covenant" in the OT Tent or Tabernacle (Leviticus 16:2).

But when Christ came to earth, He brought His "glory" along with Him; any remnant of that former cloud lost its glory. How do we know? John 1:14 states: "And the Word [Jesus] became flesh and lived ['tabernacled'; 'tented'] among us, and we saw His 'glory,' the glory of the Father's one and only Son—He is full of grace and truth."

Where does that leave us as to our "cloud" and "clouds" inquiry?

Here's my answer.

From the disciples' *earthbound* perspective in Acts 1:9, they only saw what appeared to be a single cloud. But what did the *other side* of the cloud appear to be; or, what was it really?

Consider this: As the ascension scene entered eternity, timewise, God's heavenly angels may have been the ones—in the form of "clouds" (cp. Daniel 7:13)—who escorted Jesus to the throne of the Ancient of Days. As angels appeared at Christ's birth, I suspect they now participated in His ascension. This "ascension" assumption is solely my interpretation; I cautiously offer it as my personal opinion or interpretation. I contend that the "clouds" on the heavenly side were holy angels (cp. Matthew 16:27a with Acts 1:11b and Matthew 25:31).

A. My conclusion demands that Bible observers become cognizant of several things:

1. Angels take various forms in Scripture. Remember our discussion of this (e.g., my conclusion that the Christmas "star" was an angel; see Chapter 7).

2. Angels are a big part of the Daniel 7:9–10 context. It numbers the angels in God's heavenly courtroom as being "thousands upon thousands" and "ten thousand times ten thousand; you do the math. I like the way the Complete Jewish Bible (CJB) puts it: "millions and millions" (v. 10).

(The number of heavenly angels appears to be symbolic since it is composed of multiples of the number 10, the Bible's number for "completeness.")

An interpreter could see Daniel 7:2–12 as one vision and verses 13 and 14 as a second vision. I view them as *four* visions (vv. 2–8, 9 and 10, 11 and 12, 13 and 14). The first three could be single, consecutive visions. The various events seem to follow one another, but as previously concluded, verses 13 and 14 seem to leave Jesus out of the Judgment setting of verses 11 and 12.

This would contradict Jesus, who taught: "For the Father does not judge anyone but has entrusted the judgment *entirely* to the Son . . . . He has also given Him authority to execute judgment because He is the Son of Man" (John 5:22, 27).

On this basis, investigative clues become very conclusive: Chronologically, Daniel 7:13 and 14 cannot follow the Final Judgment scene of verses 11 and 12, if these latter verses do, in fact, refer to the Last Judgment. *(Of course, a "Final Judgment" occurrence in verses 11 and 12 would raise the question of whether Daniel 7:13 and 14 really portray Jesus's Ascension Day event. That should elevate our clue-search when we tackle it a little later in this appendix.)*

3. At this point, I interject the Daniel 7:9 mention of the setting up of "thrones." Possibly there were *three*—one for each of the Persons of the Trinity. The angels are described as "standing" in verse 10, so the thrones were not for them. *(In terms of Revelation 4:4, maybe there were twenty-four more "thrones" for the "24 elders," who symbolically represent OT and NT believers.)*

4. Question: How do faithful Bible detectives fit the visions of Daniel 7:1–14 together coherently? The answer demands the following section. *(Remember that Daniel 7:1 and 13 do use the designation "visions" in the plural.)*

My "Transparencies" Layovers Explanation

Way back before classroom "smartboards," there were projectors that used plastic transparencies. These transparencies contained data for teaching. Less detailed ones were first laid down on the projector's illumined glass for examination. After this, another more detailed one was laid over the top of the former transparency; it added even more significant details—and so on.

For me, this application explains the visions of Daniel 7. More and more details are given by each vision that follows the former—but Daniel 7:13 and 14 do not seem to be in *chronological* sequence; rather, as in transparency presentation, it *overlays* the former judgment scene details.

At first glance, the arrival of Jesus, the One "like a Son of Man" appears to come *after* the Ancient of Days has already dished out final judgments upon the kingdoms of this world. But that does not fit Scriptural teachings concerning the Last Judgment, as the above-quoted John 5:22 showed: "the Father . . . has entrusted the judgment *entirely* to the Son."

All this would suggest that any Final Judgment scene of Daniel 7:11–12 could not have occurred *before* "the Son of Man" arrived in heaven. In fact, the Final Judgment is to occur when Christ returns to earth, not to heaven. Thus, the demand for *simultaneous* happenings, not chronological ones, in terms of the events of Daniel 7! (Examine verses 11 and 12 in connection with verses 13 and 14; maybe the "judgment" of verses 11 and 12 are just an *initial* sentencing of the Roman Empire, not the Final Judgment against Satan and the two antichrists (see Revelation 12 and 13 for a context).

However, one big obstacle still seems to stand in the way: the word *until* in Psalm 110, the most quoted OT text in the NT.

Just a Momentary Roadblock

Psalm 110:1, 6 ("A Psalm by David") reads:

> The LORD [God the Father] says to my [David's] Lord [Jesus],
>> "Sit at My right *until* I make Your enemies Your footstool."
> From Zion the LORD will send out the scepter of Your power:
>> "Rule in the middle of Your enemies.
> He [Christ] will rout the nations and fill valleys with dead bodies;
>> He will smash the rulers over the wide earth.

This sounds like Jesus would not be able to assume kingly power *until after* God the Father Himself defeated all enemies of the Kingdom—and then Jesus could be crowned King, be enthroned, and finally receive His eternal Kingdom. Additional *time* factors also *seem* to demand the postponement of the kingship of Jesus to a period way later than the Ascension Day of Acts 1:9. (Several other passages seem to confirm this: Revelation 11:15; 12:10–12; 17:9–18; 19:11–21. Possibly the multi-interpreted 1 Corinthians 15:24–28 belongs in this category.)

But such conclusion would contradict several other Scriptural texts:

Matthew 28:18: "When Jesus came near, He spoke to them. He said, 'All authority *has been given [my emphasis]* to Me in heaven and on earth.'"

Ephesians 1:20–23: "He [God the Father] worked with that same power in Christ when He raised Him [Christ] from the dead, and made Him [Christ] sit at His right hand in heaven, far above all rulers, authorities, powers, lords, and any name that can be mentioned, not only in this age but also in the next. And He [God the Father] put everything under His feet, and established Him as the Head of everything for the good of the Church, which is His body, completely filled by Him who fills everything in every way." *(This passage is of utmost importance to the conclusion to be reached below.)*

Colossians 2:9-10: "In Him, that is, in His body, lives all the fullness of the Deity. And in Him, who is the Head of all rulers and powers, you are complete."

1 Peter 3:21c–22: "Jesus Christ, who has gone to heaven and is at the right hand of God, where angels, rulers, and powers *have been put* under Him."

Hebrews 2:7–8 (cp. Psalm 8:5–7): "You made Him [Christ] lower than the angels for a little while, then crowned Him with glory and honor and made Him Ruler over what Your hands have made and put everything under His feet. When God put everything under His feet, He left nothing outside His control." [Extremely decisive!]

Revelation 1:4–5c: "Jesus Christ—He *is* the faithful Witness, the First of the dead to live again, and the Ruler over the kings of the earth."

How should one handle this whole dilemma of *seemingly* unsolvable contradictory passages of Scripture? It's the old "now" and "not yet" mystery of Scripture that provides a pathway to a viable solution.

Let's go back to Romans 16:20: "The God of peace will soon crush Satan under your feet."

There is a passage that absolutely demands a "now" and "not yet" interpretation. Already "now" Satan has been defeated and judged according to the words and actions of the crucified and risen Lord Jesus, who expressed this in John 19:30, by declaring: "It is finished."

But from another point of view, Paul realized that God has "not yet" decided to stop Satan's ongoing use of evil power (Revelation 20:3c–d). The reason: All humans are still living during a period of *testing* that will run right up to the Last Coming of Christ.

So what is the application to our so-called "ascension" dilemma? As the last set of Bible proof passages above decisively indicates, Jesus already according to His human nature has all power and is in complete control over His Kingdoms of power and grace here on earth, while at the same time, He also exercises total control over His Kingdom of glory in the world above (cp. the comfort of Matthew 28:20b).

There is security in this certainty. Koehler assures believers that Christ already uses His power "in the interest and for the benefit of His friends." He then adds that the exalted Christ "manages the affairs of the world so all things work together for the good of His Christians (Romans 8:28)," right in the "now" of their pre-eternal timeframe (K, *SCD*, p.156).

By means of another former grouping of Bible proof passages above, we noted that there is also a "not yet" time factor. We have "not yet" experienced the reality and full finality of the "It is finished" truth. That will come on the Last Day when "time" screeches to a halt (Revelation 10:6e), eternity welcomes us, and the total effects of Jesus's Calvary and resurrection victories are revealed for all to see. Then Christ will *visibly* rule over all forever and ever (Philippians 2:9–11).

If one views Daniel 7:13–14 from the double perspective of a "now" and also a "not yet," it becomes easier to realize that Daniel's vision needs two "transparency" overlays to grasp the whole picture of Jesus's ascension coronation. One took place forty days after Easter. Another ultimate enthronement of Jesus will follow; that is, in terms of an eternal timeless framework.

Dr. Steinmann says it this way: "It seems that the vision given Daniel in 7:9–14, which is interpreted in 7:15–28, pictures in one scene the entire sweep of salvation history that includes Christ's first advent, the church age, and Christ's second advent" (S, *D*, pp. 329–330).

Welcome to biblical tough stuff.

In any event, I believe that Daniel 7:13 and 14 refer to Christ's ascension, and as such, they indicate what took place on the other side of the "cloud" of Acts 1:9—forty days after His resurrection.

APPENDIX 13

NUMERIC SEPARATIONS

Biblical chronology is a fascinating thing, but as the late Dr. Raymond Surburg, noted biblical scholar, related privately, "Biblical chronology is not an *absolute* science." Therefore, many dates and conclusions determined as certain, may not be that certain after all.

Many are the biblical chronologists who are known for their meticulous calculations: William Foxwell Albright, Sir Robert Anderson, Jack Finegan, Floyd Nolen Jones, Sir Isaac Newton, Andrew E. Steinmann, Edwin R. Thiele, and Archbishop James Ussher, just to name a few. Their works are extremely valuable when analyzing Scripture.

I was most privileged to have known and studied with such a chronologist, named Eugene W. Faulstich, previously mentioned. For well over twenty-five years, Faulstich compiled dates of biblical events. His side specialty was determining "days and years of separation" between one Bible event and another. He did this via computer in the earlier days of computer science. Many of his findings were intriguing, to say the least.

Faulstich earned his fortune as an industrialist, inventing machinery as a mechanical engineer. His acumen with *numbers* enabled him to apply his talent to biblical data. (Faulstich's monies earned earlier in life permitted him to dedicate himself *full time* to the study of Scriptural chronology.)

One of his conclusions, whether valid or not, deserves mention. Readers will need to decide whether that conclusion has merit. It may seem "off the wall"; then again, it may be *"Evidence Just Too Coincidental to Be Accidental!!!"*

The Bible *directly* indicates three "ascension" events, involving Enoch, "the seventh from Adam" (Genesis 5:24; Jude 14), Elijah the prophet (2 Kings 2:11), and Jesus (Acts 1:9). (The ascension of Moses is only by way of induction, based on conclusions derived from a comparison of Jude 9 and Matthew 17:3. That complexity was dealt with in Chapter 15 of this book).

Faulstich recorded some very interesting data about the "days" of separation between the ascensions of Enoch, Elijah, and Jesus. His calculations:

> 1,111,111 *days* between Enoch's ascension and that of Jesus;
> 777,777 *days* between Enoch's ascension and that of Elijah;
> 333,333 *days* between Elijah's ascension and that of Jesus!
> (G, *ALD*, p. 2).

These tabulations *only* calculate if Jesus ascended in AD 30, not in AD 33. See Faulstich's tables of comparison for the two above-mentioned years (F, *HKC*, p. 11). An AD 33 date is adopted by Steinmann (S, *AP*, p. 281; cp. L, *EC*, pp. 401-402, fn. 17). He notes that both years (AD 30 and 33) had Passovers that fell on "Fridays." Floyd Nolen Jones, a most detailed chronologist, opts for an AD 30 crucifixion and ascension date (J, *COT*, p. 254).

Faulstich's evaluations also calculated unique "weeks" of separation between certain Bible events. Two are as follows:

> 77,770   *weeks* between Moses's "Burning Bush" *call* and Jesus's death;
>
> 77,777   *weeks* between Moses's "Burning Bush" call and Christians' Pentecost *call* (F/G, *"BL/SD,"* pp. 3, 15).

All this may seem "over the edge," but how could any chronologist stack the numbers to make them come out like this? Just "one day" off would destroy the whole calculated conclusion. Coincidental? You decide.

When chronology is revealed in heaven as an absolute science (all data being revealed), we will all be amazed with the calculations of the great Master Mathematician of Creation and history. Should be exciting!

> Disagreements developed between Faulstich and myself over his interpretations of passages such as Isaiah 66:8 and others, as he eventually started to computerize dates pertaining to *future* events, like the possibility of Jesus returning to earth on Ascension Day, AD 1995—on His presumed two thousandth birthday—when the age of the earth, as Faulstich calculated, would be 5,995 years old.
>
> Sticking one's nose into God's timing and future plans never turns out good for "daters" in the long run. Best to stick to telling others about Jesus's forgiveness and the future that Christians will have in eternity after death. Why would we in our weakened humanity know something that not even the holy angels know (Matthew 24:36)?
>
> Deuteronomy 4:2; 29:19–20 and the application of Proverbs 23:10a provide instructions that guide investigators to stay within Scriptural boundaries—very faithfully and carefully.

APPENDIX 14

ODDS AND ENDS

About the "Trinity" in Creation

On the Dedication page in the front of this book, strange things were said of the Father, Son, and Holy Spirit. They are based on Hebrews 3:4: "Every house is built by someone, but He who built everything is God." This teaches that God created the world, despite what evolution teaches. (By the way, the theory of evolution is being dismantled, piece by piece, day by day, by scientists, non-Christian and Christian. Within several years, it can be predicted, macro-evolutionists will be "outdated dinosaurs.")

Believing that there is a Creator-God, I have tried to communicate how the Three Persons of the Trinity functioned, that is, interacted with one another in the creation process. It can prove helpful.

When a building is envisioned, its construction begins with an *architect* who draws up its size, materials to be used, placement of doors and windows, and all the other things necessary to fit the later needs of occupants. God the Father served as the Trinity's Creation "Architect."

But an architect does *not* go out and do the actual building.

This is where God the Son came in. He became the Trinity's "Building Contractor" of Creation.

When construction ends, occupants do not move in until the government sends out a building inspector. That was much like the procedure followed in the Creation. The Holy Spirit became the Trinity's "Building Inspector" at the creation of the world.

This fits the Creation account in Genesis 1:1–3. As Architect, God the Father is the basis of all creation, being the Creator behind it all, "of the heavens and the earth." The Spirit "hovered," like a bird, over every created entity, making sure it was according to the Father's specifications and suitable for later occupation by trees, fish, and humans, to name a few. While hovering, He was doing His job as Building Inspector. In the meantime, for six days, Jesus the Son was busy as General Contractor, creating all that His Father had laid out in His original architectural plan.

Remembering that John's Gospel starts with the same words as Genesis ("In the beginning"), echoes a Creation theme, and indicates that the mighty Creator Jesus has now entered His own Creation in the "flesh" to salvage [redeem] it, it records of Jesus: "not one thing that was made was made without Him" (1:3b).

Scripture's Usage of *Gender*

What should Scriptural examiners think when reading that the Apostle Peter addressed that *mixed* crowd of Jews at Pentecost with the designation "*Men* of Israel" (Acts 2:22)? That "gender" notation certainly raises a *red flag* in the minds of many moderns. What a touchy subject! Just google words like "Why God Is Often a 'She'" or, after that, "When God Was a 'She'"—and observe some sane comments, as well as some opinions that are *off the wall*, so to speak. (Some modern Bible translations are gender-neutral, opting to making the Greek text fit today's cultural preferences—and that is contrary to the Bible's original meaning.)

Peter's *male* expression certainly calls for a biblical inspection; and surprisingly, the conclusions are simple if one stays with Scripture—and not with mere emotional, human opinion.

First, realize that God is neither male nor female. The Bible says, "God is a spirit" and *spirits* do not have "flesh and bones" (John 4:24; Luke 24:39). In fact, Jesus in His divine nature, before He was made flesh, is referred to as a "Being" or "Thing" (*neuter* gender) (Luke 1:35b).

So if that is true, why does Scripture repeatedly refer to God with *male* terms, terms like "He, Him, Himself, Father, Son"?

Good question.

However, some have not realized that God is also denoted by *female* terms and phrases, indicators like "hen" and as One who has *mother love* toward humankind (Matthew 23:37; Isaiah 66:13).

Here's the lowdown on the whole matter, and it is so simple.

In Scriptural terms, *male* terminology indicates "responsibility"; *feminine* terms convey "endearment"! Application: God the *Father* took "responsibility" to send His Son to earth to deal with the problem of sin; His *Son* accepted the "responsibility" to enter our earthly realm to die for our iniquities. Thus, the *male* designations "Father" and "Son"!

Conversely, when God desires to love His people, the Church, He sometimes uses a term like "mother" to express "tenderness" and "endearment" for us, the children of God.

Just that simple!

Second, let's consider Peter's Pentecost reference: "Men of Israel"; it can serve as a case in point. Peter is calling upon the Jewish crowd before him (both males and females) to take "responsibility" for the crucifixion of Jesus (Acts 2:38a)—as they did (Acts 2:41) and as all sinners should also do and as many so do. They take "responsibility" for their wrongdoings when making confession and asking the heavenly "Father" to act *responsibly* and forgive, as He did at that initial Christian Pentecost—and still does (1 John 1:9).

In addition, the "endearment" aspect is revealed when God's *mother*-like forgiving love is poured out on earth's created human creatures (see 1 John 4:8, 16b). As a result, these forgiven people (both males and females) are then told to pour out that godly love of "endearing" forgiveness and kindness upon other created beings who desperately need it too (Ephesians 4:31–32).

Thus, some examples; others can be researched by those interested in the usage of *gender* in God's Holy Bible!

> As to *female* usages in Scripture, recall that all *male* believers (as well as *female* believers) are called the "brides" of Christ (Revelation 21:2, 9d; 22:17; cp. *Song of Solomon*), and then, also note that the followers of Jesus Christ are called the "Church" [Greek.: *ekklēsia*], which is *feminine* as to gender.

What about Angels?

Angels are *created* messengers of God. Since there was *nothing* before Creation began and *nothing* created after God "finished" creating at the end of the sixth day, angels must have been created *during* the six days of Creation. God does not say on which day. A good option would be Day One. Why? Job 38:7 says "the morning stars sang together" at the Creation, meaning they praised every magnificent creative action of God while He created. These "morning stars" are interpreted as referring to angels. Could it be that these "light" bearers (cp. Acts 12:7, even 2 Corinthians 11:14) were part of the creation that was generated when Jesus, the "Light of the world," commanded, "Let there be light." Just a thought.

Remember, regular "stars" were not created until Day #4 (Genesis 1:16).

> Ray Comfort has penned one of the most remarkable books on science and the Bible (C, *SFB*, 101 pages; note p. 28 in particular)—a must read!

"Threesomeness"

Forgive me. I am hereby creating a new word for Webster's dictionary. (Like we need a bigger dictionary, right?) This new term is my *hapax legomenon*, a one-time used word: "threesomeness"! Here's how it can be used. God is *three*—Father, Son, and Holy Spirit; this is part of His "image." And remember, humans were created in the "*image* of God"! Would it then not be natural for God to put His "threesomeness" into His created world?

It seems He did.

Think about the Apostle Paul's claim in 1 Thessalonians 5:23: He says humans possess *threesomeness*. Here we are reminded that we humans are a threesome, made in the image of God (Genesis 1:27). Like God, we have *three* parts—"spirit, soul, and body," just as God is Father, Son, and Holy Spirit. And as He is *not* three Gods, but one God in Three Persons, so we are not three human beings, rather one human being, having three entities.

Your "body" is your *physical* part; your "soul" is *you* yourself—your *personality* and *traits*; your "spirit" is your *belief system* or *worldview*. Concerning the latter, are you a believer in the God of the Bible or a believer in some other god, or do you only have belief in yourself?

A further observation for what it may be worth. Evaluate. Investigators, do you think it is coincidental that the big threesome of the OT, holding its theological history of the promise of Jesus together, are Abraham, Isaac, and Jacob? Could they be labeled "the *human* trinity of the Bible"? There is Abraham the father, Isaac the son, and Jacob the representative of the "work" of the Holy Spirit. Note: Jacob the deceiver becomes a changed man at the River Jabbok (Genesis 32:24–32). Never again does the OT present him as "deceiving"; now he becomes the "deceived" when his sons "deceive" him concerning the apparent death of Joseph his son. The Holy Spirit had changed Jacob in a most unique way (cp. 1 Corinthians 12:3). Jacob comes to represent the "work" of the Holy Spirit.

Other "threesomes" are observable: Apples equal "skin, core, meat"; the "heavens" of Genesis 1:1 are comprised of atmosphere, outer space, and "the third heaven" (the latter region being spoken of in 2 Corinthians 12:2). Missionary James May likes to term these latter three categories as "our space, outer space, and God space." Playing off May's terminology, I term these spaces as "our space, outer space, and angel space" (possibly "Paradise" or "paradise"), teaching that "God space" is everywhere, since His omnipresence finds Him in heaven, on earth, and yes, even in hell with His angry face. Psalm 139:7 asks,

> Where can I go from Your Spirit?
> Where can I flee from your presence?

Both analogies are sound; readers can choose their preference.

God's "Private Eyes"

This should interest those readers who have enjoyed this book's "detective" motif. In a roundabout way, the term "private eye" comes from Zechariah 3:9b: "Seven *eyes* are on one stone."

The context of that passage is this: God's people have returned from their exile in Babylon. They are rebuilding the Jerusalem Temple. God's protection is needed since the Jews are surrounded by enemies. Therefore, God the Father sends His Holy Spirit to keep an "eye" on things. That Spirit is called the "Seven Eyes" of God in the Zechariah text.

(This same Spirit is called the "Seven Spirits" in Revelation 1:4. No, that does not mean there are seven Holy Spirits any more than Zechariah the prophet means the Holy Spirit has seven literal eyes. "God is a spirit" [John 4:24]; He does not have a body and eyes. The Zechariah text is symbolic. *Seven* is the most used symbolic number in the Bible; it stands for *holiness* or *perfection*. Thus, "Seven Spirits" indicates "Holy" Spirit. "Seven Eyes" means the "holy" watching of the Holy Spirit.)

Why does God have Zechariah refer to the Third Person of the Trinity as the "Seven Eyes"? It was a takeoff on a Persian governmental agency of that day and age. The Jews were now under the Persians, the Persians being world rulers at that time. The secret service of the Persians was called "The Persian Eyes and Ears of the King" (google the same). The king's "private eyes" [inspectors] were everywhere in the Persian kingdom, reporting back to their king. In this way, the king could keep his eyes on everything.

It was similar with God; the Spirit kept His "eyes" on things to make sure God's plans were succeeding. The rebuilding of the Temple had to succeed or Jesus would not be able to "suddenly come to His Temple" (Malachi 3:1) at the right times to be "presented" (Luke 2:22–23), to cleanse that Temple with His whip (John 2:14–17), to stand trial before the Sanhedrin (Matthew 26:57), or to die so the Temple curtain could be "torn in two" (Matthew 27:51).

(It is assumed that the term *private eye* came into modern usage on the basis of Zechariah 3:9b. Bible probers are God's *private eyes* today, finding truths in the Scriptures to share with others.)

The Real Meaning of the "David and Goliath" Account

This appendix section is designed to initiate action in Africa to be able to teach Sunday school lessons in a *Christ-centered* way.

Here's the dilemma. Almost all Bible teachers know the story of David and Goliath. (Goliath the giant was approximately nine feet, six inches tall, being able to slam dunk a basketball without leaving his feet. Read the account in 1 Samuel 17, a very long chapter.)

What do Sunday school teachers generally do with this narrative?

They tell the story and get the children all excited with the fact that the little guy David defeated the big, big giant Goliath, even cutting off his head. (Kids love gore!) Then their teachers emphatically emphasize that "the little guy killed the big guy," and then say, "Amen," and direct the children to start "craft time."

Wait a minute! Was this meant to be a *Christian* classroom? Where was *Christ* in the story? He was left out as the teacher forgot to move the story into terms of the NT.

How was that teacher supposed to do that? Here the "how"!

First, David was not yet married when he battled Goliath. He had no children, but he held the key to the bloodline of the genealogical trail to Jesus. If he is killed in battle, then kiss Bethlehem, Calvary, the empty tomb, and heaven goodbye. There will be no *Jesus!*

Second, if David does not later become king, then he cannot become a "kingly type" of Jesus, who would later become the greater "Ruler" (Micah 5:2).

Third, God's people would not have Psalm 23 and all those messianic psalms that David wrote foretelling the death and resurrection of Jesus.

Oops! Guess that "Goliath" story is more than "the little guy beat the really, really big guy"! It is!

It's about a parallel battle to come, the battle of Calvary! Here the beaten, bloody, and weak Jesus would fight the giant of hell, Satan—and would win to save, yes, to save those children in that above-mentioned classroom who need Jesus, not "the little guy" David. In spiritual reality, Jesus is the only warrior who can forgive these children's wrongdoings and get them to heaven.

As you now sense, the whole David and Goliath account must be connected to the coming Messiah Jesus!

How Long Is Eternity?

What if there is a God and some do not agree? What if there is a *hell*, even though some doubt it? What if those *persons* end up in the wrong place? How long will they be there?

A Potent Illustration: Imagine a hard ball of marble or granite the size of planet Earth. Once every year a little bird lands and takes one peck. Peck! He does this once a year, year after year on the same spot. After 1,000 years of repeated pecking on the same spot, a tiny nick appears. Finally, when he pecks away the whole globe of earth, then eternity will be over. *Not!* Then he could start pecking all over again. Why? Because eternity lasts forever; it never ends.

Moral: During our stay on earth, it would be wise to ready ourselves by evaluating biblical *truth*; for "if" there is an existence in the hereafter, it would be good to end up in the right place, because eternity lasts a lot longer than anyone's short existence here on earth.

Persons who bet on *"No* existence beyond death" put "all their eggs in one basket." That's okay, if there is *"No* afterlife"! *However,* it's disaster if there *is* a judging God and a real *hell* for eternity. As the former hit song by Blood, Sweat & Tears reverberated, "I can swear there ain't no heaven but I pray there ain't no hell." Not so sure, huh? Or as Dante's *Inferno* depicted *hell*'s welcoming sign: "Abandon all hope, ye who enter here."

Think of this: If atheists or agnostics die *without* the conviction that there "is" a God—and there is none, they are home safe, but so are Christians, since there will be "no" God to judge them wrong for having believed in "One" who did not exist.

On the other hand, if there "is" a God, the believing Christian has a chance before an existing, judging God since he believed in Him; whereas, the "No God" person is in deep trouble as to *eternal* placement.

If you have never taken time to analyze this, Google "Pascal's Wager"—and consider. Hebrews 9:29 indicates that Bible information must be comprehended *before* death. It states: "... people are appointed to die *once* and after that comes judgment." No "second chances"; all receive those chances here on earth. That is why Hebrews 3:7–19 says "today" is a good day to embrace Christ Jesus before it is tomorrow—and maybe too late. "Today" is the time to get a true "perspective" on God, who is both a God of love and wrath (G, *RL*, pp. 78–79).

APPENDIX 15

I WOULD NEVER GO THERE, EVER!

What an intriguing setting. Simon Peter is out spreading the word as Jesus instructed. We find him at the seaside town of Joppa, located on the Mediterranean. He is a visitor of another Simon, Simon the tanner or leather worker. It is getting near lunchtime; Peter decides to take a nap till lunch is served. He falls asleep which gives God opportunity to send him a message via three identical visions.

Peter sees a big king-sized bed sheet coming down from heaven. All kinds of unclean animals are in the sheet, animals forbidden to Jews as food, as defined in the OT book of Leviticus. A voice from heaven says, "Get up, Peter. Kill and eat!" Peter protests and refuses, stating he has never broken Jewish food laws—and does not intend to start now.

The sheet is withdrawn, but returns twice more with the same animals and commands; Peter gives his same obstinate refusal a second and third time. The sheets are pulled back into heaven.

What could this all mean? Peter will soon find out.

Peter is puzzled by the vision. Simon the tanner wakes Peter and tells him three men are at the door. Go with them; "do not hesitate," says the Spirit.

(Three visitors are at the door wanting to speak with Peter? Three? Umm! Three sheets; three visitors. Might not be a coincidence. Hello!)

Peter goes down to the door. The three messengers inform him their master Cornelius (No, not the one from the Planet of the Apes movie!) has been told by an angel to "summon" him to come to his home.

The next day Peter travels with them to Caesarea. Cornelius had a whole congregation of "relatives, close friends," probably servants too, ready to hear Peter preach.

Cornelius and his friends were Gentiles. Now it dawns on dense Peter. When he enters a Gentile house, God will not declare him unclean. These Gentiles can kill unclean animals, and Peter can now eat and preach in a home considered ceremonially "unclean" by Jews, certainly by those who had also accompanied Peter from Joppa. (God has a big teaching lesson going on here.)

The long and short of it all is that Peter preached, and while he was speaking the Holy Spirit fell on the people. It was Pentecost #2! Baptism followed. God had voted in favor of Gentile conversion, as He had formerly accepted Jews fifty days after Passover.

The resurrected Christ was blessing His Church with growth.

(The above is a condensed form of Acts 9:43–10:48.)

Now the connective. Have you OT and NT searchers spotted it?

The key lies in the *name* of the city of "Joppa," where the whole episode begins. Was the city of Joppa ever mentioned in the OT? It was. Jonah 1:3 tells us the prophet Jonah ran to "Joppa" to board a ship going west when God had told him to go east to the capital city of Nineveh. No way was the Jewish prophet Jonah going to go and preach salvation to rotten Gentiles. If saved, these Assyrian Gentiles could live and later attack the Jews in the Holy Land of Canaan. Jonah was a true Jewish patriot. No way was he going to be a traitor.

God had other ideas, as He did with the reluctant Peter. During a violent storm on the Mediterranean, a big fish was prepared by God. To stop the storm, Jonah was thrown overboard the ship carrying him; the fish swooped him up and then "vomited" him up on an eastern shore. From there, Jonah traveled to Nineveh, preached there, and a *mass* conversion among the "120,000" people of Nineveh took place (Jonah 3:1–10; 4:11). Wow, would modern preachers, evangelists, and missionaries like the kind of results Jonah experienced!

The final clue to be nailed down was given to me by missionary James May of Nairobi, Kenya, Africa. I was teaching this story when May directed my attention to Matthew 16:17 where Jesus calls Peter, "Simon son of Jonah." (You will read, "Simon son of John," "John" being the Greek form of the Hebrew "Jonah.")

> There you have it—another connective ("*Evidence Just Too Coincidental to Be Accidental!!!*") to solve more *New Testament Mysteries* with *Old Testament Clues*. Peter is the new "Jonah" of the NT era. Like Jonah, he preached to Gentiles—and also had *great* success by the blessing of the Holy Spirit.

Final Comment

Thank you for reading this book; may you benefit much as the Spirit leads you to Jesus and His Father, more and more, each day.

FURTHER PERSONAL ACKNOWLEDGEMENTS

Many are the persons who in one way or another are responsible for the contents and publication of this book, first and foremost—the Holy Spirit.

Since it is not customary to thank a huge list of persons and organizations on Dedication and Acknowledgement pages at the front of a written work, I have chosen to accomplish my desires at the end of this book. I owe so much—to so many people over the seven decades of my life—from my parochial day school teachers, Sunday school teachers, and professors in the halls of higher learning, to my several sacrificial donors who have made my numerous foreign missionary journeys possible.

Thank you, thank you, and thank you!

Publication and initial distribution costs have been made possible by the generosity of my *spiritually* adopted son, Dr. Solomon Praveen Samuel from the country of India, who has been a top benefactor as relates to the missionary efforts of Team-Jesus for Africa. (Solomon has been Research Head at the Einstein Medical Center in Philadelphia, PA, USA, where he is still retained as a consultant. Presently, Dr. Samuel is the assistant director of research in Philadelphia at the Shriner Children's Hospital. He also teaches courses at Temple University and Philadelphia University.)

The William F. Beck family has graciously granted permission for me to use the two translations mentioned on the copyright page, the AAT and the NET. Dr. William F. Beck developed that former combined translation over a period of thirty years. It has undergone a series of careful revisions over the years of 1976 to the present. (Tedious textual revision care has been provided by Reu Beck, son of "Bible Bill" Beck.)

The NT NET is a major revision of the translation work of Dr. William F. Beck, mentioned above. The key revisers were Drs. Siegbert W. Becker, Phillip B. Giessler, Robert G. Hoerber, and emeritus professor David Kuske.

The NET's major contributions to the world of modern translations relate to: (1) updates of modern language for "ease of English reading"; (2) unique poetic layout, especially in the book of Revelation by Rev. Jack Michael Cascione, containing a totally unique "*kai*" [Greek: "and"] format; (3) built-in outlines that divide the texts of the various twenty-seven books of the NT; (4) brilliant maps by Dr. John C. Lawrenz; (5) superb informational appendices; and (6) other front and back data of significance.

Heartfelt Gratitude to:

Inez, my multi-capable and willing wife, analogous to Proverbs 31:10–31, covering many areas of need to the glory of Christ's Kingdom.

"Ginnie" Renkel, my career-long biblical literary consultant.

Janet Guda, one who is always there with words and actions of encouragement.

The enduring friendships of Dan and Janice Buzz that have enhanced my various ministries.

"Andy" and Bernice Bilich, former college classmates, have paved spiritual and financial pathways, as have other numerous American and Ecuadorian contributors, donors too many to name individually.

Bruno Putze and wife Miriam; Dr. Ron Schultz and wife Lorraine (two most valuable couples who have attended my Bible classes for the longest duration of consecutive time and have provided great incentive to prepare and offer additional Bible studies—year after year).

Dr. John Davidson, Pastor "Rob" Foote, Pastor David Mommens, Pastor "Rick" Sweney, and The Reverend George Zehnder were five men who were under my pastoral care before they entered seminary and later the Holy Ministry of our Lord. It was my honor from the Holy Spirit to have had some *spiritual* influence in their lives on behalf of Christ. They all have given great glory to God the Father through their pastoral dedication.

Dr. Thomas Ahlersmeyer (my best seminary student ever and the epitome of scholarship and practicality mixed together), as well as missionary "Jake" and wife Michelle Gillard: all three have been constant prodders to get the thoughts of this book down into writing.

Dr. David Buegler for opening doors to teach "Christ" to multiple students through several years.

James and Kay Stanley of Ecuador, South America, for providing a writing sanctuary in their home to speed along the initial writing of this book.

Dr. Robert Rahn, who opened the doors of Africa for me to teach the Scriptures to seminary students, pastors, evangelists, and laypersons. These teaching opportunities have enhanced this present writing. (Robert is the founder of the Lutheran Heritage Foundation—Macomb,

Michigan, USA. This organization is instrumental *worldwide* for the translation of biblical and theological materials into countless foreign languages to the benefit of formerly lost souls.)

Pastor Robert Green, who unselfishly provided American preaching and teaching opportunities between my various retirements and trips to Africa. His continual encouragement to the members of Bethlehem Lutheran Church—Parma, Ohio, USA—has motivated effective prayers and tremendous financial support for missionary ventures. His wife Kathy has been a sacrificial Godsend.

The underlying scholastic reality of this present work is largely due to my former teachers and academic friends: Drs. Wm. F. Beck, Siegbert W. Becker, Eugene Bunkowske, Fred Danker, Robert G. Hoerber, "Rudy" Honsey, John Klotz, David Kuske, John Warwick Montgomery, Richard E. Muller, J. Barton Payne, J. A. O. Preus, Robert Preus, Raymond Surburg, Cornelius Van Til, Pieter A. Verhoef, Waldo Werning, Bryant G. Wood, Edward J. Young, and others. These professors have been my mentors through many decades of education.

Present biblical influences also deserve credit: Dr. A. Andrew Das (Scriptural scholar of scholars), Gioacchino Michael Cascione (insightful trailblazer of new interpretive biblical data and also a fine Christian artist), and Dr. Andrew E. Steinmann (voluminous researcher and writer, reaching into various biblical sciences).

African friends: The late Rev. Samwel Atunga (lecture translator *par excellence* from English into Swahili); Principal or President Japheth Dachi of the ELCSS seminary in Yambio, South Sudan (most humble theologian and willing protector—with a great sense of humor); Pastor Kleopa Akyoo of Meru, Tanzania (best overall congregational pastor and administrator I have encountered in Africa); Dr. Godson Maanga, president of the Lutheran College of Theology in Mwika, Tanzania (everything a religious leader should be); Dr. Wilhelm Weber, former head of Tshwane Theological Seminary in Pretoria, South Africa, and now president of the Old Latin School, Wittenberg, Germany (superb German theologian and excellent Christian administrator); Mr. Herbert Gore, financial expert for LIA in Nairobi, Kenya (possibly the most trustworthy and efficient handler of Christ's monies in all of Africa); Naphtali Mayoyo Igendia (faithful translator of many English materials into Swahili); Bishop Jerome Wamala of Kampala, Uganda (hard, hard worker in Christ's vineyard); Bishop Peter Anabati of Yambio, South Sudan (my former seminary student in South Africa); and Nisha of Uganda (a modern-day giver of hospitality to travelers in parallel to 1 Peter 4:9–11). These residents of Africa, in one way or another, have opened doors for the distribution of this present book for further learning on their continent and elsewhere.

Missionary James May of Nairobi, Kenya, Africa (the Savior's amazing servant, "standing against all odds" and proclaiming the Gospel to people in at least *four* varying languages in over twenty different countries—and providing exceptional opportunities for others to teach Christ to the nations).

Jesse and Erica Kloos, who continually provided invaluable power point program productions for the raising of funds to teach on several fronts.

Claude Winquist, who has proved my most able assistant on several African trips.

The late Marvin Schwan, founder of the Schwan Food Company and establisher of the Marvin N. Schwan Charitable Foundation, as well as Rev. Lawrence Burgdorf. Both were so instrumental in financially backing the revision work of the Bible texts presently used in this book.

The resource friendships of Ken Ham, Mark Looy, and David Menton of the Creation Museum in Petersburg, Kentucky, USA, plus that of Herman Otten of *Christian News*, are also so deserving of mention. (In the years to come, "Herm" will go down as the Christian editor who best knew and reported on *all* the various trends and theologies being championed worldwide over the past fifty-five years, while those at the Creation Museum are already Christ's champions in our present world that has forgotten to praise the Triune God as its Creator supreme.)

Once again, thanks to all the above and so many others also for making this book possible.

INDEXES

BIBLIOGRAPHY WITH REFERENCE CODES

Alphabetized according to Code Letters

A, *1PH*: Achtemeier, Paul J. *1 Peter*. Hermeneia. Minneapolis: Fortress, 1996.

A, "ER": Arnold, Thomas. Google "Thomas Arnold on resurrection"; click on "Thomas Arnold on the evidence for the Resurrection – Apologetics."

AGAGNT: *A Grammatical Analysis of the Greek New Testament*. Editors: Max Zerwick, S.J and Mary Grosvenor. Roma: Editrice Pontificio Istituto Biblico, 1996.

A, *GL*: Arndt, William F. *The Gospel according to Luke*. St. Louis, Missouri: Concordia Publishing House, 1956.

B, *BP*: Bruce, F. F. *The Books and the Parchments*. Third and revised edition. Westwood, New Jersey: Fleming H. Revell Company, 1963.

B, *CBA*: Bruce, F. F. *Commentary on the Book of the Acts. The New International Commentary on the New Testament*. Grand Rapids, Michigan: Wm. B. Eerdmans Publishing Co., 1954 (reprint 1973).

B, *CG*: Beck, William F. *The Christ of the Gospels*. Saint Louis, Missouri: Concordia Publishing House, 1959.

B, *FW*: Bray, John L. "The Fate of the Wicked" in *Biblical Perspectives; The Newsletter for Thinking Christians*. Lakeland, FL: P.O. Box 90129.

B, *NBD*: Bruce, F. F. "Hour," *The New Bible Dictionary*. Organizing editor: J. D. Douglas. Grand Rapids, Michigan: Wm. B. Eerdmans Publishing Co., 1962.

B, *R*: Brighton, Louis A. *Revelation*. Concordia Commentary Series. St. Louis, Missouri: Concordia Publishing House, 1999.

B, *RDTS*: Becker, Siegbert W. *Revelation: The Distant Triumph Song*. Milwaukee, Wisconsin: Northwestern Publishing House, 1988.

B, *ROTNC*: Bird, Chad L. *Reading OT Narratives Christologically & Christ in All the Scriptures & The Biblical Typology of Luther & the Fathers*. Parts I & II. Fort Wayne, Indiana: Concordia Theological Seminary Press, 2003.

CBD: *Compact Bible Dictionary*. Editors: Ronald F. Youngblood, F. F. Bruce, & R. K. Harrison. Nashville, Tennessee: Thomas Nelson, Inc., 2004.

C, *RB*: Cascione, Gioacchino Michael. *Repetition in the Bible*. Tucson, AZ: RedeemerPress. org, 2016.

C, *SBO*: Cascione, Gioacchino Michael. *In Search of the Biblical Order: Patterns in the Text Affirming Divine Authorship from Revelation to Genesis*. St. Clair Shores, Michigan: RedeemerPress.org, 2012.

C, *SFB*: Comfort, Ray. *Scientific Facts in the Bible*. Alachua, Florida: Bridge-Logos, 2001.

D, *BGF*: Das, A. Andrew. *Baptized into God's Family: The Doctrine of Infant Baptism for Today*. Second Edition. Milwaukee, Wisconsin: Northwestern Publishing House, 2008.

D, "BNT": Das, A. Andrew. "Baptism in the New Testament: 1 Peter 3:18-22," paper delivered to the Rocky Mountain District of the Lutheran Church-Missouri Synod, 1999; http://www.issuesetcarchive.org/issues_site/ resource/archives/das2.htm.

D, *G*: Das, A. Andrew. *Galatians*. Concordia Commentary Series. St. Louis, Missouri: Concordia Publishing House, 2014.

D, *JOG*: Das, A. Andrew. "Jesus outside the Gospels" (personal classroom teaching notes by Das, based on John P. Meier's *A Marginal Jew*, vol. 1, 1991 (see M, *MJ* below).

E, "J,"*NLBC*: Ellis, David J. *The Gospel according to John. The New Layman's Bible Commentary (in one volume)*. Editors: G. C. D. Howley, F. F. Bruce, H. L. Ellison. Grand Rapids, Michigan: Zondervan Publishing House, 1979.

E, *LTJM*: Edersheim, Alfred. *The Life and Times of Jesus the Messiah*, 2 vols. Grand Rapids, Michigan: Wm. B. Eerdmans Publishing Co., 1962.

E, *MMOT*: Ellis, Peter. *The Men and the Message of the Old Testament*. Collegeville, Minnesota: The Liturgical Press, 1963.

F, *HKC*: Faulstich, E. W. "How Can You Know for Certain?" from "It's About Time" (April 1987). Spencer, Iowa: Chronology – History Research Institute, April 1987.

F, *TS*: Fairbairn, Patrick. *The Typology of Scripture*. Two volumes in one. Grand Rapids, Michigan: Zondervan Publishing House, n.d.

F, *UB*: Fuller, Daniel P. *The Unity of the Bible: Unfolding God's Plan for Humanity*. Grand Rapids, Michigan: Zondervan Publishing House, 1992.

G, *ALD*: Giessler, Phillip B. "An Abbreviated List of Dates, Arranged Chronologically, and Interspersed with a Listing of Events, Events that Indicate the Specific Time Spans that Separate Them: A Study of 'God's Timetable' as Based on Scriptural Data." Based on the chronological research of E. W. Faulstich. Personal summary notes (1981).

G, *FOTP*: Giessler, Phillip Bruce. *The Function of the Old Testament Prophet: A Study Concerning Prophetic Forthtelling and Foretelling.* Bachelor of Divinity thesis presented to the Department of Exegesis at Concordia Theological Seminary—Springfield, Illinois (1967). 268 pages.

G, *RL*: Giessler, Phillip B. *Referred by Luke M.D.* Lima, OH: C.S.S. Publishing Company, Inc., 1976.

G, *SJL-K*: Giessler, Phillip B. *SHILOH, THE JUDAIC LION-KING: An Exegetical Study of Genesis 49:8–12.* Master of Theology thesis presented to the Faculty of the Graduate School of Westminster Theological Seminary—Philadelphia, Pennsylvania (1974).

H, *AD*: Harper, Henry A. *From Abraham to David: The Story of Their Country and Times.* New York: MacMillan and Co., 1892.

H, *COT*: Hengstenberg, E. W. *Christology of the Old Testament and a Commentary on the Messianic Predictions,* I–IV. Translated by Theod. Meyer and James Martin. 1872–78. Reprint. Grand Rapids, Michigan: Kregel, 1956.

H, "E": Hanegraaff, Hank. "Equip," Christian Research Institute's (CRI) newsletter (Volume 20, Issue 2, March 2007).

H, *EE*: Horton, R. L. *Elijah & Elisha* (Teacher Guide). Penascola, FL: mmix Pensacola Christian College, n.d.

H, *GWG*: Herberger, Valerius. *The Great Works of God* or *Jesus, the Heart and Center of Scripture.* Four volumes in two. St. Louis, Missouri: Concordia Publishing House, 2010.

H, *JW*: Hahn, Scott. *Joy to the World.* New York: Image (Crown Publishing Group), 2014.

H, *R*: Hanegraaff, Hank. *Resurrection.* Nashville, Tennessee: W Publishing Group, a unit of Thomas Nelson, Inc., 2000.

H, "RN": Holbert, John C. Google "patheos.com/Progressive-Christian/Resurrection-Another-Name-John-Holbert"; click on "Resurrection By Another Name: Reflections on Exodus 14–15" ("Lectionary Reflections Exodus 14-15 Easter Sunday April 20, 2014").

H, *RNTU*: Hoerber, Robert G. *Reading the New Testament for Understanding.* St. Louis, Missouri: Concordia Publishing House, 1986.

H, *TDOT*: Haag, H., *"ben 'ādhām,"* *Theological Dictionary of the Old Testament. The authorized and unabridged translation of Theologisches Worterbuch zum Alten Testament.* Volume II. Edited by G. J Botterweck and Helmer Ringgren and translated by John T. Willis. Grand

Rapids, Michigan: William B Eerdmans Publishing Company, 1975 (revised edition 1977 and reprinted, July 1988).

H, "WWN": Hodge, Bodie. "Who Were the Nephilim? Genesis 6 and Numbers 13—A Fresh Look. Google https://assets.answersingenesis.org/doc/articles/aid/v3/who-were-nephilim.pdf.

"I,"*ODCC*: "Irenaeus, St." *The Oxford Dictionary of the Christian Church.* Second edition. Editors: F. L. Cross and E. A. Livingstone. New York: Oxford University Press, 1974.

J, *COT*: Jones, Floyd Nolen. *The Chronology of the Old Testament.* Green Forest, AR: Master Books, 2005.

J, *G*: Jeske, John C. *Genesis.* St. Louis, Missouri: Concordia Publishing House, 1992.

J, *WJ*: Josephus, Flavius. *The Works of Josephus.* Translated by William Whiston, A.M. Peabody, MA: Hedrickson Publishers, Inc., 1987.

K, *BI*: Kuske, David. *Biblical Interpretation: The Only Right Way.* Milwaukee, Wisconsin: Northwestern Publishing House, 2003.

K, *CRT*: Krauth, Charles P. *The Conservative Reformation and Its Theology.* Reprint edition of 1871 & 1899 editions. Minneapolis, Minnesota: Augsburg Publishing House, n.d.

K, *G*: Kidner, Derek. *Genesis: An Introduction and Commentary.* Downers Grove, Illinois: Inter-Varsity Press, 1967.

K, *SCD*: Koehler, Edward. *A Summary of Christian Doctrine.* Third revised edition. St. Louis, Missouri: Concordia Publishing House, 2006.

L, "D": "Diatessaron," *Lutheran Cyclopedia.* Editor: Edwin L. Lueker. St. Louis, Missouri: Concordia Publishing House, 1954.

L, *EC*: Limbaugh, David. *The Emmaus Code: Finding Jesus in the Old Testament.* Washington, DC: Regnery Publishing, 2015.

L, *EG*: Leupold, H. C. *Exposition of Genesis*, I. Grand Rapids, Michigan: Baker Book House, 1942.

L, *IEPJJ*: Lenski, R. C. H. *The Interpretation of the Epistles of St. Peter, St. John and St. Jude.* Minneapolis, Minnesota: Augsburg Publishing House, 1966.

L, *J*: Laetsch, Theo. *Jeremiah.* Saint Louis, Missouri: Concordia Publishing House, 1952.

L, *LP*: Lightfoot, Neil R. *Lessons from the Parables.* Grand Rapids, Michigan: Baker Book House, 1965.

L, *LW*: Luther, Martin. *Luther's Works*, I. St. Louis, Missouri: Concordia Publishing House, 1958.

LSB: *Lutheran Service Book*. Saint Louis: Concordia Publishing House, 2006.

M, *EDV*: McDowell, Josh. *Evidence That Demands a Verdict: Historical Evidences for the Christian Faith*. Revised edition. San Bernardino, CA: Here's Life Publishers, Inc., 1979.

M, *MJ*: Meier, John P. *A Marginal Jew: Rethinking the Historical Jesus*. Vol. One: *The Roots of the Problem and the Person*. New York, New York: Doubleday, 1991.

M/S, *HTR*: McDowell, Josh and Stewart, Don. *Handbook of Today's Religions*. Nashville, Tennessee: Thomas Nelson Publishers, 1983.

M, *WMS*: Morison, Frank. *Who Moved the Stone?* Grand Rapids, Michigan: Zondervan Publishing House, 1930/1958.

NET: *God's Word to the Nations: New Evangelical Translation* (NET); *New Testament*. Cleveland, OH: NET Publishing, 1990.

N, *JT*: Natan, Yoel. *The Jewish Trinity: When Rabbis Believed in the Father, Son and Holy Spirit*. Chula Vista, CA: Aventine Press, LLC, 2003.

N, *JTS*: Natan, Yoel. *The Jewish Trinity Sourcebook: Trinitarian Readings from the Old Testament with B&W Text*. Yoel Natan, 2003).

P, *CD*: Pieper, Francis. *Christian Dogmatics*, I–IV. St. Louis, Missouri: Concordia Publishing House, 1951.

P, *CJ*: Pitre, Brant. *The Case for Jesus: the Biblical and Historical Evidence for Christ*. New York: Image (Crown Publishing Group), 2016.

P, *EBP*: Payne, J. Barton. *Encyclopedia of Biblical Prophecy*. Grand Rapids, Michigan: Baker Book House, 1962.

P, *R*: Panning, Armin J. *Romans*. Milwaukee, Wisconsin: Northwestern Publishing House, 2001.

R, *DB*: Roark, Dallas M. *Makers of the Modern Theological Mind: Dietrich Bonhoeffer*. Peabody, Massachusetts: Hendrickson Publishers Marketing, LLC, 1972.

"R,"*ODCC*: "Recapitulation," *The Oxford Dictionary of the Christian Church*. Second edition. Editors: F. L. Cross and E. A. Livingstone. New York: Oxford University Press, 1974.

S, *AP*: Steinmann, Andrew E. *From Abraham to Paul: A Biblical Chronology*. St. Louis, Missouri: Concordia Publishing House, 2011.

S, *BHNT*: Stoeckhardt, G. *The Biblical History of the New Testament*. Swanville, Minn: Wisdom for Today, 1966. (Reprint from St. Louis: Concordia Publishing House German edition, 1906. Translated by Arthur E. Beck.)

S, *D*: Steinmann, Andrew E. *Daniel*. St. Louis, Missouri: Concordia Publishing House, 2008.

S, *E*: Stephenson, John R. H. C. *Eschatology*. Robert Preus, General Editor. Fort Wayne: The Luther Academy, 1993.

S, *FESP*: Selwyn, Edward Gordon. *The First Epistle of St. Peter*. London: Macmillan & CO LTD, 1958.

S, *HCC*: Schaff, Philip. *History of the Christian Church*, I–VIII. Grand Rapids, Michigan: Wm. B. Eerdmans Publishing Company, 1950.

S, *IIP*: Surburg, Raymond F. *Introduction to the Intertestamental Period*. St. Louis, Missouri: Concordia Publishing House, 1975.

S, *MMP*: Schwartz, Rob. *Miracles of Messianic Prophecy: From Elijah and Elisha*. Xulon Press, 2011.

S, *PP*: Schonfield, Hugh J. *The Passover Plot: New Light on the History of Jesus*. New York, N.Y.: Bantam Books, Inc., a subsidiary of Grosset & Dunlap, Inc., 1967 (Bantam edition).

S, *RC*: Sarfati, Jonathan. *Refuting Compromise*. Green Forest, AR: Master Books, Inc., 2004.

T, *AOL*: Toon, Peter. *The Ascension of Our Lord*. Nashville, Tennessee: Thomas Nelson Publishers, 1984.

***TGPGS*:** *The Greatest Part of the Greatest Story: The History of Jesus from Cross to Crown*. Cleveland, OH: NET Publishing, 1990.

V, *EDNTW*: Vine, W. E. *An Expository Dictionary of New Testament Words (with their Precise Meanings for English Readers)*. Westwood, N.J.: Fleming H. Revell Company, 1940.

Y, *PD*: Young, Edward J. *The Prophecy of Daniel—A Commentary*. Grand Rapids, Michigan: Wm. B. Eerdmans Publishing Co., 1949.

Z, *JOG*: Zacharias, Ravi. *Jesus among Other Gods: The Absolute Claims of the Christian Message*. Nashville: Word Publishing (A Thomas Nelson Company), 2000.

AUTHORS/SOURCES/BIBLE VERSIONS

BIBLE PERSONALITIES
Selected

SUBJECT INDEX
Selected

REFERENCED SCRIPTURES
(Over 1,500 citations)

1 KINGS

8:27—257
8:63—133
17—100
17:1–2 Kings 13—101
17:8-9—52
17:10-24—100
19:8-9—197
22:19—255
22:19-22—256 f.

2 KINGS

2–13—108
2:8, 13-14—98
2:9-12—101
2:11—256
2:18-22—108
4:42-44—95
5:1-27—99
5:15—100
6:1-7—101
9:36-37—90
13:20-21—166

1 CHRONICLES

5:1-2—42, 209
5:2—75
6:17—144
21—131
21:1—131
21:15—132
24—226
24:15—226

2 CHRONICLES

1:3—132
3:1—33, 132
28:16-19—159

JOB

1:6—238, 241
1:6-7—256
2:1—241

19:23-27—209
19:25—174
19:25-26—30
19:25-27—193
38:7—241, 257, 278

PSALMS—5

2—199, 209
2:1-12—208
2:4—42
2:7-9—53
2:12—115, 119
8—209
8:4—16
8:5-7—272
14:7—30
16—168, 209
16:8-11—168
16:9-10—231
16:10—244
22—152, 160, 161, 209
22:1—153
22:1-31—208
22:18—136
23—281
23:6—263
34—209
34:20—167
40—209
41—209
45—209
45:7—208
51:5—48, 206
68—209
68:17—51
68:17-18—257
68:18—238, 267
69—209
69:21—154
72—209
78—209
86:13—244

3:1-10—209
3:8—56
3:9—4, 114, 117, 152, 170, 208, 214, 219, 279, 280
6:12-13—209
9:9-10—209
9:9-12—78
11:12-13—209
12—141, 144-146
12:9-14—209
12:10—167, 209
12:10-14—140
13:7-9—209
14:3-5—209
14:4—198

MALACHI
3:1—32, 280
3:1-3—209
3 Kings
17:23 (LXX)—100
1 Enoch
1:9—242
xx.1-7—106
10:10—242
15:2-5—242
15:3—242
20:1-8—244
67:8-13—238
2 Enoch
18:2-5—242

MATTHEW
1—17, 216
1:1-17—210, 212
1:1–28:20—60 & 61
1:16—141, 210
1:17—214
1:18—41
1:22—217
1:23—41
1:25—142
2:1—42, 52, 75

2:1-11—50
2:3—50
2:8—54
2:12—54
2:13—52, 53
2:15—52
2:16—50
2:18—54
2:19-22—55 f.
2: 23—56
3:15—66
3:16-17—8
3:17—18, 153, 158, 203
4:11—66
4:13—82
4:15-16—83
4:17—83
4:19—67
4:23—83, 86
4:24—83
4:23-24—83
5–7—59
5:18, 35—148
5:22—237
5:44—93, 137
6—199
8:12—257, 261
9:6—19, 198
9:6-8—19
9:22—20
10:1-4—67
10:4—122
10:16—187
11:2-3—85
11:3—40
11:11—223-225
11:27—203
11:28—78
12:5-6—171
12:40—33, 170, 178
12:41-42—87